Hitchcock's Lar

Hitchcock's Ear

Music and the Director's Art

DAVID SCHROEDER

continuum

The Continuum International Publishing Group

80 Maiden Lane   The Tower Building
New York   11 York Road
NY 10038   London SE1 7NX

www.continuumbooks.com

Library of Congress Cataloging-in-Publication Data
A catalog record for this book is available from the Library of Congress

ISBN: HB: 978-1-4411-1458-7
PB: 978-1-4411-8216-6

Typeset by Fakenham Prepress Solutions, Fakenham, Norfolk NR21 8NN
Printed and bound in the United States of America

To Daniel, Emily and Linda,
with love.

Contents

List of illustrations

Preface

As a youth in the 1950s and 60s, I could not escape the name Alfred Hitchcock, on television, in newspapers, and of course at the movies. In my student years it soon struck me that his films belonged in the same class as those of Eisenstein, Bergman, and Fellini, and that, like these directors, music played a key role in making his films what they were. When I became an active writer sometime later, I assiduously avoided Hitchcock, not quite knowing how to approach this role of music in his films. That changed in the late 1990s, when visiting my daughter Emily at university in Montreal, and we spent an afternoon at the exhibition "Hitchcock and Art: Fatal Coincidences" at the Montreal Museum of Fine Arts. This exhibition powerfully illustrated the effect of artworks on Hitchcock's visual images, and it occurred to me then that music did something similar for him as a director, not so much the music by the numerous composers used for his films, but instead music as an underlying force in generating the type of aura he wished to capture, as a way of prompting visual images, and even having a possible bearing on structure for parts or the whole of a film. While still finishing a couple of other books, I acquired all of his 52 known feature films (some of which were difficult to find until very recently, such as *The Pleasure Garden*, *Downhill*, and *Waltzes from Vienna*), watched them carefully, and read avidly.

As with any book, it took some time to determine its scope. Much has been written about Hitchcock and music in the past few decades, although a fair amount of this is fairly inaccessible to Hitchcock enthusiasts. Until a few years ago there was only one monograph on the subject in English (along with two in German and one in French), the very fine *The Silent Scream: Alfred Hitchcock's Sound Track* by Elisabeth Weis (1982), which, as the title implies, considers not only music but also sound in general. This book has long been out of print, and by no means covers the subject in its fullest possible range. I wondered if I would need to discuss the actual music from all the films, but that fortunately became unnecessary with the appearance of Jack Sullivan's *Hitchcock's Music* (2006), a book that does exactly that, starting with the first sound film *Blackmail* (1929). Sullivan covers the ground well, and his book allowed me to focus on the parts of the subject that interest me most; my endorsements of and differences with him turn up in the course of the book.

While the films themselves yield much of the necessary resources, large amounts of unpublished material also proved necessary, especially early drafts of scripts that show the evolution of the thought going into a film, some of which directly concerns music, and many other documents as well, such as letters, telegrams, inter-office memos, dubbing notes, music cues, Hitchcock's music notes, continuity notes, and the like. I also needed to view the silent version of *Blackmail*, which is not available in any commercial format. To see this material much travel was required, and for getting me to these archives I would like to thank the Social Sciences and Humanities Research Council of Canada for a research grant. Not only did the Council cover this and other expenses, but the grant also allowed a teaching release for one term, the cost of which was shared by the Faculty of Arts and Social Sciences at Dalhousie University. Numerous research facilities made their resources available to me, and one stands out among these, the Margaret Herrick Library in Los Angeles, where I happily spent many weeks over a number of years; Barbara Hall, whose knowledge of film is prodigious, went out of her way to make my time there productive. Other archives I visited include the Cinema-Television Library and Archives of Performing Arts at USC in Los Angeles, the UCLA Film and Television Archive, the Film Study Center of the Museum of Modern Art in New York, the British Film Institute in London, the Swedish Film Institute in Stockholm, and the Bernard Herrmann Collection at UC Santa Barbara. Numerous of these unpublished items are cited throughout the book, and all of these are identified in the notes.

I also owe thanks to Katie Gallof at Continuum for her interest in the project, and for steering it through to publication. One of the readers she consulted, Sidney Gottlieb, critiqued the proposal in an especially constructive and helpful way.

This is now the fifth book for which I have the privilege of thanking the person who cares most about what I write, my wife Linda. She reads and re-reads, will discuss endlessly, and never tires of this. As a musician of the highest order she also brings a keen sense of hearing which I can only stand back and admire.

Introduction

The basis of the cinema's appeal is emotional. Music's appeal is to a great extent emotional, too. To neglect music, I think, is to surrender, willfully or not, a chance to progress in filmmaking.[1]

(ALFRED HITCHCOCK, 1933)

Psycho has a very interesting construction and that game with the audience was fascinating. I was directing the viewers. You might say I was playing them, like an organ.[2]

(ALFRED HITCHCOCK, 1962)

In 1933, still in the early part of his career, although with 15 feature films already under his expanding belt, Alfred Hitchcock linked progress in filmmaking directly with music. Three decades later, with only six more films to go, he still saw music as having a bearing on filmmaking and the effect his films should have on an audience, which he quipped that he could play like an organ. Just after making *The Birds* in 1963, he added more to what he had in mind about construction, explaining to an interviewer from the magazine *Cinema* that "construction to me, it's like music. You start with your allegro, your andante, and you build up."[3] A year earlier, when speaking with François Truffaut, he made an analogy with music which sounds much more like his observation in 1933, bringing emotion and construction together: "The main objective is to arouse the audience's emotion, and that emotion arises from the way in which the story unfolds, from the way in which sequences are juxtaposed. At times, I have the feeling I'm an orchestra conductor, a trumpet sound corresponding to a close shot and a distant shot suggesting an entire orchestra performing a muted accompaniment."[4]

Hitchcock especially liked to compare filmmaking with orchestration, making these observations after completing *Marnie*:

> It is how the director handles his images that creates the state of mind, of emotion, in the audience. That is to say, the impact of the image is directly on emotions. Sometimes the director goes quietly along in a mood of simple, normal photography, and the eye is pleased as it follows the story. Then suddenly the director wishes to hit hard. Now the pictorial presentation changes. There is a bursting impact of images, like a change in orchestration. Indeed, orchestration is perhaps the best simile for a film, even to the parallel or recurrent themes and rhythms. And the director is, as it were, the conductor.[5]

Throughout his life Hitchcock made numerous similar comments about music and film, although not in any consistent or organized fashion. With his explanations about rhythm and montage, or "the visual substitution for sound"[6] in *The Lodger*, he also made no attempt to build this into a coherent theory in the way that Sergei Eisenstein or Vsevolod I. Pudovkin had. Hitchcock in fact had little stomach for exegesis of any kind, and took great delight in leg-pulling, not only in speeches and articles but presumably in interviews as well. His interviews with Truffaut and Peter Bogdanovich are so riddled with problems, often used for self-promotion or fostering the notion of himself as an *auteur*, that we may be inclined to dismiss them out of hand, if not as entirely bogus then at best in the way that one writer characterizes the exchanges with Truffaut: "exhaustive in scope but perfunctory in depth."[7] Perhaps so. Of course one could not imagine Hitchcock agreeing to answer the 500 questions Truffaut proposed to ask him unless he saw benefit for himself, notably in controlling the image of himself that the publication of these conversations could achieve.

If anything, we should be happy that Hitchcock did not share Eisenstein's predilection for theory, at least concerning music, since he does not trip us up with theories that may or may not hold. He gives us hints about music, many of them, certainly enough to suggest something worth exploring. The proof will lie in the films themselves, and some of them have such a strong musical essence that the question arises if the full depth of the film can be plumbed without taking the musical considerations into account. By this I do not mean the score that a particular composer has written for the film, although that certainly may be an important factor. Instead I refer to Hitchcock himself and his musical conception of a given film, which he expected his composer to grasp and augment. When the composer can meet him on this level, as Bernard Herrmann, for example, did fully in understanding Hitchcock's Wagnerian conception of *Vertigo*, the results could be stunning, yielding one of the most extraordinary films ever made. For Hitchcock, like his idol Edgar Allan Poe in speaking about Tennyson, it was possible to "see with his ear."

If Hitchcock took this underlying notion of music to be a useful principle for his films or used musical urges as the structural basis for some films, as well as to create aura and atmosphere, we would, of course, like to know how sophisticated his knowledge of music was or if he had actual musical skills. To the best of my knowledge he had no performance skills on any musical instrument, and he had minimal musical education beyond the rudimentary appreciation taught at his Catholic boarding school, St Ignatius College. Some directors who used musical principles in their films had fairly sophisticated musical backgrounds, or had at least reached some accomplishment on an instrument, such as Luis Buñuel as a talented violinist, Orson Welles on the piano, and William Wyler as a professionally trained violinist, but more often than not the most musically experimental directors had no such skills, and this freed them from the inhibitions musicians would have. Eisenstein stands out most notably, explaining his conception of montage with musical vocabulary, flagrantly using musical terminology in ways that would make a musician cringe. D. W. Griffith falls into a similar category, invoking musical principles to achieve emotions and pace in his films, and he formulated principles in the making of silent films from which Eisenstein, Hitchcock, and others could learn.

While not musicians, Eisenstein and Griffith listened to music avidly, developing sophisticated listening skills. Hitchcock got an early start as a concert-goer, attending regularly during his youth in London, especially at the Royal Albert Hall (where the crucial scenes

0.1 Hitchcock with sound device from *The Birds* (Painful sounds)

from both versions of *The Man Who Knew Too Much* would take place) and the Queen's Hall. Among his favorite composers at the time he could list Roussel, Elgar, and Wagner, and he singled out Dohnanyi's *Variations on a Nursery Suite* "because it opens like the most grandiose, huge, spectacular movie, probably by De Mille, and then reduces itself to a little twinkling on the piano; it always appealed to my sense of humor."[8] He also had a fond memory of Artur Rubinstein playing Robert Schumann's *Carnaval*, and from this work he would later strategically insert material into *Notorious*. Although he did not study music he did take some lessons in dance while still in his youth, learning the waltz and ballroom dancing.

His love of listening remained throughout his life, although in the United States he generally did not go to concerts or to the opera, preferring to listen to recorded music on his home sound system. He shared this enthusiasm with friends and colleagues while still in England, such as Charles Laughton, whom he left rapt at one point listening to his new hi-fi gramophone at his flat in Cromwell Road.[9] On another occasion, while spending a weekend with John Galsworthy, he declared Wagner to be his favorite composer, a claim which seemed to send a shudder through Galsworthy's wife, who preferred J. S. Bach.[10] In California the amount of listening he did if anything increased from that of England, and in fact studio documentation of his LP and tape purchases have survived for the late 1950s and 1960s;[11] often he would take these LPs to his ranch home near Santa Cruz when he could get away from Los Angeles. Many of these recordings, which numbered in the hundreds, cover the less well-known classics, and one can safely assume that he acquired these because he already owned all of the standard repertory. When important new recordings of the warhorses came out, such as Tchaikovsky's *Swan Lake* and the *Pathétique Symphony*, or Berlioz's *Symphonie Fantastique* performed by the Philadelphia Orchestra under Eugene Ormandy, along with many others, he instructed studio staff to order them. Without question Hitchcock knew the classical repertory well, and he often made the choices of the musical works to be heard in his films.

Hitchcock belongs to a generation of directors thoroughly grounded in the silent era before the advent of sound, and with the majority of these directors, who include DeMille, Eisenstein, Lang, Lubitsch, Stroheim, Sternberg, Pabst, Renoir, Clair, Vidor, Ford, Hawks, Chaplin, Wyler, and Curtiz, he shared a distinctive vision of cinema shaped by the absence of spoken dialogue in their early films. When sound arrived at the end of the 1920s, some of these directors regarded it as a mixed blessing, providing an opportunity to synchronize music with their films but introducing dialogue which some of them found unappealing. For those like Hitchcock who crossed the line and had to come to terms with dialogue, the principles of silent film remained firmly planted, and more often than not they would not allow spoken words to dominate their films. For these directors the theater played a fairly insignificant role in their development as filmmakers, since the most fundamental feature of the theater, words spoken by actors, did not exist for them before the late 1920s. They saw cinema as a visual medium, and all visual components needed to be governed by temporal considerations, certainly montage, but also other variations of pace. For many of them evoking emotional responses became directly linked with these variations of pace, and to achieve the desired goal they often borrowed from an art form that already functioned in this way, that being music—both vocal and instrumental. We should not be surprised that Eisenstein took his terminology for montage from music.

Many of these directors made their views on the matter fairly clear, and that includes Hitchcock. As an adolescent he attended the theater as frequently as concerts, but it did not take him long to see which of the two would have the greater effect on cinema; Patrick McGilligan points out that as a young director he "began to feel that film should be a different experience, almost 'anti-theater'."[12] McGilligan makes the point later in his biography as well, noting that "as a man with one foot always in the silent era, he preferred not to articulate every last meaning with words."[13] In the Truffaut interviews from 1962 the same issue came up, and in response to Truffaut's observation that, "as I see it, Mr. Hitchcock, your approach is anti-literary and purely cinematic," Hitchcock replied, "That's about the size of it."[14] The advent of sound resulted in great enthusiasm from some directors for dialogue, and at the time Hitchcock wished to distance himself from this group, clarifying this in his 1933 interview with Stephen Watts: "The arrival of talkies, as you know, temporarily killed action in pictures, but it did just as much damage to music. Producers and directors were obsessed by words ... But music as an artistic asset of the film is still sadly neglected."[15]

These comments from 1933 remain some of Hitchcock's most thorough public pronouncements on music and film, and despite the fact that the interview coincided with one of his least successful films, *Waltzes from Vienna*, the views held for his finest films as well, from his earliest to the latest. Some of this relates to the background music the viewer hears, and the effect that this can have. As important as film music may be, Hitchcock in the end wished to elucidate something else at this time, although the right words often eluded him. He started to get at this other phenomenon with a comment directly after explaining how music can express the unspoken: "It may sound far-fetched to compare a dramatic talkie with opera, but there is something in common. In opera quite frequently the music echoes the words that have just been spoken."[16] He knew perfectly well that this is the least important thing that happens in opera, especially his favorite Wagner, where the words themselves play a much less important role than the music. He also knew from earlier directors how potent a force opera or music could be in the formulation of cinematic principles, and one senses that in invoking opera here he hoped to get at something much broader, going beyond the mixing of words and music. In fact, the ensuing discussion in this interview takes us there.

Earlier when he spoke of music bolstering excitement in the build-up to a physical climax, he had added that this could be done "just as effectively as cutting," and promised more on that later. That comes, and in describing a musical scene from *Waltzes from Vienna*, he explained that he had "arranged the cutting to match the rhythm of the music. It is difficult to describe in words. You must visualize the film moving in time with the music. In the slow passages the cutting is slow, when the music quickens the mood of the melody is followed by the quick cutting." He takes this further: "Film music and cutting have a great deal in common. The purpose of both is to create the *tempo* and mood of the scene. And, just as the ideal cutting is the kind you don't notice *as* cutting, so with music."[17] The comparison of music and cutting takes us directly into that larger area, difficult to describe in words, and with implications far beyond a particular scene in *Waltzes from Vienna* with music in it. As a director of silent films Hitchcock had been using this technique all along, allowing the pacing or rhythm of these films to be envisaged in musical terms, and the chapter on *Blackmail* will explore this in greater detail, invoking the influence of the Russians Pudovkin and Eisenstein so admired by Hitchcock.

In sound films too he uses the technique, not strictly for pacing and rhythm but for other purposes as well. One notices throughout his career that many of the most effective moments in his films lack dialogue altogether, especially striking in *Vertigo* in the final transformation of Judy back into Madeleine at the Empire Hotel, and in numerous wonderful scenes in other films as well. For the remake of *The Man Who Knew Too Much*, the "Script Outline" dated 14 March 1955 clarifies that during the performance of Arthur Benjamin's "Storm Cloud" cantata at the Albert Hall, leading up to the famous cymbal crash, that "all these moves are rhythm."[18] This outline, with the strong hand of the director evident, refers to how the cutting should follow the music, and in a detailed essay on this, Murray Pomerance demonstrates exactly how that happens.[19] Generally the scenes in question have powerful musical accompaniments, causing a spectacular fusion of music and visual images, but something else may also be at work in these films, where specific music, possibly hinted at in the score, not unlike Hitchcock's own cameos in his films, alerts us to an underlying musical essence for the entire film, in some cases possibly providing the film with its structure. This appears to happen in *Shadow of a Doubt*.

Excellent and detailed studies exist on the music that we hear in Hitchcock's films,[20] and the focus in these tends to be on the effectiveness of this music by the numerous composers with whom he collaborated in achieving the various functions of film music. Hitchcock's own judgments may be called into question here, but more often than not the focus of these studies has been on the composers themselves and the quality and effectiveness of their music. Exceptions to this of course exist, most notably the books and articles by Elisabeth Weis, which look at music as one aspect of the larger spectrum of sound in the films, and therefore take a much broader view of Hitchcock's involvement.[21] This book will not avoid discussion of the composers and the music they provide, but when this happens, the emphasis will be on Hitchcock himself, certainly his judgment about the music, but even more on the role he intended the music to have in supporting his structural objectives or his ways of enhancing tone and atmosphere. These matters, though, are not the focus of this book; instead, I attempt to get at Hitchcock's own musical impulses, not ones that necessarily result in audible music, but ones that help to shape his conception of film as something visual.

Some of this will deal with matters of technique, but in no way should that obscure the attempt to get at the broader themes and approaches of his films—those things that he wished to get across to audiences through stirring their emotions or making them aware, often through subliminal means, of a larger sense of the world. At the heart of this lies the tension in the films between facets of stability and order on the one hand and on the other the chaotic or irrational forces that seek to undermine these. This conflict has been the focus of many studies of Hitchcock's films for a very long time, articulated clearly by Robin Wood as early as 1965; in pulling together some of the main themes in the films, Wood includes "the theme of the struggle of a personality torn between order and chaos (perhaps the most constant Hitchcock theme)."[22] In his discussion of individual films Wood shows how this works, with phrases such as "the chaos of our unknown," "descent into hell," "all is chaos," "whirling uncontrolled into chaos," "chaos abruptly takes over," "plunge into chaos is set in the supreme symbol of potential world order," and many more.[23] In some films, recovery from the chaos at the end does not come, while in others it may appear that order has returned but in fact in has not, since the cheerful ending offers nothing more than a ruse, in no way removing the dark forces evident throughout the film. In these the words that actors say will give the impression of order restored, but the visual images may tell a very different tale.

Frequently these visual images of ambiguity connect directly with music, although not necessarily the music we hear, but instead music that can act as an implied underlying force of disorder. Royal S. Brown discusses in his essay "Herrmann, Hitchcock, and the Music of the Irrational"[24] how the actual music can reinforce this, and Jack Sullivan gets at the same idea in reference to the collaboration between Herrmann and Hitchcock: "Both men saw life as a treacherous chaos fleetingly ordered by art."[25] The word "fleeting" may at times be overstating the case. Even more fascinating is the way music can work to achieve this in an underlying way, as a force that Hitchcock harnesses by transferring the energy into visual images. The chapters that follow will focus on the ways in which this can be achieved, and this of course happened initially in the silent films, which found musical parallels in shot construction and in the rhythm and tempo of cutting. Hitchcock discovered these possibilities in the works of Murnau, Griffith, Eisenstein, Pudovkin, and others, and these influences will be outlined before looking at *The Lodger* (1926) and *Blackmail* (1929), the early films that apply these principles most effectively.

Throughout his 53 feature films, certain musical images recur with remarkable consistency, and Hitchcock fully understood their capacity to invoke ambiguity. One of these, the waltz (or other types of dancing), can be found in over a third of the films, starting with silent pictures such as *The Lodger* and *The Ring*, and despite the enormous popularity of the waltz as a social vehicle, it also had a darker side, which moralists in the United States quickly pointed out. Most films that include the waltz exploit its dual nature, to the point that in a good number of cases it can act as a dance of death. This takes on an especially poignant sense in *Shadow of a Doubt*, in which a specific waltz connects directly to death and the breakdown of order. While the readily audible waltz in that film immediately captures our attention, a more subtle possibility emerges through a linkage with a waltz that directly charts a course of destruction leading to chaos, Ravel's *La Valse*; not only do we hear this work quoted in the score (which also happens in *Strangers on a Train*), but the fact that the structure of *Shadow of a Doubt* precisely parallels Ravel's work seems not to be coincidental. Another musical image, the piano, turns up in close to half of Hitchcock's films, and like the waltz it can be used ambiguously; we may think of the piano as an innocuous household furnishing, but it has associations that suggest other possibilities. In the ways that Hitchcock uses pianos in his films, both heard or unheard, he amply reveals these ambiguous qualities, as pianos often have a special relationship with the camera.

Rear Window has an entire chapter dedicated to it since this film sets up a parallel between the composition of a song and the unfolding of the film itself. Sullivan has written at some length about this film as well,[26] but my view moves in a different direction from his. Hitchcock seemed unsatisfied with Franz Waxman's song, and Sullivan thinks Hitchcock simply did not appreciate its quality. I explore what Hitchcock hoped to get from this song in relation to the often dark visual images in the film, images that suggest something Waxman missed almost entirely in his song, and point directly to the heart of Hitchcock's displeasure. Actual music becomes part of the consideration here, but since it misrepresented the tone of the film, it raises the matter of Hitchcock's own musical ideas, and specifically his judgment about the quality and nature of the music for a film. In fact, he knew what he wanted, and what he did want, as early drafts of the script make clear, was music that would address the tension between stability and disorder, something that Waxman seemed unable to provide.

The role of early drafts of scripts can play a significant part in considering Hitchcock's inclination to think of some of his films in musical terms, with his procedures for script development ensuring a high level of personal involvement; the ever-flowing stream of script revisions frequently tells us much about Hitchcock's musical objectives. Despite some testimony by his writers to the contrary, we know that Hitchcock never simply turned his writers loose, but as a rule met with them daily in order to shape a new script. As the scripts developed, new versions were typed up on a regular basis, and there could be numerous typed versions from the earliest drafts to the final shooting script. Many of these scripts have been preserved, mostly in the Hitchcock Collection at the Margaret Herrick Library in Los Angeles, and comparing drafts at various stages of development, with periodic title and author changes, can be very revealing. With *Suspicion*, for example, we discover in an early draft that Lina (Joan Fontaine) at one point plays the *Wiener Blut* waltz on the piano in the style of Ravel's *La Valse*, confirming that Hitchcock knew this piece and considered including it (although he did not) in a film just two years before its insinuated invocation in *Shadow of a Doubt*. Similarly with *Vertigo*, we discover in an early draft that Scottie (James Stewart) should first see Madeleine (Kim Novak) at a performance of an opera, and even though Hitchcock dropped this elaborate scene, it confirms the essence of this most operatic of all his films.

The operatic essence of *Vertigo*, as many commentators have recognized, has everything to do with Wagner, especially *Tristan und Isolde*, and even Herrmann's score all but borrows from that opera. Wagner's music can be heard directly in some films, for example *Murder!* and *Lifeboat*, and in others he invokes it, as in *The Birds* with the LP jacket of *Tristan* in plain view at Bodega Bay. Not only a favorite composer for Hitchcock, Wagner represented for him a way of getting at irrational and chaotic elements, and in a film such as *Vertigo* this happens not only in Herrmann's score, but in other facets of the film as well, including the narrative, which has much in common with *Tristan*. Aspects of Wagner's music allow the association with irrationality to occur, and in contrast to this, other composers can be used to represent order, as Mozart and J. C. Bach are in *Vertigo*, in ways though that make it clear that their attempts at order cannot tame the darker Wagnerian elements. Similar juxtapositions of source music play out in other films as well, not necessarily with these composers, but with others who fall into the respective camps, allowing source music to underlie the most basic thematic conflicts in Hitchcock's films. Especially with Wagner, Hitchcock himself had a role in the selection of the music.

In showing displeasure with Waxman's song for *Rear Window*, Hitchcock raised the matter of his judgment of his own works, and in fact revealed it to be entirely sound. In that case the music needed to serve a structural function as well as capturing the right tone, and to achieve that, ambiguity needed to be present. Similar issues arose in the next decade as well, and in the 1960s an additional complication loomed concerning the use of popular music in films. *Torn Curtain* brought about an irreconcilable split between Hitchcock and Herrmann, and Hitchcock used the argument to Herrmann that he needed a score with a beat; Herrmann doubted this, and based on the score Hitchcock received from John Addison and the scores for his subsequent films, Herrmann's hunch turned out to be correct. Much has been written about the breakdown of this highly productive collaboration, with very spirited and often partisan opinions expressed, most often casting the blame on Hitchcock's failure to recognize a good thing or to be loyal to someone who had a major role in his success during the previous decade.

Human relations certainly did not stand out as Hitchcock's strong point, but this may have obscured the real issue in this case. Pressure from the studio bosses appears to have played an inconsequential part in this drama, since, along with his good friend Lew Wasserman, Hitchcock was the studio boss, at this point holding a significant share of the MCA stocks. But even more important than the ruse about pressure for a popular score was the matter of understanding the nature of the film itself, and Hitchcock's judgment about this in relation to the type of score the film should have. Some of Herrmann's score has been recorded, and from this we can determine which of the two got it right. Herrmann of course had persuaded Hitchcock to change his mind about music for the shower scene in *Psycho*, undoubtedly the best-known piece of film music ever written; he assumed that he could do the same in this case—that he knew better than the director what the music should be. The book ends with this focus on Hitchcock's ability after four decades of directing to make sound decisions about his own films. The themes of order and disorder come into play here more obliquely than in many films, since the script for *Torn Curtain* provided little opportunity for a classic Hitchcock film. Despite that, it had classic Hitchcock touches, most notably a sense of humor—even surrounding some of its darkest moments, and that needed to be respected. This book explores the uncanny ability of a director not only to make good judgments but often to think as a composer would think, and transfer an underlying musical energy to his visual approach, helping to make these films extraordinary.

1

The sway of America and Europe

In the mid-1920s, the young Hitchcock remained susceptible to the influence of other filmmakers, and over the next few years we can see his debt to certain American, German, and Russian directors emerging noticeably in his films. At the heart of this lay notions of film construction—how to build a shot in both space and time, and how to put shots together to generate the rhythm and tempo of the film. Not simply esoteric technical matters that filmmakers ponder, these were the essential elements of designing how an audience would respond, especially at an emotional level. Some of these directors spoke about their film techniques using musical terminology, not merely putting music forward as a simile but in fact as something actually tied to their procedures: Hitchcock did not hesitate to follow their lead. By no means did that influence come only from other filmmakers. As a young man interested in all the arts, regularly attending concerts and the theater, taking dance lessons, and reading avidly, Hitchcock found elements in all these activities that could be applied to filmmaking.

Edgar Allan Poe

One of the influences Hitchcock seemed most prepared to talk about was that not of another director, but of a writer, Edgar Allan Poe. In his essay "Why I Am Afraid of the Dark" he posed the question: "Was I influenced by Edgar Allan Poe? To be frank, I couldn't affirm it with certainty. Of course, subconsciously, we are always influenced by the books that we've read. The novels, the paintings, the music, and all the works of art, in general, form our intellectual culture from which we can't get away."[1] In this essay, first published in French in 1960, he says much about Poe and himself, and considering the French had been fascinated with Poe for over a century by that point, his enthusiasm may have been directed to the receptive audience of *Arts: Lettres, Spectacles*. Of course he gives us much more, including a short history of his reading of Poe, and perhaps most notable here is what he does not say about Poe's effect on him. Starting with his early reading of Poe, he points out, "It was only when I was sixteen that I discovered his work. I read first, at random, his biography, and the sadness of his life made a real impression on me." In the next few years he devoured Poe's works: "When I would come back from the office where I worked, I would hurry to my room, take a cheap edition of his *Tales of the Grotesque and Arabesque*, and begin reading. I still remember my feelings when I finished 'The Murders in the Rue Morgue.' I was afraid, but this fear made me in fact discover something that I haven't since forgotten." He also includes "The Gold Bug" among the works making a strong impression on him, and as Dennis Perry reminds us, neither this nor "The Murders in the Rue Morgue" appear in *Tales of the Grotesque and Arabesque*, suggesting he read Poe much more widely than the volume mentioned.[2]

Focusing mainly on fear, horror, and suspense, he answers with little hesitation the question about influence:

> In my opinion, the reader is exactly in the same situation as the cinema spectator. And, very probably, it's because I like Edgar Allan Poe's stories so much that I began to make suspense films. Without wanting to seem immodest, I can't help but compare

what I try to put in my films with what Poe put in his stories: a perfectly unbelievable story recounted to readers with such a hallucinatory logic that one has the impression that this same story can happen to you tomorrow.

Near the end of the article he backs away from the comparison between himself and Poe, calling Poe a *poete maudit*, and himself a mere commercial filmmaker, although he certainly would not expect French readers to think of him in that way; they should fill in the blank, recognizing him as an artistic director. In broaching a more difficult comparison between himself and Poe, despite both of them liking to make people shiver, he concluded that Poe lacked a sense of humor: "for me, 'suspense' doesn't have any value if it's not balanced by humor." Nevertheless, "Poe and I certainly have a common point. We are both prisoners of a genre: 'suspense.' You know the story that one has recounted many, many times: if I was making 'Cinderella,' everyone would look for the corpse. And if Edgar Allan Poe had written 'Sleeping Beauty,' one would look for the murderer."[3]

Of course we can all see the connection between the two of them concerning fear and suspense, but the most important facets they have in common Hitchcock notes so briefly that they may pass unnoticed, and this lies in the two words "hallucinatory logic." Normally one would not place these two words together, since one implies the opposite of the other, but for Hitchcock they get at two fundamental elements of his films and Poe's writing, one having to do with the images that generate their aura and atmosphere, while the other, logic, considers the methods of control and construction to make them most effective. We do not know if Hitchcock read any of Poe's theoretical writing, such as his "Philosophy of Composition" or *The Brevities*, but it seems entirely possible even if he had not that he could have intuited much of what Poe had to say about his writing. The parallels between Hitchcock and Poe in the area of construction have not gone unnoticed;[4] both of them were calculating to the point of being mathematical in their approach to designing a work. In Poe's words,

Most writers—poets in especial—prefer having it understood that they compose by a species of fine frenzy—and ecstatic intuition—and would positively shudder at letting the public take a peep behind the scenes ... at the wheels and pinions—the tackle for scene-shifting—the step-ladders and demontraps—the cock's feathers, the red paint and the black patches, which in ninety-nine cases out of a hundred, constitute the properties of the literary *histrio*.[5]

Hitchcock went in the same direction as a filmmaker, according to Truffaut "universally acknowledged to be the world's foremost technician." Perry backs this up with the observation that "his pre-cut productions are planned to the point that, as Hitchcock himself said, 'I can hear [the audience] screaming when I'm making the picture.'"[6] In later years Hitchcock would drive producers such as David O. Selznick to distraction by shooting his films with such precision that the producer/editor could do nothing with the takes other than what Hitchcock intended.

While some of Hitchcock's own comments on construction from articles and interviews sound similar to Poe's, the influence of Poe's writing on atmosphere and emotion proves much more difficult to pin down; music possibly plays an important role here. Musical images abound in Poe's writing, and Hitchcock would certainly have been aware of them, such as these from *Ligeia*: "enthralling eloquence of her low musical language," or "by the almost magical melody, modulation, distinctness, and placidity of her very low voice." In *Loss of Breath* he gives a subtitle "Moore's Melodies," or *The Tell-Tale Heart* has the line "I arose and argued about trifles, in a high key and with violent gesticulations." His fondness for this type of image may seem to be somewhat superficial, but in fact it points to something beneath the surface, the way in which music permeates his writing at the deepest possible level, the element that Baudelaire and the later French symbolists found so appealing about his works. In *The Brevities* Poe has much to say about the bearing of music on his writing, and while we have no evidence that Hitchcock ever read these essays, some of Poe's ideas seem remarkably similar to comments made by Hitchcock or approaches he uses in his films.

A large number of Hitchcock's films use the piano as a striking and ambiguous image, as Chapter 7 will make clear, sometimes seen and played, at other times seen and heard with no one actually playing it, and often seen but not heard. For Poe, "The great variety of melodious expression which is given out from the keys of a piano, might be made, in proper hands, the basis of an excellent fairy-tale. Let the poet press his finger steadily upon each key, keeping it down, and imagine each prolonged series of undulations the history, of joy or of sorrow, related by a good or evil spirit imprisoned within."[7] Here he discusses not only music for the piano with its melodious expression, but also the wave of sounds that can emanate from the instrument simply by holding down the keys, the instrument's tone now becoming comparable to emotions or even an aura of good or evil. In fact, that aura appears trapped within the sound, but the sound can release it for others to experience, inciting the reader in a way that normal prose cannot. Poe's piano works very much like Hitchcock's organ noted in the Introduction, which allowed him, he claimed, to direct his viewers and play them, "like an organ."[8] He referred to this as a game with the audience, but it went much further, linking this musical image with construction and his ability to achieve the desired result with viewers.

In "Why Am I Afraid of the Dark" Hitchcock made much of Poe's place in literature, calling him "without the shadow of a doubt, a romantic and a precursor of modern literature." In placing him historically, he notes that Poe went to school in England "when Goethe had already published *Faust* and when the first stories by Hoffmann had just come out. This romanticism is perhaps even more apparent in the translation done by Baudelaire, which is the one you use."[9] Following this he links Poe and Baudelaire closely together, calling Baudelaire the "French Poe." The details may not always be correct (part one of *Faust* had been published by 1818, but not part two) but the perceptions are interesting, including evoking the name E. T. A. Hoffmann. Hoffmann stood as one of the most influential of the early romantic German writers, and for him music played an essential role in his way of defining the essence of romanticism, something that came easily to him as a prominent composer as well as being a leading writer. That essential quality of music to romanticism for him lay in the capacity of music to find a level of expression not bound by fixed images, invoking a sense of the indefinite and even the infinite, a capacity he believed that words on their own lacked. For poets, according to Hoffmann,

1.1 Hitchcock with Shirley MacLean (Directing from the piano)

music became the best possible model for images, and poets should aspire to the state of instrumental music.

In writing about Tennyson, Poe takes a position similar to that of Hoffmann's, making this comment in relation to the "Lady of Shalott": "If the author did not deliberately propose to himself a suggestive indefinitiveness of meaning, with the view of bringing about a definitiveness of vague and therefore of spiritual *effect*—this, at least, arose from the silent analytical promptings of that poetic genius which, in its supreme development, embodies all orders of intellectual capacity."[10] To understand this, one must switch to a discussion of music, and Poe does this directly, proceeding immediately with the following:

I *know* that indefinitiveness is an element of the true music—I mean of the true musical expression. Give to it an undue decision—imbue it with any very determinate tone—and you deprive it, at once, of its ethereal, its ideal, its intrinsic and essential character. You dispel its luxury of dream. You dissolve the atmosphere of the mystic upon which it floats. You exhaust it of its breath of fäery. It now becomes a tangible and easily appreciable idea—a thing of the earth, earthy. It has not, indeed, lost its power to please, but all which I consider the distinctiveness of that power.[11]

He rails at music which fails in this, singling out a late eighteenth-century piece by Franz Kotzwara, the *Battle of Prague*, laughing at "the interminable drums, trumpets, blunderbusses, and thunder." Here he even gets into matters of orchestration, one of Hitchcock's favorite musical subjects, although now he shows how ludicrous it can be if handled badly, becoming prosaically non-musical (blunderbusses and thunder). Music, he says, should not attempt to imitate anything, and if it does, that should be limited to what the Italian poet Gian Vincenzo Gravina believed possible, "to imitate the natural language of the human feelings and passions."

After this discussion of music he returns to Tennyson, now to matters that could apply most directly to cinematography for Hitchcock: "Tennyson's shorter pieces abound in minute rhythmical lapses sufficient to assure me that—in common with all poets living or dead—he has neglected to make precise investigation of the principle of metre; but, on the other hand, so perfect is his rhythmical instinct in general, that, like the present Viscount Canterbury, he seems to *see with his ear*."[12] Rhythm and meter for both Poe and Hitchcock lie at the center of their views of their respective arts, and Poe's censure here exactly parallels Hitchcock's own disparagement of other directors whose style he claimed he did not like, such as Cecil B. DeMille. Most striking though is Poe's comment that Tennyson could "*see with his ear*" (his emphasis). Here lay the impulse that Hitchcock and Poe had most deeply in common, expressed by Poe in a way that sounds even more apropos to cinema than to poetry. The chapter which follows will attempt to get at this notion—how a film can be thought of as a symphony in a genuine way; the directors Hitchcock encountered in Germany revealed a large part of how it could be possible to see with the ear.

German expressionism

In an interview with Bob Thomas in 1973, Hitchcock recalled the years he spent in Berlin, and emphasized the importance of this experience to his future career—especially the film made immediately after his return: *The Lodger*. In his words, "in 1924 I went to Berlin. These were the great days of German pictures. Ernst Lubitsch was directing Pola Negri, Fritz Lang was making films like *Metropolis*, and F. W. Murnau was making his classic films. The studio where I worked was tremendous, bigger than Universal is today. They had a complete railroad station built on the back lot. For a version of *Siegfried* they built the whole forest of the *Nieblungenlied*."[13] Later in the interview he mentioned one of Murnau's films by name, and in fact while working on *The Blackguard* in 1924, he met Murnau and watched on the set during the shooting of *Der letzte Mann* (*The Last Man*, but titled *The Last Laugh* in the UK and US). It impressed him especially that the "Germans in those times placed great emphasis on telling the story visually; if possible with no titles or at least with very few … In *The Last Laugh* Murnau was able to do that, to dispense with titles altogether except in an epilogue."[14] "Telling the story visually" sounds fairly innocent, but exceptionally complex issues come together here, and one can see him attempting to coordinate these in *The Lodger*, despite his bombardment of it with titles. Perhaps he did not trust his British audiences, steeped in a culture of the written word, to recognize that they did not need titles.

Well aware of that tension between the verbal British and the visual Germans, Hitchcock stated his own position: "I've always believed that you can tell as much visually as you can with words. That's what I learned from the Germans." Early cinema in Britain developed as an extension of the theater, using West End plays and the same actors who appeared on the stage, with the obvious problem for silent films, clearly recognized by Hitchcock, that "when people opened their mouths, nothing came out."[15] Titles had to compensate for the lack of sound, and as a titles man during his earliest film apprenticeship, Hitchcock assumed before he went to Germany that cinema had to be that way. Of course the Germans did not invent cinema any more than the British did, and filmmakers such as Wiene, Lubitsch, Ruttmann, Lang, and Murnau took their inspiration from another medium; the one they chose appears to have been music. We see that in titles calling films symphonies, such as Walter Ruttmann's *Berlin, die Symphonie der Grossstadt* (*Berlin, Symphony of a Great City*, 1927) and Murnau's *Nosferatu, eine Symphonie des Grauens* (*Nosferatu, a Symphony of Horror*, 1922); to that we can add Murnau's first American film *Sunrise: A Song of Two Humans* (1927). Other aspects of the underlying musical urge lie even deeper, and Murnau tries to explain this by drawing a parallel between visual architecture and music:

> What I refer to is the fluid architecture of bodies with blood in their veins moving through mobile space; the interplay of lines rising, falling, disappearing; the encounter of surfaces, stimulation and its opposite, calm; construction and collapse; the formation and destruction of a hitherto almost unsuspected life; all this adds up to a symphony made up of the harmony of bodies and the rhythm of space; the *play of pure movement*, vigorous and abundant.[16]

This idea of pure cinema inspired by music had not yet been achieved, despite his innovations with the moveable camera: "All this we shall be able to create when the camera has at last been de-materialized."

Again he uses the word "symphony," but his sense of a musical model appeared to go well beyond that genre. No one had a stronger influence on all the arts in early twentieth-century Germany than Richard Wagner, and Murnau, along with Lang and other filmmakers, saw much in Wagner that they could apply to film. Lang for one used subject matter closely related to Wagner in his *Nibelungen* films, noted by Hitchcock above, although he adapted it in a way that achieves different ends than Wagner does in the *Ring* cycle.[17]

While Murnau does not use any legends as close to Wagner's as Lang had, elements of Wagnerian subject matter make themselves evident in his films, and perhaps none more starkly than the effect of *Der fliegende Hollender* on *Nosferatu*. In her book *From Wagner to Murnau*, Jo Leslie Collier argues that Wagner permeates Murnau's vision of film at just about every possible level, and for the most part she does this convincingly. This includes parallels in subject matter, although here her persuasiveness slips a little, for example in drawing doubtful connections between *Die Meistersinger* and *Der letzte Mann*. More successfully she shows that "the cycle of anti-realistic-romantic theatrical expression which had its roots in Richard Wagner ultimately reached its peak in the work of Friedrich Wilhelm Murnau," and here she includes "Murnau's long-takes, deep-focus photography, his use of the moving camera, his preference for the long shot rather than the close-up, his chiaroscuro, his arresting use of shadow and silhouette," and various other features.[18] Perhaps most interesting is her demonstration of the role of music in Murnau's treatment of *mise en scène*, suggesting that "he strived as his theatrical predecessors had before him to create a visual equivalent of music," often using "the movement of actors and objects within the frame to establish rhythm and tempo." Going beyond the description of a film as a symphony, he used more specific musical terminology, describing the function of blocking as an attempt "to convey the film's 'tonal chords' or 'dramatic chords in space'."[19]

Eisenstein, Pudovkin, and others would similarly use musical terminology to describe aspects of film technique, and so of course does Hitchcock, to be discussed in some detail later in this chapter. As for Wagner, Hitchcock's own strong interest in his music may very well have been solidified in Germany during the mid-1920s, where no lack of exposure existed, and he could observe the effect of Wagner on other filmmakers. As noted in the Introduction, on at least one occasion he declared Wagner to be his favorite composer,[20] and Wagner played, as Chapter 8 will argue, a decisive role in his films throughout his career.

Lang and Murnau appeared to be among the first to recognize the great potential that Wagner had for filmmaking, although some of this came not directly from Germany but via America, in the work of D. W. Griffith, himself an avid Wagnerian. For Griffith and others this worked primarily at an emotional level, but for the Germans this also included the sense of Wagner's notion of the *Gesamtkunstwerk* (the all-embracing artwork). Heinrich C. Richter, the designer for *Der Januskopf* and *Der Gang in die Nacht*, wrote that "Murnau concerned himself with lighting effects because he did all he could to make a film a total work of art."[21] Wagner attempted on his own to pull together as much as possible the various facets that make up an opera, and while Murnau concerned himself deeply with all aspects of making a film, he relied heavily on his excellent collaborators, such as Richter, Carl Mayer, Robert Herlth, Walter Röhrig, Erich Pommer, and Emil Jannings in *Der letzte Mann*, making innovations as a result of their collective efforts.[22] The same can be said of Hitchcock, although after the French new wave critics discovered him and bestowed on him the mantle of *auteur*, his comments about collaboration turned out to be much less generous. Part of the process in creating the *Gesamtkunstwerk* for Murnau involved the elaborate planning of every aspect of the film, and that could take months of preparation. Hitchcock surely learned much about this type of meticulous construction in Germany as well, and we find it reflected in his often-repeated comment that he enjoyed planning shots, but not executing them.[23]

D. W. Griffith

By 1929 Hitchcock had become much more aware of the achievements of Griffith, and that awareness reflected on some of his own procedures. Truffaut reminded him of his frequent quotation, that, "like all directors, I was influenced by Griffith."[24] Hitchcock added that "I especially remember *Intolerance* and *The Birth of a Nation*," and while he no doubt did, in his usual reluctance to give credit where it is due, he failed to mention how he probably gained his first exposure to Griffith. This almost certainly came from his future wife Alma, who had worked on Griffith's production of *Heart of the World* in 1918, shot in London using Twickenham personnel. Like Hitchcock with Murnau, Alma met Griffith while doing this work, and in the words of her daughter Pat Hitchcock O'Connell, "how stimulating it must have been to Alma to be part of such an exciting project— and how inspiring for her to be a witness to the production, even in a very modest position." To put it into an up-to-date perspective, she compared it to working on a Steven Spielberg movie today, and reflected "that my mother was in essence being exposed to American filmmakers and receiving an education from people who were far more advanced than their British counterparts."[25] In fact, as early as 1931, Hitchcock wrote an essay on Griffith, with the title "A Columbus of the Screen," published in *Film Weekly*, with exceptionally high praise for Griffith, giving him credit for "revolution-izing Motion Picture drama and founding the modern technique of the art." Sidney Gottlieb, who discovered this essay, takes the view that Griffith's own admiration for Poe undoubtedly assisted Hitchcock in discovering how to transform aspects of Poe into cinematic form.[26]

As the most talented maker of silent films in the world, Griffith exerted an extraordinary influence in every possible country, certainly on the Russians, and also in Britain, where Hitchcock, through Alma, whom he would marry not long after her employment under Griffith, would incorporate some of his techniques into his own films. In his 1965 *Encyclopaedia Britannica* entry "Film Production," Hitchcock made his views on Griffith clear—this director "who contributed more than almost any other single individual to the establishment of the technique of filmmaking." His importance to Hitchcock lay in treating film as something other than theater, taking the camera and moving "it in from its position at the proscenium arch ... to a close-up of the actors." But more importantly, "Griffith began to set the strips of film together in a sequence and rhythm that came to be known as montage; it took the action outside the confines of time and space, even as they apply to the theater."[27] He used almost identical words in his interview with Truffaut: "The next major step was when Griffith, improving on the earlier efforts of the British G. A. Smith and the American Edwin S. Porter, began to get the strips of film together in sequence. This was the beginning of cinematographic rhythm through the use of montage."[28]

Just as Griffith had recounted the deficiency of sound film in relation to music, Hitchcock took a very similar view, lamenting that along with the harm done by the talkies to action, "it did just as much damage to music." With their obsession for words, producers and directors "forgot that one of the greatest emotional factors in the silent cinema was the musical accompaniment."[29] Clearly he does not mean this in the obvious way of the Wurlitzer organist improvising an accompaniment as the film rolls; in that respect a soundtrack provided a great advantage, of coordinating the accompa-niment with the picture, and giving the director control over what the music would be. Hitchcock embraced this possibility wholeheartedly, and used the soundtrack effectively in his earlier sound films, for example the shaving scene in *Murder!* (1930) with the music from

Wagner's *Tristan und Isolde*, and he would continue this brilliantly in. all of his subsequent films. He comes closer to what he has in mind when describing a certain type of scene, where

> music makes it possible to express the unspoken. For instance, two people may be saying one thing and thinking something very different. Their looks match their words, not their thoughts. They may be talking politely and quietly, but there may be a storm coming. You cannot express the mood of that situation by word and photograph. But I think you could get at the underlying idea with the right background music.[30]

Here he speaks of the effect of audible music, but that could also work the other way round, where music gives rise to the actual visual presentation.

V. I. Pudovkin

In speaking about Griffith and montage, Hitchcock always included the word "rhythm" to qualify what he meant by montage, and while he could perceive this in the films of Griffith, his specific understanding of it owes much more to the Russian directors, who themselves had learned from Griffith. Discovering the Russians in the late 1920s in London proved to be not all that difficult, in part through the recently formed Film Society of London—eagerly joined by Hitchcock, and most directly through activities and promotion by Ivor Montagu. An urbane youth (five years younger than Hitchcock) with a Cambridge education, Montagu entered the film scene as much a critic as filmmaker, and the respect accorded him by people such as Hitchcock's boss Michael Balcon drew him into direct contact with the industry. Montagu became one of the most active members of the Film Society, and Balcon hired him to work on Hitchcock films, first on *The Lodger* to do editing and titles, then as an editorial consultant on *Downhill*, and again as editor on *Easy Virtue*. By 1927 Hitchcock knew him well and respected him, even accepting the criticism that Montagu offered on *The Lodger*.

Fairly fluent in Russian, Montagu had visited the Soviet Union where he met Eisenstein and discussed principles of editing with him,[31] and he probably met V. I. Pudovkin on the same trip. Almost certainly at Montagu's urging, Pudovkin came to London in 1929 and gave a lecture at the Film Society on 3 February,[32] a lecture Hitchcock would not have missed. At the same time Montagu began to translate Pudovkin's writing, and Victor Gollancz published his *Pudovkin on Film Technique* in English in 1929. In his own essays and interviews Hitchcock often referred to Pudovkin along with the other Russians, as in his essay for the *Encyclopaedia Britannica*: "The Russian filmmakers, Eisenstein, Pudovkin, and their contemporaries, in the late 1920s developed creative editing, or montage, as they called it, by way of the juxtaposition not just of sequences but also of individual shots or frames, to illustrate character, to convey ideas or even to create motion by the juxtaposition of static objects."[33] In his own descriptions of various aspects of editing, one often finds Hitchcock using terms or analogies very similar to those of Pudovkin.

Montage for Pudovkin and the other Russians became the most important principle in filmmaking, not only as a technique but as that which gave a film its expressive and emotional essence. With montage the filmmaker did not simply let the camera roll, putting theater on the screen, but instead got at the essence of perception, finding the difference between the world itself and the fractured way we experience it. They regarded variance of time as central to this distinction, and that variance can best be expressed with musical terminology, especially rhythm and tempo in their different fluctuations. Pudovkin explains this sense of perception and its bearing on emotions in this way:

> Always there exist two rhythms, the rhythmic course of the objective world and the tempo and rhythm with which man observes the world. The world is a whole rhythm, while man receives only partial impressions of this world through his eyes and ears and to a lesser extent through his very skin. The tempo of his impressions varies with the rousing and calming of his emotions, while the rhythm of the objective world he perceives continues in unchanged tempo.

Many philosophers have discussed these contrasting types of time, using terms such as "a priori" or ontological time for one type, and psychological time for the other, but Pudovkin wishes to apply these specifically to the art of the filmmaker, continuing his discourse with this: "The course of man's perceptions is like editing, the arrangement of which can make corresponding variations in speed, with sound just as with image."[34] At the heart of this notion of perception lay the way in which the camera would be used; through the maneuvering of the camera it became possible for a new expressiveness to be achieved, and he credits this discovery to the Americans. In this way the camera becomes charged with life, and through movement it can be transformed from a motionless spectator to an active observer, since the director's control of it "could not merely enable the spectator to see the object shot, but could induce him to apprehend it. It was at this moment that the concepts *close-up*, *mid-shot*, and *long-shot* first appeared in cinematography, concepts that later played an enormous part in the creative craft of editing, the basis of the work of film direction."[35] More than anywhere he defines the contrast with the theater here, clarifying the role of the moving camera in the editing process, and the bearing of the camera and editing on emotions and perception.

Constructive editing, then, allows the director to shape the world for the benefit of the audience at a much deeper and more sophisticated level than the images themselves, giving an underlying essence to the images that parallel our most fundamental modes of perception. This of course involves much more than merely tinkering with tempos or rhythms to generate psychological time, or time that passes in accordance with the variables of our emotions; at its best it goes to an even deeper level, one that has an underlying idea behind it. This underlying idea more often than not cannot be described with words, but requires other modes of expression to make sense of it, the same types that give us poetry or music. Pudovkin tries to get at this notion at various points in his discourse, and he usually does a better job of saying what it is not than what it is. He cannot imagine it in films with star actors, who command most of the attention of the film, but only in a different type of film:

To the second group belong those films that are underlain by some definite idea or thought. These scenarios are not written for an actor, but actors must be found for their realisation when written. Thus works David Griffith. It is not, therefore, remarkable that in several of his pictures Griffith rejects such brilliant names as Pickford, Mae Marsh, and others ... To that extent to which a film is basically inspired by some thought, by some definite idea—and not merely by the display of clever technique or a pretty face—the relationship between the actor and the material of the film receives a special and specific character, proper only to the film.[36]

This type of filmmaking requires "work on the formation of the 'essence' of the picture, the necessity for an organic dependence between the developing action and the surrounding."[37] Not always able to explain this essence, he sometimes realized what it was when he saw it on the screen: "After the actual shooting, I edited it differently—more complexly, using shots taken at various speeds. With each separate set-up were new, more finely graduated speeds. When I saw the result upon the screen I realised that the idea was sound."[38] With this, he could reach to that deeper level, and in part it could be explained with musical terminology, as he continues: "The new rhythm, independent of the real, deriving from the combination of shots at a variety of speeds, yielded a deepened, one might say remarkably enriched, sense of the process portrayed upon the screen."

The attempts to explain montage and the deeper essence of film for Pudovkin run parallel to music in the strongest possible ways, and even when he makes analogies to literature (and Hitchcock used the same ones), he generally brings them back to music, invoking writers such as Poe who themselves thought in musical terms. In fact, in discussing Griffith's working out of a scenario, he puts it into operatic terms, something Griffith (as an aspiring singer) would have appreciated, pointing out that "written though it may be in purely literary phraseology, such a treatment will provide the libretto, as it were."[39] In his essay On Film Technique, which Hitchcock read probably in 1929, he makes numerous explanations of the filmmaker's art in musical terms, and he draws some of his colleagues into the discussion as well: "From our contemporary point of view, Kuleshov's ideas were extremely simple. All he said was this: 'In every art there must be firstly a material, and secondly a method of composing this material specifically adapted to this art.' The musician has sounds as material and composes them in time."[40] Elsewhere he uses descriptions that Hitchcock would repeat in almost identical form, such as this description of his work on parts of *Deserter*: "Here I had a real musical task, and was obliged to 'feel' the length of each strip in the same spirit as a musician 'feels' the accent necessary for each note."[41] In a later essay he wrote that "a film, a work the material of which includes the acting of actors, can attain, in the exactitude and precision of its rhythmic construction, the exactitude of the rhythmic construction of a musical composition."[42]

Of the musical terminology Pudovkin uses to elucidate montage, no word comes up as often as "rhythm," and this he reinforces over and over "as the means of emotionally influencing the spectator."[43] On this of course he agrees fully with Eisenstein, for whom "rhythmic montage" stands as the most fundamental of his different types of montage, and the two of them also agree on the usefulness of the term "counterpoint" to represent juxtapositions that may seem contradictory. Pudovkin also readily uses musical terms such as "crescendo," "diminuendo," and "staccato" to describe various types of accentuation or the possibilities of building toward climaxes or the reduction of tension. Hitchcock undoubtedly picked up his favorite analogy with an orchestra from Pudovkin, who spoke of orchestrating sound effects in sound films, editing the sound in an attempt "to use the pieces like the separate instruments that combine to form an orchestra." And earlier in the anticipation of sound in cinema, he speculated that "the real future belongs to sound films of another kind. I visualise a film in which sounds and human speech are wedded to the visual images on the screen in the same way as that in which two or more melodies can be combined by an orchestra."[44]

The connection between Hitchcock's own comments and Pudovkin's cannot be mistaken, as in this one by Hitchcock already cited: "Film music and cutting have a great deal in common. The purpose of both is to create the tempo and mood of the scene." Like Pudovkin he gave the credit to Griffith, who "began to set the strips of film together in a sequence and rhythm that came to be known as montage."[45] Extending that notion to music, he told Peter Bogdanovich that "pure cinema is complementary pieces of film put together, like notes of music make a melody. There are two primary uses of cutting or montage in film: montage to create ideas, and montage to create violence and emotions."[46] In speaking to Truffaut about an effect used near the end of *The Trouble with Harry*, he called it "the equivalent of the crescendo or the coda in my other films."[47] In comparing editing with the activity of a musician, it mystified Hitchcock "why so many other filmmakers need to see things on the screen before they edit, whereas a musician can hear his music simply by looking at the notes and lines of his score."[48] Following up on Pudovkin's ideas about camera motion, Hitchcock gave it specific musical significance, this time in reference to *Psycho*: "From a high angle to a big close-up. It's orchestration again, you see?"[49] Sharing Pudovkin's view that cinema had to be fundamentally different from the theater, Hitchcock noted how in being "anti-literary and purely cinematic," that "cinema, approached in this way, becomes a truly abstract art, like music."[50] Hitchcock had no particular interest in this type of theory for its own sake; for him these formulations get at the heart of what he hoped to accomplish as a practical filmmaker, and no two films illustrate these attempts at this point in his career as clearly as *The Lodger* and *Blackmail*.

2

The Lodger: A London symphony

Immediately after his two-year sojourn in Germany, where he worked at the Ufa Babelsberg studio just outside Berlin, Hitchcock, back in London, started work in 1926 on his third film, with the full title *The Lodger, A Story of the London Fog*. Looking back on the achievement almost four decades later, he made these comments to François Truffaut: "*The Lodger* is the first picture possibly influenced by my period in Germany. The whole approach to this film was instinctive with me. It was the first time I exercised my style. In truth, you might almost say that *The Lodger* was my first picture … As a matter of fact, I took a pure narrative and, for the first time, presented ideas in purely visual terms."[1] Despite the difficulties of sorting out fact from fiction in these interviews, much of what he says here rings true, certainly concerning the German influence, and the distinctiveness of *The Lodger* in relation to the earlier *The Pleasure Garden* and *The Mountain Eagle*. More troublesome are words such as "instinctive with me," "I exercised my style," and "presented ideas in purely visual terms," which put him firmly in control, taking all the credit for the film that the British press hailed as the best British film to date, no doubt following Truffaut's prompting about him being an *auteur*. A highly visual film to be sure, but Hitchcock, despite his two years in Germany and contact with F. W. Murnau, lacked the sense not to clutter it with intertitles. Ivor

Montagu, who later had the task for getting rid of most of the titles, claimed it originally had "in the region of 350 to 500,"[2] although he surely exaggerated, since that number would have added 30 minutes to the film. Presumably he meant it contained far too many, a failing that could certainly be attributed to the fact that Hitchcock had previously been a writer of titles for the films of others, and apparently remained mired in an excessive need for that type of narrative. Hitchcock worked with very good people on this film, which aside from Montagu (editing and titles) included Alma Reville (assistant director), Michael Balcon (producer), Eliot Stannard (screenplay), and Baron [Gaetano] Ventimiglia (photography); thanks to all of them the film turned out as it did. In this case they together represent the "corporate" Hitchcock; he was only as good as the people that worked with him, although certainly many of the best ideas he could claim as his own.

Something special did happen in *The Lodger*, and despite its full title, a title more descriptive of its actual essence might be *The Lodger: A London Symphony*. Hitchcock told Peter Bogdanovich that since 1928 he had wanted to make a film of London which he would call *Life of a City*, something that would cover the city from dawn to dawn, getting at "the backstage of a city." Sidney Gottlieb rightly compares this project with Walter Ruttmann's 1927 film *Berlin, die Symphonie der Grossstadt* (*Berlin, Symphony of a Great City*) "which told the life of a people by a rhythmic and stylized presentation of their comings and goings, their environment, their shapes and spaces, and so on."[3] To a limited extent Hitchcock achieved this type of symphonic approach in *The Lodger*, and he would take that much further with *Blackmail* a few years later. Ruttmann had not yet made his film in 1926, but Hitchcock's idol Murnau had made his "symphony" *Nosferatu, eine Symphonie des Grauens* (*Nosferatu, a Symphony of Horror*, 1922) well before that point. Hitchcock's notion of the symphony in *The Lodger* combines the city and horror, and certain parallels with *Nosferatu* cannot be mistaken.

Calling a film a symphony may at first strike one as nothing more than a convenient label, but there appears to be more to it. At this point in the 1920s film still remained at a stage of relative infancy, which Hitchcock himself compared in 1927 to the theater: "The stage drama has been 2,000 years in reaching its present state of perfection—or imperfection! The film show, in less than 20 years, has made much quicker strides."[4] By no coincidence does he refer to the imperfections of the theater, especially when comparing the theater with film. Of both silent and sound pictures he consistently felt throughout his life that the theater provided a poor model for film, and his own films that merely adapted plays, such as the silent *The Farmer's Wife* or the sound *Juno and the Paycock*, he considered among his poorest efforts. He liked comparisons with the other arts, and in the same 1927 article, "Films We Could Make," he takes this further, pointing out that film "differs from the novel, the play, music, and the ballet. Perhaps it approaches nearest to music and the ballet. It can play on the emotions and can delight the eye."[5] Writing this in November 1927, only a year after the release of *The Lodger*, he tried to get at one of the most basic of his notions of filmmaking: the role that music could play in providing the underlying impulse for a film.

Not only does he suggest a general role for music, and rhythm in particular, but he even points to the possibility of a specific musical work doing this: "But suppose we *could* make really artistic films for the artistically minded minority. Could we not then make as beautiful a film about rain as Debussy did a tone poem in his '*Jardins sous la pluie*'? And what a lovely film of rhythmic movement and light and shade we could make out of cloud studies—a sort of film interpretation of Shelley's "The Cloud'."[6] Here he suggests a literary representation of clouds, but while thinking about Debussy, he could also have referred to "Les Neiges" from *Les Preludes*. Hitchcock's wistful thinking about art films may have resulted from his unfortunate experience with *The Lodger*, shelved temporarily by the studio brass who doubted it would have any audience appeal, although by the time of the writing of this article, the brass had been proved wrong. In fact the possibility of combining "art" and "popular" ultimately proved to be entirely viable, although at this point it seemed unlikely to be a trend in the UK: "Such things have been attempted on the Continent, where they frequently make pictures for love rather than profit; one German producer even makes film studies of cubes and circles which change their shape as they move over the screen in rhythmic form like a Cubist painting in motion. But those things are not for the present, though they suggest how the film may become an artistic medium." In the same article he makes much of tempo in films, and tempo creates the mood: "We call it 'tempo,' and by paying careful attention to the speed with which we act our little plays we do attempt to guide the observing minds into the right mood."[7]

With this emphasis on music, and especially rhythm and tempo, he may very well have been talking about *The Lodger*, in which musical ideas may have helped him in his formulation of visual constructions. His attempts to describe this phenomenon, as early as 1927 and at every point throughout his life, get at the principle, which also includes references to orchestration, harmony, and melody, but without a descriptive precision that a more musically literate person would use. In fact, had he been more musically literate, he may have been less inclined to make musical references the way he did. With his non-professional knowledge of music and enduring love of music, it seemed the perfect medium to bring into play in building his conception of cinema, and here he stood in very good company, since the German directors he admired, along with D. W. Griffith, had done the same. The Russians, such as Eisenstein, Pudovkin, Kuleshov, and Dovzhenko, would add another large piece to the equation, but for Hitchcock, knowledge of that and application of their musical principles of montage would come a couple of years later. That is not to say that *The Lodger* lacks montage, but in this case other techniques play a greater role in transferring musical principles into visual ones; for now, those other forces predominated. The key role that music (and ballet) plays in the film shows up in a number of choices, both on and below the surface. The murders of the Avenger unfold against the background (in fact backstage) of a West End musical, "Golden Curls," with the actresses as primary and likely victims because of the Avenger's preference for blondes, although they do not always take the threat seriously. The central scene of the murder of the Lodger's sister happens at her coming out ball, where everyone dances. The central character, the Lodger, is played by Ivor Novello, a prominent musician, who, like Geraldine Farrar in DeMille's early films, could put his considerable musical talent to work in generating the appropriate moods and emotions. Farrar had in a sense transferred her operatic voice to the silent screen,[8] and Novello may have had similar expectations placed on him.

Mise en scène and orchestration

When Hitchcock spoke of the Germans telling a story visually and of the importance of construction, he surely had shots by those such as Murnau and others that he knew in mind. Putting this into more specific terms than Murnau had, he said, as I noted in the Introduction, "construction to me, it's like music." If he had stopped with that, we could put it down to a nice comparison with no great significance, but he does not. Here and elsewhere he gets fairly specific about what he means, in the case of this quotation following with "you start with your allegro, your andante, and you build up."[9] In this instance he uses tempo indicators, but elsewhere he applies a full spectrum of musical terminology, covering orchestration, dynamics, pitch, rhythm, and tempo. In some cases he drew a specific parallel between musical elements and a certain type of shot, such as this comment also noted in the Introduction: "At times, I have the feeling I'm an orchestra conductor, a trumpet sound corresponding to a close shot and a distant shot suggesting an entire orchestra performing a muted accompaniment."[10] In this way the film becomes decidedly orchestral, and in the case of *Psycho*, he suggested how this could work: "But the main reason for raising the camera so high was to get the contrast between the long shot and the close-up of the big head as the knife came down at him [Arbogast at the top of the stairs]. It was like music, you see, the high shot with the violins, and suddenly the big head with the brass instruments clashing."[11] His description here has nothing to do with Bernard Herrmann's music for the film, which does not use any instruments other than strings; instead of the actual music, this refers to the musical ideal in the director's own mind which gives the essence to the visual images. Not only did he make these comments to Truffaut, but he said something almost identical to Peter Bogdanovich: "From a high angle to a big close-up. It's orchestration again, you see."[12]

Of course he does not give us a catalog of correspondences here, merely a prompting, but if we follow his prompting, it leads to a fascinating view of how he may have thought. That would change in the late 1920s when montage became a more significant part of the equation, but for the moment, with the German influences that contributed to his conception of *The Lodger*, the musical parallels apply primarily to *mise en scène*. He refers specifically to the parallels between orchestral instruments and long shots or close-ups, but other aspects of spatial construction and motion in a shot can also have musical parallels. Similarly, when Murnau spoke of construction as "the harmony of bodies and the rhythm of space" together creating a symphony, he appears to have had more than musical imagery in mind, thinking of shot construction in the way that a composer uses the various elements of music to combine the actual sounds, and then places these sounds in motion. Murnau does little more than tease us with this possibility, and in fact we discover much more directly from Hitchcock how this may have been conceived. To get some sense of this, certain shots are worth describing in detail to consider the various elements of the filmmakers' craft that they embrace.

Numerous shots could be used as outstanding examples, but sometimes because of the placement of a shot it will gain special importance. In the case of Murnau, that can happen with the first shot of a film following the titles, since that shot, like the prelude or overture to an opera, may set the tone for the entire film that follows in the intricate way that it engages the eye. Here we could use just about any film by Murnau, but I will limit this to two films made before *The Lodger*, films that Hitchcock knew well: *Nosferatu* and *Der letzte Mann*. *Nosferatu* begins with a composition shot that lasts only about three seconds, giving a church roof and steeple in the foreground, and a square in the town of Bremen in the background. The steeple dominates the center of the shot, and divides our view of the town non-symmetrically, with an open square (except for a small rotunda) on the left, partly obscured by trees, and a concentration of houses and other buildings on either side, houses and shops on the left and more official buildings to the right. Through the steeple's vaulting in the center of the shot we can see a small portion of the square and the bottoms of buildings. The nature of the shot creates something of its own motion in the way it prompts the eye to move, taking in the steeple and then moving back on either side, but another element of motion also comes into play as a few people can be seen in the square, walking in both directions at varying speeds. They especially catch our attention seen through the steeple's vaulting, giving us a bird's-eye view of people through the prism of the church.

Light, or chiaroscuro, plays a key role in the shot, brightest on the square in the center, and then darkening around the perimeter of the shot, fading into obscurity and creating some sense of menace as the eye moves from the stability of the light to the eeriness of the darkness. The position of the camera also comes into play, with its vantage point high above the town, making the church loom prominently while diminishing humans in the background. As the film proceeds, the church and religion have little or no direct role, but as the central part of the first image we see, the church sticks subconsciously in the mind as a perspective for the mysterious things that unfold for which religion cannot account. In the opening scene, the church steeple stands out in the foreground, as a single instrument does in a concerto, or as an obligato instrument in an orchestral work. In this case foreground and background intermingle, as we can see through the open vaulted space of the steeple a portion of the town square and people walking, and here we have the thematic interplay of the of the soloist and orchestra, sharing and exchanging thematic or motivic material. Foreground and background will be a factor in just about every shot, and in general that balance can be similar to the relationship of melody and harmony. An almost infinite number of ways exist to combine these, for example in film using or not using deep focus (a later technique); similarly in music melody and harmony can be closely related or starkly separated.

While spatial composition dominates the opening shot of *Nosferatu*, Murnau features motion in the more complex opening of *Der letzte Mann*, a film made a few years later. The opening shot lasts about 12 seconds, and the most visually striking element lies in the motion of the camera, in a descending elevator, with the outer cage of the elevator framing everything we see, especially the horizontal supports which create a metric pulse as they go by. Since the elevator starts fairly high up, the people on the hotel lobby floor appear from a long shot at the beginning of the shot, but they move through a middle shot to a close-up (figures from the back) as the elevator approaches the floor level. On the floor the movement of the hotel patrons establishes a fairly complex series of tempos, with people moving in all directions at paces ranging from barely moving to almost running. The fluid motion here gives a different sense of space, with the motion itself determining our response to that space, and again light plays a key role. The darkened frame of the elevator cage provides the frame for the shot, and the brightness of the floor stands in marked contrast. This shot does much more than merely give us the principal setting for the film, the Hotel Atlantic, a bustling city hotel with a tempo exceeding what the old doorman (Emil Jannings) can manage. Throughout the film we see Jannings moving very slowly, and his tempo stands in extreme contrast to the pace of the job that provides his identity and on which his reputation and social credibility depend.

Mise en scène most often involves a combination of spatial design and motion, with many possible gradations, and the potential for either one to take the lead. The elements that make up the spatial design may themselves be the objects in motion, as would be true in a dance scene or the door scene in *Der letzte Mann*, making it all but impossible to separate space and motion as distinctive elements. Music, especially for orchestra, similarly can be divided in this way, and in both cases the spatial element must be experienced in passing time. The spatial component of music comes from the sound itself, generated by the instruments of the orchestra in their various combinations. This can be fairly static if one hears the same combination of instruments for a short or longer period of time, or it can be highly active if the orchestration itself fluctuates constantly. Some composers will occasionally make orchestration the central feature of a work, minimizing the other elements such as thematic material, harmony, or rhythm, allowing the progression of the work to unfold through its changing orchestration. Ravel does this in *Bolero*, using a repetitive theme and rhythm throughout, providing development by way of the changing orchestration of the theme and its background. Arnold Schoenberg goes even further in the third movement of his Five Pieces for Orchestra, Op. 16, "Farben" (Colors), avoiding thematic material altogether, and instead providing the shifts of color through frequently changing orchestration. Here we have the ultimate fusion in music of spatial elements and motion, although in an unusual way; most music will combine the changes in orchestration with the development of themes, harmony, tonality, and rhythm.

Hitchcock returns frequently to the analogy of orchestrating his shots, and one can see why he would. The density of a shot, for example one combining numerous objects, could be the parallel of full orchestration, merging all or many instruments that make up an orchestra, although typically not all will be heard at the same time, allowing for the variations of color. While orchestration remained central to the quality of all nineteenth-century orchestral music, certain composers took it to new heights late in the century and early in the twentieth century, most notable among them Rimsky-Korsakov, Debussy, Ravel, Richard Strauss, and Gustav Mahler, all of whom could use orchestration as another facet of virtuosity. As a keen concert attendee, Hitchcock knew works by all of them, and occasionally mentions them. Even in their piano works he seemed able to recognize shifts in color, as he did with Debussy's "Jardins sous la Pluie" from *Estampes* (although he may have heard an orchestrated version of this piece, that being a popular practice at the time). Brilliance in complex shot-making could certainly be related to the virtuosity we find in the orchestrations by these composers. Shots of course could also be very simple, focusing on a single object or person, and here too orchestration could be a prompter, in the use of a single instrument or a small combination of instruments.

The all-important treatment of light in a shot can also be related to orchestration. At the time, of course, film used only black and white, but the balance of these, through chiaroscuro, took on the quality of color. While orchestration plays a role here, so do the other facets of music, with low instruments (especially in their low registers) suggesting something dark or indefinite, while light relates to the clarity that arises from well-defined melody and harmony in a medium or higher range. Light and darkness can also become part of the motion, most obviously in the searching flashlight beam, for example, of the night watchman in *Der letzte Mann*, but it can work much more subtly as well, such as with shimmering water, as happens in the sailing scenes in *Nosferatu* or the lake scenes in *Sunrise.* In both of these the shimmering beauty of the water suggests an element of menace, allowing the sparkling blend of darkness and light to carry a complex emotional message. Two composers just prior to this time had brought a shimmering effect in music to perfection, first Ravel and then Debussy, finding extraordinary beauty in some of their piano works with this approach, and then extending it to orchestral works, as Debussy does in *La Mer*. Some of these piano works simply stand as objects of great beauty, such as Ravel's *Jeux d'eau*, but others can be menacing, as the programme for Ravel's *Gaspard de la Nuit* implies. The association with water, as with the impressionist painters, can be very strong, for example in *Jeux d'eau*, and the German filmmakers did not have to look to the French for musical model here but could embrace one of their own. Franz Schubert had already achieved it early in the nineteenth century, in the shimmering representation of the brook in his song cycle *Die schöne Müllerin*, and in piano works as well, such as the inner voice motion in his Impromptu in G Flat. In fact, Schubert stood as one of the great avant-garde composers of his time, influencing composers a century later with his modulations and other procedures that seemed out of place early in the nineteenth century.

Certain objects or their representation appealed especially to filmmakers in the early 1920s, and none more than the use of stairways. One can see this in the films by Murnau already noted, and Hitchcock takes this even further in *The Lodger*, as a remarkable amount of the film takes place on stairs. Stairways become almost a fetish in his subsequent films, and in part that goes back to his silent films, where they could be used for intense emotional representation. Stairways are transitional, linking the high and the low or things between these, and the movement of someone on a stairway often becomes indicative of an emotional state; sometimes the stairs themselves can do this without the presence of a person. The linkage of high and low has an obvious musical analogy, where rising and falling pitch can play with our emotions in the extreme and can also represent complex narrative matters. Murnau even uses a musical instrument to illustrate the upward motion of sound, in *Der letzte Mann* showing a trumpet whose sound reaches the doorman during the wedding reception, achieving the sense of motion with a moving camera in the courtyard (run in reverse because the camera could only go downward). For the filmmaker, a stairway can be a type of unheard music, representing pitches that rise and fall, and can even have an element of orchestration in the manner of the stairway's representation, both in its actual look (or the shadows that it may cast, including banisters), and in the placement or motion of people on the stairs. Not only does pitch come into play here but so do tempo and rhythm. The stairs themselves may be as simple as the notes of a scale, but scales provide little more than musical building blocks; composers usually do not present scales in their rawest form in musical works, but the music rises and falls to patterns designed by the composers that may very well be underpinned by scales. That rising and falling can happen very quickly, or it can give an entire work its form, as happens in the prelude to *Lohengrin*, making orchestration, thematic working, and dynamics part of the equation. Here Wagner gives us not only emotion but he encapsulates the entire narrative, with everything from brutal strife to the reaching of ecstatic heights. A stairway as central to a film as happens in *The Lodger* can also work both emotionally and formally, by association giving the work a type of musical essence.

While in many respects spatial design and movement cannot be separated, either in film or in music, certain aspects of movement within shots nevertheless require special attention. Murnau highlights the contrast of stasis and frenetic motion in *Der letzte Mann*, showing the beleaguered doorman slumped in a chair in contrast to the whirlwind motion of the hotel lobby and the even more extreme motion of people and cars on the street. Various types of musical analogies for this exist, the most obvious being the contrasts of adagio and allegro (or presto), although these are probably the least useful since as designations they cannot happen simultaneously in music. In film shots not only do these tempos occur simultaneously, but there can be an entire range of tempo options within the same shot, creating a counterpoint of tempos; "counterpoint" turns out to be another of Hitchcock's favorite terms. Music of course has a large range of sophisticated means for achieving this, at a simple level placing two things against each other, or in layers that can be so dense the ear may have difficulty recognizing all the layers. At the simplest level, stasis and motion can occur simultaneously with one note or chord being held while the rest of the music moves actively around it.

The Lodger shots

With the first title image we see in *The Lodger*, Hitchcock pays his debt to the German filmmakers whose works he now knew. The title appears on the left on a dark background diagonally crossing the screen. To the right in a light V-shaped area looms a shadowy figure, giving a composition entirely in the German style. Before the rest of the title comes on, the V-shape closes over the shadowy figure, and when the title finishes, the V re-opens. This stands as one of many acknowledgments to the Germans throughout the film, others including shadows cast by the stairway rails, the Lodger's hands contorted like Nosferatu's, the discomforting light cast on the ceiling through the window of Daisy's mother's room, and the shot composition at the lamp where a murder occurs and where the Lodger and Daisy meet. Along with these fairly obvious signs of indebtedness, many others can be found, primarily in designs within shots of spatial elements and motion. Comparing Hitchcock with Murnau at this stage, especially *Der letzte Mann* which he had observed in the making, Hitchcock's work seems a little unrefined, as one would expect, considering that *The Lodger* offered one of his first opportunities to experiment with style, while Murnau now stood at the height of his career. Seldom do we find the same levels of complexity in Hitchcock's shots, either in spatial terms or the use of motion so common in Murnau's, yet there seems little question that he nudged his shot construction in this direction. He seemed to get his best results using actors to create motion, and the fact that he constructed less elaborate plastic compositions may have something to do with the conditions under which he worked in the UK.

Near the beginning of *The Lodger* he tries to create shots with different levels of motion in them, such as the discovery of the first murder by the Avenger, where a woman witness and two policemen can be seen in one shot followed by a surging crowd in another. The attempt to then put them together in one shot does not work well, since the crowd more or less obliterates our view of the principals; instead of well-defined motion within the shot, we end up seeing a general surge of motion. At this point a type of montage works better, cutting quickly from individuals to the crowd, and finally to newspaper reporters who will set the early context of the film as a story of how the press works. With the shot of the newsroom immediately after the lengthy teletype message, Hitchcock achieves a combination of set and motion comparable to some of Murnau's, with an editor sitting at a desk in the foreground separated from the activity of the newsroom by layers of windows; in the passageways beyond the first set of windows employees can be seen working at desks, some darting in either direction, and others moving more slowly and occasionally stopping. In this nine-second shot he complements the movement of the people with a turning fan-like device, achieving an overall complexity in the counterpoint of motion similar to what composers achieve with counterpoint, along with interesting spatial textures with the separation of layers sustained by the banks of windows. Here then orchestration comes into play in that the visual layers give varying tones and textures, light with persons and objects clearly visible in the foreground, and fading into darker tones further back. We can envisage all of this activity producing something that will end up on the editor's desk, and will gradually progress to the next shot, to a huge press rolling out the newsprint.

Much more motion comes into play as the papers come off the press, are packed into trucks for distribution, and the trucks head out to the newsstands. Hitchcock had some fun with these shots, making the back of one of the trucks look like a human face,[13] but in the most effective of these shots, lasting 19 seconds, he places the camera in the back of a truck, giving a type of moving camera as the truck weaves its way through London streets. Now the motion takes on a new level of complexity as we see people walking on the sidewalks, others crossing the street in front of the truck, and other vehicles driving or standing on the street; all this gains a different type of relativity from the fact that we experience the motion from a perspective of motion—a moving camera. The city streets provide the set, and the set itself moves because of the camera. Here we have the young Hitchcock at his best, experimenting with rhythm and meter within the shot, and also finding orchestrational textures with the proximity of objects of varying sizes to the camera, with moments of tension as swerves prove necessary to avoid collisions.

Numerous other shots throughout the film achieve a formalized type of motion, combining motion and stasis or giving us motion at contrasting tempos. After the newspaper story, Hitchcock takes us backstage at the musical "Golden Curls," showing a woman looking at a newspaper as the girls from the show run toward her and gather round to look at the paper. In contrast to the more generalized motion backstage at the musical, Hitchcock creates motion of an individualized nature in the fashion show in which Daisy (June Tripp) takes part. Here a more elaborate shot construction comes into play, as we see two arched doorways for the models to enter and exit, a broad stairway lined by lamps leading down to the promenade circle, and stationary viewers and attendants around the circle. The models enter through the arch, descend the stairs, walk around the circle doing a full rotation at the end of the circle, go back up the stairs, and leave. Hitchcock also uses some montage to get the full effect, alternating between close-up and medium shots to show different levels of motion. With a medium shot that takes in the entire scene we have a fairly equalized sense of pace, but that changes in the close-up which puts the models at the end of the circle in the foreground walking across the screen, while those on the stairs in the background appear to be moving at a different pace. Hitchcock compares long shots with certain instruments, and in these contrasting shots he achieves a similar effect, both with textures through depth and motion that can vary according to the camera's angle.

Many other shots could be described, including a stage door scene as actors leave, some getting into a car; the aftermath of the murder at the lamp with police, witnesses, and the crowd; people walking back and forth as seen from the window in the lower level of Daisy house; or even the rain on a window. The most discussed scene in the film, of the Lodger seen pacing in his room through a glass floor, of course also involves motion, with the steps that we see in either direction establishing a meter and tempo. When speaking with Truffaut, Hitchcock explained this as a visual representation of sound: "You must remember that we had no sound in those days, so I had a plate-glass floor made through which you could see the Lodger moving back and forth, causing the chandelier in the room below to move with him. Naturally, many of these visual devices would be absolutely superfluous today because we would use sound effects instead. The sound of the steps and so on."[14] Often for Hitchcock little difference existed between sound effects and music, and here music in a sense takes over because of the meter and tempo established; something similar happens when we see a row of policemen marching in line, not entirely in step and thus creating a type of rhythmic/metric tension (on that occasion they do not get their man).

While music underlies these scenes in an indirect way, that changes late in the film as the Lodger describes to Daisy the murder of his sister at her coming out ball, a scene that focuses on brother and sister and all the guests dancing. For the first dance shot the camera fades from the portrait of the sister to the dancing in progress, brother and sister in the foreground surrounded by many dancing couples. A few shots make up this sequence, the first the longest, followed by a second shot that puts brother and sister much more into the foreground. The third shot places more emphasis on composition as the camera withdraws to a lower level, the dancing now seen through a doorway at the top of a short flight of stairs; two women leave the dance floor and descend these stairs. The next shot in fact shows a hand flicking the light switches, creating darkness for the murder, and we immediately get the same shot as before, now with dancing in the dark. At least one commentator has suggested that the Lodger himself may have murdered his sister,[15] although it seems highly unlikely that the Lodger would incriminate himself in his own flashback description for Daisy. The parallel of motion and implied music here may very well help to strengthen the musical essence of the many other scenes involving spatial design and motion.

In the dance scene just described the stairs appear to play an important function, as people are seen descending them just before the lights go out and the murder occurs. Dancing takes place on the elevated level, while the preparation for the murder happens below, and the downward motion we see on the stairs prepares us for the fall of the victim. If one image trumps all others in this film it is that of stairways, most often the same one in Daisy's house leading from the front door foyer to the Lodger's room, but others as well, including those at the fashion show and the curved stairway in the Lodger's opulent house seen at the end of the film. Literally dozens of shots take place on the stairs in Daisy's house, and as in Murnau's films, we know much about characters' emotions by the way they move up or down stairs. When the Lodger first goes to his room, he climbs the stairs slowly, as if apprehensively. Daisy usually bounds up the stairs at a fast or medium pace, with lightness of

2.1 *The Lodger* (Ivor Novello dancing) (The Lodger and his sister in a dance of death)

step as though she is soaring joyously upward. As she forms her first impressions of the Lodger we see her moving down the stairs slowly, clearly in a state of thought.

The levels of the house increasingly come to represent stages of happiness for Daisy, with the kitchen on the bottom level giving the prosaic activities of her family, as well as the usual meeting place with Joe (the policeman Daisy is engaged to). The Lodger's room at the top of the stairs comes to represent first a place of interest and pleasure, but eventually much more than that, even ecstasy as it is here that they first kiss passionately. The Lodger's room for Daisy takes on an almost Wagnerian essence, and her movement up the stairs becomes something akin to the rising pitch and growing orchestration that Senta experiences with the Dutchman, Elizabeth with Tannhäuser, Elsa with Lohengrin, or Isolde with Tristan. With this visual sense of rising and growth, Hitchcock achieves something of that sound impression in pictures, allowing her to soar above her family and Joe in the arms of the Lodger. Since Hitchcock maintains the possibility of the Lodger being the Avenger for much of the film, Daisy's ecstasy may become elevated even higher through an element of danger, at least in the minds of her parents and Joe. Again the parallels with Wagner hold, since love and death are almost always inseparable in his operas; heroines do not always survive to the end of the opera, and the extremes of their love happen because of actions such as taking a love potion when they think it is a death potion (as Tristan and Isolde do).

The stairway that leads to bliss eventually takes Daisy and her parents to the Lodger's house, with all its wealth and high social status. The Lodger has been a type of Lohengrin, descending from his lofty heights to the more common areas of London, on a mission to avenge his sister, but in the process finding love with Daisy and rescuing her from the dismal existence of her small-minded parents and a subservient marriage to Joe. At his house he stands at the top of the curved stairway, now virtually the stairway to heaven for Daisy. Like Lohengrin, he descends to earth, to the prosaic world of returned toothbrushes, and as he and Daisy kiss, the stairs loom prominently in the background, carrying them upward, although we do not see them ascend. They embrace in another room, in front of a window with London fog in the background, and even the lit sign "To-Night, Golden Curls." Like the kiss in the Lodger's room, the camera focuses on them, dollying in so as to make the London background fade out of sight, vanquished from their sanctuary.

Hitchcock also uses montage in this film, for example in the mob chase scene near the end, quickly intercutting between the Lodger fleeing and the crowd in pursuit, placing one against the many, although even here he builds more to a climax through the construction of shots than acceleration generated from montage. The shots of the Lodger suspended from the fence tend to be fairly lengthy, and motion comes from the actions of the crowd. That distinction here holds generally for the film, with its far greater emphasis on *mise en scène* than montage, as was true of the type of construction used by the Germans. Returning to his comments in the interview "On Style" from 1963, in response to what he felt was a lack of shape in Truffaut's *Jules and Jim*, he compared construction in a film to a musical build-up, and we should not "forget even a symphony breaks itself into movements ..." What he describes here may apply more to montage than *mise en scène*, but it certainly addresses both. It was the Germans who called their films symphonies, and in part that sense of a symphony emerged from the components of shots that make it up, most notably in the parallels with orchestration and rhythm. His own attempts to describe the procedure with musical analogies give an interesting insight into the way he thought about these procedures, that he too thought of a silent film as a type of symphony. No interference in this case could arise from the music an audience would hear in the film; the only music that mattered was that which the filmmaker himself would hear and could prompt some of his visual images.

3

The music of montage: *Blackmail*

Only three years elapsed between *The Lodger* and *Blackmail* (1929), but during that time Hitchcock worked at a steady pace, with three films in 1927 (*Downhill*, *Easy Virtue*, and *The Ring*) and three more in 1928 (*The Manxman*, *The Farmer's Wife*, and *Champagne*). As appealing as some of these films may be, with the exception of *The Ring* they generally offered limited opportunities to try new experiments with visual techniques, and one finds fewer of the elaborately constructed shots in these that characterized *The Lodger*, although by no means do they lack them.[1] In 1929 two extraordinarily important things happened that had the profoundest possible effect on Hitchcock as a filmmaker, and he made the most of the new possibilities. The most obvious of the two was the advent of sound, initiated in the United States with technology such as the Vitaphone (a sound disk that would run simultaneously with the film), and then the soundtrack, which allowed actual dialogue as well as music and sound effects to be precisely synchronized with the pictures. The other development, less obvious but every bit as important, was Hitchcock's awareness of what D. W. Griffith and the Russians such as Eisenstein, Pudovkin, Dovzhenko, and Kuleshov achieved with montage, or constructive editing, in their films; with some of these he also took note of their theorizing about film.

Filmgoers of the twenty-first century sometimes think of silent movies as an unfortunate primitive stage that the industry had to traverse before real film arrived with sound. This misguided view tends most of all to be associated with Hollywood, where studios found that the best way to sell their product to the public was to create stars, with the primary role of the camera being to give the best possible shots of these icons. With sound this took a large step forward, since audiences could now not only see their beloved stars but hear them as well, and it should not surprise us that the Americans preceded the Europeans not only in sound technology but also in the inclination to use it. An audible Al Jolson or John Barrymore proved immensely more appealing to the public than a silent one. Not everyone, though, embraced sound with open arms, and while most directors made the transition without too much difficulty, a few, including some of the best, remained somewhat ambivalent about the virtues of sound. Griffith stands out most notably among these; his two final films, *Abraham Lincoln* (1930) and *The Struggle* (1931), both with sound, stand as two of the weakest of his career, although curiously Hitchcock gave high praise to the former.[2] Expressing his preference decidedly for silent film, Griffith contended that "the very nature of the films forgoes not only the necessity for but the propriety of the spoken voice. Music—fine music—will always be the voice of the silent drama ... We do not want now and we never shall want the human voice with our films."[3] This may seem a little ingenuous, but probably contains an element of truth. His earlier films had set the standard and had been a beacon around the world for how technique could profoundly affect an audience; with sound he appeared to be out of his element.

Having made nine silent films by this time, and still very much at the beginning of his career, Hitchcock, a great admirer of Griffith, had to decide his own strategy on the matter, and *Blackmail* thrust him into the fray in a most unusual way. *Blackmail* generally receives the credit for being the first sound film in Britain,[4] and since not all theaters in the UK would be able to present the sound version in 1929, he made both sound and silent versions of it. The expectation was that he would essentially make a silent film with music on the soundtrack and then add dialogue to the final reel, but that very clearly did not happen. Hitchcock actually made two substantially different versions of the film, not simply dubbing the silent one with dialogue,[5] and his curious way of presenting the sound version at times gives the sense of being a comparison between the two, showing both the advantages and disadvantages of sound. His most famous experiment with sound here, the knife sequence, showing a neighborhood busybody repeating the word "knife" with accentuation and rhythmic acceleration, demonstrated a virtue of sound that few would have suspected possible. But not entirely convinced of the value of dialogue, Hitchcock also reveals it as responsible for the possible breakdown of intelligibility, adding more than a humorous misunderstanding, as the landlady gives information to the police inspector on the phone which he manages to get all wrong. Hitchcock may be taking a poke at verbal narrative itself here. When Frank (John Longden), the police detective fiancé of Alice (Anny Ondra), speaks to Alice in a phone booth, and Tracy (Donald Calthrop) gets the drift of the conversation—not by way of audible words but lip reading through the glass wall of the booth—Hitchcock reminds us that we do not need to hear dialogue to understand the action.

Whether or not Hitchcock took on the controversy of sound in the film itself, he certainly had things to say on the subject, and his comments reveal the fine line he had to walk, showing his sympathy for Griffith's position. In comparing the two, he ventured that "the only trouble with silent pictures was that when people opened their mouths, nothing came out. The trouble with talking pictures is that too many of them are merely pictures of people talking."[6] As the phone booth scene and many others reveal, it may not matter all that much if nothing comes out. Nothing could be worse than simply showing talking heads, and like Griffith, he could imagine no useful value in that. As early as 1933 he saw the problem, commenting ruefully about the obsession of producers and directors with words, and that "the arrival of talkies ... temporarily killed action in pictures."[7] By action he means motion within the shot or motion generated by constructive editing. That type of editing must necessarily give way to sustained shots to coordinate the motion of the actors' lips with the words that we hear, and even in his sound version of *Blackmail* some of the richness of that type of editing had to be sacrificed.[8] Despite the achievement with *Blackmail* and its international influence, including on films in the US, it would take a few more years for Hitchcock to become entirely comfortable with sound and to use it to its best advantage, as happened with *The Man Who Knew Too Much* (1934).

Music and montage

As with *mise en scène*, one can use musical imagery to get at the essence of montage, but showing how it actually may work proves much more difficult, if montage in fact takes its technical cues from music. Eisenstein tried to classify types of montage with the terms "rhythmic," "tempo," "tonal," and "overtonal" montage, and the application of some of these terms is by no means straightforward. Part of the problem here lies in the fact that different types of montage can be all but impossible to distinguish, something Eisenstein probably would have been the first to admit, and his terms become just about as unclear as the differences between types. Having little or no actual musical background, Eisenstein could use his terms with a kind of naiveté and impunity that musicians simply cannot. The flow of montage can be as varied as the flow of music itself, and in this way classification proves not to be very useful. Nevertheless certain types do stand apart from others, and I will attempt to show the possible musical foundation of some of these.

Perhaps the most common type of montage involves an acceleration of motion, used specifically at points in a film that lead directly to a climax. Certainly Hitchcock uses this type with great frequency, although one should not always expect the rate of increase to be constant, since it can vary, often working in conjunction with motion within a specific shot. There may, for example, be an overall acceleration to the climax, but in some shots the motion within the shot can replace the pace of the cutting, causing the shot itself to be extended, allowing montage and *mise en scène* to work in tandem in building to the climax, as happens in montage sequences in *Blackmail*. One could associate this type of building with accelerando or even crescendo in music, but in fact these are fairly crude and imprecise descriptions of what actually happens. Crescendo involves building, but in music the volume increases, so other factors would need to play a part in film for the analogy to hold, for example an increase in the density or elaborateness of shots. Accelerando comes closer to what actually happens in accelerating montage, but in fact composers use accelerando fairly sparingly, since it requires a departure from the metric stability of the piece, and composers generally prefer not to forgo that, in part because of the difficulty it creates for performers, especially those playing in ensemble.

A much better way exists in music to achieve this, a procedure that leaves the meter intact but still allows a building toward a climax. Also, just as with montage which remains at least partially subliminal in that most viewers will not be conscious of the actual cutting but only the effect that it has on them in bending their sense of perception, the musical technique in question has a similar subliminal effect, unlike accelerando which will be completely apparent to all listeners. The most usual variety of this is known as harmonic rhythm, involving the rate at which the harmony changes. In some musical works we find passages either short or long in which the harmonic rhythm changes so as to create acceleration, starting with fairly infrequent chord changes and then gradually speeding up that change, so that by the end of the passage the changes will be happening very rapidly. As the pace of the harmonic change accelerates, one experiences a building toward a climax, although most listeners would not be able to identify specifically why they experience that. By the end of the passage the climax will come, and it will usually be reinforced by other musical elements such as dynamics, pitch, and possibly orchestration, although these elements need not be in full cooperation, causing a type of counterpoint of climaxes. One finds this type of acceleration of harmonic rhythm with some frequency in the works of Beethoven, and the opening eight bars of his first Piano Sonata (in F minor, Op. 2, no. 1) provide an especially good example (see Appendix 1a); in fact, this has different types of climaxes within the phrase. The listener will be especially aware of the rising gestures and dynamic build-up both leading to the *ff* chord in the right hand at bar 7; the rate at which the harmony changes runs parallel to this, but not precisely. Along with the divisions in the phrasing pattern, the harmony also subdivides, starting with two bars of the tonic (i, the home key) followed by two bars of the dominant (V, the most closely related key). The next four bars do anything but follow this pattern: for the next two bars the harmony changes every bar, in bar 7 it changes twice within the bar, and this propels it to the *appoggiatura* (a dissonant note that resolves to a consonant position) at the beginning of bar 8, which resolves to the dominant chord.

The rate of harmonic change, then, follows this pattern, the numbers representing the length of time in bars (or fractions of bars) that each chord is sustained (the top line of Appendix 1b): 2, 2, 1, 1, ½, ½, ¼ (*appoggiatura*), ¼. This climax drives to the end of the phrase, not halting at the loud chord at the beginning of bar 7, and in fact makes the *appoggiatura* in bar 8 stand out as the climax. The real climax is not the tonic chord at bar 7, no matter how loud it may be, but instead the subversive non-harmonic chord at bar 8, much quieter, but with the capacity to upset the harmonic stability of the phrase; in the next phrase that instability immediately sets in. Beethoven, then, introduces the most dangerous element of the phrase through the most subliminal process, one most listeners will not actually hear since they will be distracted by thematic material and dynamics. Here we have musical constructive editing at its best, where the most important element becomes the least obvious through the camouflage of harmonic change. Along with harmonic rhythm, other elements can achieve a similar effect, such as an accelerating change in rhythmic patterns or even the same type of motion in the progression of a single note, possibly within a chromatic sequence, as happens in Ravel's *La Valse* (to be described in Chapter 5).

Acceleration in montage can work hand in hand with *mise en scène*, with a building of intensity in shots as the pace of the cutting increases, and this runs parallel to what some composers do with acceleration in figuration supported by broadening or variance in orchestration. One of the best musical examples of this happens in the work that Hitchcock used only one year after *Blackmail*, Wagner's prelude to *Tristan und Isolde*, to accompany Sir John while he shaves, in *Murder!* Shaving tells us very little, even with a voice-over (which may even somewhat mislead us), but Wagner's music tells us much about the intensity of Sir John's thoughts and even some of the content of those thoughts, since the leitmotifs in the prelude evoke a series of emotions including desire, sorrow, longing, and death (to be discussed in Chapter 8). As a musical model for the combination of montage and *mise en scène*, the prelude starts very slowly with the barest possible orchestration, the leitmotifs in oboes and cellos only, with very sparse backup from clarinets, English horn, and bassoons. Long held notes carry these leitmotifs, with a small amount of chromatic motion in quarter notes, motion that seems slow because of the tempo. As the prelude continues, the level of the motion picks up momentum, with the dotted rhythm leitmotif and figuration in eighth notes and sixteenth notes, and Wagner sustains this increase in the pace with a thickening of the orchestration and increases in the dynamics. Occasionally he allows for variance in the tempo (with *poco rall.*, *riten.*, or *belebt*), but often he puts in warnings not to let the tempo run away (*nicht eilen, ohne zu eilen*, and even *niemals eilen*—never hurry), allowing the acceleration for the most part to come from the figuration and orchestration, not from shifts in tempo. By the time the full orchestra has entered, the figuration in the strings includes thirty-second notes in triplets, now giving the sense of a great rush, but still with cautions to remain in tempo. The climax comes with a final rush of thirty-second notes in triplets leading to the huge fortissimo chord at bar 83, and after the climax he returns to the sparse orchestration and slow figuration. Hitchcock surely knew this prelude well, prompting him to use it in *Murder!*; it can stir the emotions as few pieces of music can.

Regardless of the type of montage used it will probably lead to some type of climax, although generally the climax will be most accentuated at the end of an acceleration. As well as the possibility of working in tandem with an intensification of motion in individual shots, the acceleration can also be intermixed with something static, for example a scene of increasing motion intercut with shots of a person who remains entirely static, as happens in the chase scene leading to the British Museum late in *Blackmail*, the rapid motion now intercut with the anxious but statically frozen face of Alice. The surrounding motion in this case heightens the moral dilemma she finds herself facing, knowing that someone else may be forced to pay for the deed she committed (whether justified or not), and here her own mind races with the chase in the eye of the audience. Musical parallels to this type of combination of stasis and motion abound, and Chopin's Prelude No. 15 in D flat ("The Raindrop") provides one of the best examples in a well-known work (see Appendix 2). The motion in this case happens in the melody line in the right hand as well as the harmonic progressions, while the stasis resides in the repeated A flat in the left hand, a note repeated 39 times in the first eight bars (closer to 50 if we include the right hand A flats). Of course we consciously hear the repetition, but at no time does it become boring, since the activity around it modifies it, making it sound different with changing melody and harmony. The motion in this piece may not be rapid, but the contrast between motion and stasis has a striking effect. Beethoven sets up the same type of contrast at the beginning of his Piano Sonata in D, Op. 28, here obsessively repeating the static note D in the left hand three times per bar for each of the first 24 bars, and just about as often until bar 29 (see Appendix 3). The harmonic and melodic motion of the right hand gains its distinctive quality in relation to the repeated note in the left hand. A similar type of piece, "Chopin" from Schumann's *Carnaval*, was well known to Hitchcock since he uses it in *Notorious*; we hear it played in the background the first time Alicia Huberman enters Alexander Sebastian's home just outside Rio de Janeiro. This piece, marked *agitato*, has a sedate although not entirely static melody, set against a torrent of motion in the accompaniment, and the application of this to *Notorious* will be discussed in Chapter 7. In the music of this type and the motion/stasis montage that it parallels, there can be varying levels of both motion and stasis.

Another type of montage, every bit as common as accelerating montage, I will call variance montage, since it has no perceptible standardization of tempo or acceleration as it alternates fairly quickly among varying paces, but still reaches some type of climax at the end of the montage. The climax in this case will not necessarily come as an inherent result of the montage, as in accelerating montage, but could almost come as something of a surprise, as happens in *Blackmail* in the late-night London walk montage, which ends in the parallel scream of Alice on the street and the landlady discovering the corpse. There can be many sorts of musical models for this type of montage, using harmonic rhythm, tempo changes, or other devices to generate the variance, and some of these happen in musical works specifically referred to by Hitchcock. In his 1927 essay "Films We Could Make" he singled out, as I noted in the previous chapter, Debussy's "Jardins sous la Pluie" from *Estampes*, an essay very much about rhythm and tempo in film,[9] and even the rain may have invoked rhythm in his mind. The piece starts entirely in the bass clef, with staccato low sixteenth notes, four per bar that represent raindrops, and an accompaniment of higher sixteenth notes creating a gloss of sound with the tempo of *vif* (lively or animated). The combination of running bass and accompaniment generates a harmonic rhythm, and unlike the Beethoven sonata noted in Appendix 1, this one turns out to be varied. The number of beats for each chord change yields an accelerating pattern for the first eight bars (see Appendix 4). While this gives fluctuation within these bars, so do the hairpin expression marks (extended wedges), especially the long one over bars 8 and 9, signs that indicate more of a broadening gesture than dynamic change (the piece starts *pp*, and after the long hairpin is still *pp*, suggesting that dynamically change has not occurred).[10] The broadening along with the rising pattern allows an arrival or small-scale climax at the beginning of bar 9. Compared to the Beethoven Sonata in F minor, the harmonic rhythm here proves to be an even more subtle way of building to a climax, partly since little climax is called for. If a climax occurs at bar 9, it seems almost incidental.

Another type of music that generates variance in a more perceptible way, the fantasy, occurs mainly in the eighteenth century but also in nineteenth-century music. Mozart's little Fantasy in D Minor (K397) offers a useful example, starting andante, and then moving through adagio, presto, tempo primo, presto, tempo primo, allegretto, and finally a tempo (original tempo) again at the end. Eight different tempos may seem a lot of changes for a short work just over 100 bars, and the figuration at times allows for other tempo variance (Mozart at least once writes this in with *rallent.*, or slowing down). Composers such as Schumann continued this tradition in the nineteenth century, with, for example, his *Phantasiestücke*, but also within individual sections of some of his character pieces. One of these, *Carnaval*, Hitchcock knew well from a performance by Artur Rubenstein, as Patrick McGilligan reports,[11] and as I just noted, he used it in *Notorious*. This semi-autobiographical work by Schumann starts with a Préambule (prelude) that makes a number of tempo shifts, through quasi maestoso, più moto, accelerando, animato, vivo, and presto. This may remind us of Hitchcock's comment that "construction to me, it's like music. You start with your allegro, your andante, and you build up,"[12] although curiously he reverses the likely slow to fast tempo sequence. The type of construction he has in mind here is surely montage.

Other types of models for montage also exist in *Carnaval*, as in the juxtapositions of greatly contrasting movements side by side which form a type of incongruous pair, such as the sedately moderato "Pierrot" beside the energetically vivo "Arlequin," reflecting accurately the differences between these *commedia dell'arte* (and carnival) characters. This juxtaposition stands even more starkly in the characters of Schumann's own invention, also used by him in his music journalism to represent two radically different views of music and for that matter the world, "Eusebius" (adagio) and "Florestan" (passionato). This type of adjacent contrast may also occasionally be used in montage.

Unlike variance, montage may at times be characterized by stability, or stasis on its own without the motion, and here one would expect regularity in the cutting, with each shot more or less the same length. In musical works one does not generally find this type of stasis in long extended passages or an entire movement, although even to that exceptions exist. Ravel's *Bolero* achieves a type of thematic stasis, although in this case, as described in Chapter 2, another property such as orchestration can carry the motion. Short periods of stasis within a musical work happen with some frequency, as we find further along in "Jardins sous la Pluie" (bars 24–5 and also 40–1).

Another very interesting type of montage occurs from the placing together of still shots, and while the shots themselves may have no motion, the cutting can generate motion, radically altering the way we perceive these stills. A notable example of this type occurs in Eisenstein's *Alexander Nevsky*, in the much-discussed 12-shot montage of the Russians on the battlefield just before the Germans attack. Eisenstein described this sequence at great length in relation to the music composed for it by Sergei Prokofiev, something that occurred to him after the fact—that a spatial comparison can be made between the content of the shots and the shape of the music. Certainly not all have been prepared to buy into his theory on this, but whether one does or not, the results are fascinating. Perhaps the most significant facet of this description lies in the fact that Eisenstein attempted to link music and this type of montage, supporting the overall depth of Prokofiev's music, according to Eisenstein, in realizing the underlying basis of this film.[13]

Montage in *Blackmail*: silent version

Blackmail introduced Hitchcock's most sophisticated attempts at montage to date, but the need to make *Blackmail* as both sound and silent versions added a level of unforeseen complication. In comparing the two versions,[14] one notes substantial differences, for example in the assault on Alice—the scene in which she changes out of the costume and finds that Crewe (Cyril Richard) has taken her dress. Since this is building to a climax in the assault, one expects montage here, and in the silent version we get it, with a carefully constructed series of shots leading up to Crewe grabbing Alice. In the sound version, something very different happens, since the music performed by Crewe makes the montage both unnecessary and untenable. In his article comparing the versions, Charles Barr rightly notes that "when the characters converse at any length, or sing, movement stops, and cinematic time (constructed and compressed by editing) gives way to real time."[15] Some have been inclined to find the silent version superior to its counterpart in sound, but in fact Hitchcock reveals his brilliance in both, discovering the unique qualities of sound that allowed it to match the technical mastery of montage. In fact, many of the montage scenes are identical in both versions, made possible by the fact that speaking does not occur in these scenes. This section focuses on those scenes which are different in the silent version.

The opening scenes of the police making an arrest are identical in both versions, as is the attempt of Frank and Alice to dine at the Lyon's Corner House, with the obvious difference that titles needed to be added to the silent version. The most notable change takes place in Crewe's studio, and initially involves his piano, which becomes an active participant in the sound version, including Alice's engagement with it, as she plays a few notes before sampling other fixtures of the studio. In the silent version Crewe leans on the piano as Alice changes into the costume which he would like her to wear in posing for him to sketch, and after that, the piano ceases to be a factor. Alice is clearly in the mood for flirting, and in the silent version she takes that much further than in the somewhat more prudent sound version. After she emerges from behind the screen and neither of them can get the back zipper up, she pretends to be a ballerina in this tutu-like costume, to which he provides mock applause and adoration. She dances closer to him, falls into his arms giving him a quick kiss, and only at this point do the tables turn, as he attempts a full embrace, which she rejects. With the lack of her flirtatious moves in the sound version, we have less context for his actions, flirtation which in the silent version helps to get him aroused, and contributes to the moral dilemma she faces later in the film. The responsibility she feels, along with her overwhelming urge to confess, has more substance in this version.

Instead of the song "Miss up to date" played and sung by Crewe to accompany Alice's clothes-changing scenes behind the screen, which of course would not have been possible in the silent version, Hitchcock uses a series of montages. Each one of these builds up to some level of climax, and occasionally he achieves this with accelerating montage. In the first of these Alice stands behind the screen and changes while Crewe leans on the piano, waiting for her to emerge. Instead of shots that show both of them simultaneously, the shots present them individually in fairly rapid succession, Alice struggling with the costume and Crewe drinking and smiling. The sequence ends when she emerges and enlists his help with the stubborn zipper, now with both of them in the same shot, with some acceleration in the sequence (in seconds, approximately: 23, 5, 5, 2, 2, 3, 2). A small climax occurs as Crewe fails to move the zipper, no doubt strategic to his plan to have her as unclothed as possible. This leads directly into the mock ballet scene and kiss, where the motion occurs in the *mise en scène*, and culminates in the menacing image of the aroused Crewe with sinister shadows on his face.

The next montage runs parallel to the first, with Alice retreating behind the screen to put her own dress back on, which she cannot find because he has taken it. Once again the camera shows them individually, with Crewe's smiles transformed to leers, and the sequence ends with both of them again together in the same shot; matters now become more intense as he grabs her and pulls her by the arm. Among the rapidly alternating shots stands one of about ten seconds, the first of them together, in which he advances toward her before clasping her; it also includes a shot of a policeman walking on the street below, just before the struggle begins, in shadows, using a type of variance montage. The struggle behind the curtain, which results in Crewe's death, is achieved entirely with motion within one long shot—the same shot used in both silent and sound versions.

Other scenes that use sound in special ways in the sound version also revert to montage in the silent version, starting with Alice back in her own room dressing for breakfast, after the montages of her walking London streets. A bird singing obnoxiously loudly dominates the sound version, but the silent version gives us an accelerating montage at this point. With Alice once again changing her clothes, a direct parallel with the earlier montages at Crewe's studio holds. The most striking use of sound, involving the word "knife," also receives accelerating montage in the silent version, reaching the obvious climax as she inadvertently flings the bread knife. The admonition from her father comes in the title that immediately follows this montage: "You really ought to be more careful with knifes, Alice." Other montage sequences do not involve speaking or diegetic music, and therefore are identical in both versions.

Montage in *Blackmail*: sound

The scenes just described required heightened drama in which the emotions can be intensified through montage, and the necessity to remove that montage would have been completely discouraging to some directors, finding what they cared most about in film wiped out by sound. Hitchcock appears to have considered the problem and resolved it in a way that allowed him to proceed with sound. The solution lay in the fact that in his best films dialogue would be minimized, and in those sections without dialogue montage could be used. To some extent it could also be applied in dialogue scenes, since one did not necessarily have to see the speakers' lips move, and that happens occasionally in this film. In scenes with diegetic music, such as the one in Crewe's studio with him playing the piano and singing, the need for montage was very much diminished since the musical effect of montage could be replaced by real music with audible rhythm, and in the longer sustained shots *mise en scène* could also be used to achieve the intended rhythm leading to a climax.

Unlike his films to follow, Hitchcock had it both ways in the sound version of *Blackmail*, treating it as a silent film at the beginning, where he used montage in the opening sequence with the police making the arrest, illustrating in a sense how he would like to treat sound films. Since he now had sound available to him, he could place it in this early silent sequence, using the non-diegetic music on the soundtrack in the most effective synchronized way. His treatment here seemed at odds with the manifesto issued jointly by Eisenstein, Pudovkin, and Alexandrov, published in *Close Up* in 1928, that the "first experimental work with sound must be directed along the lines of its distinct non-synchronisation with the visual images."[16] They did not want sound to be used merely to achieve "photographed performances of a theatrical sort," and in this respect Hitchcock took them seriously, as in the much-discussed knife sequence, which so ably revealed his embrace of sound. Music, though, was another matter, where synchronization could be useful in intensifying the impact of rhythm, although even here counterpoint could be effective. Certainly the music and the pace of the action could be coordinated, but this was less likely for music and the montage; in generating its own pace in contrast to the music, montage would continue to have a life of its own. If the two did coincide, the effect of the montage would be disguised by the music, making it even more subliminal.

Just as *The Lodger* started with a sequence showing the function of the press, which plays an important subsequent role in the film, *Blackmail* does the same thing with the police, who rush to the residence of a suspect, make the arrest, and put him behind bars. Again the function of the police will play an important role as the film unfolds, in fact subverted by Frank who does everything he can to hide Alice's complicity. We hear no spoken voices until almost eight minutes into the film, after the substantial part of the police sequence has ended—with a couple of officers chatting about inconsequential personal matters, shown from the back so we cannot observe any coordination of speech and lip movement. Hitchcock does offer sound during the opening eight minutes, music from the soundtrack, and he appears to be making a statement about sound here, that music provides the most important sound. The music clearly works on our emotions along with the treatment of visual images; when we finally hear spoken dialogue, it is too insignificant to concern us, and it makes no difference if we hear it or not. The music starts at the beginning of the opening titles, and within 18 seconds its frenetic pattern emerges, giving us the driving music and preparing us for the motion of the first visual image: a close-up of a spinning van wheel.

Motion characterizes the opening sequence, certainly within the individual shots, and more importantly, in the cutting. In this his first sound picture, Hitchcock starts with montage accompanied by music, showing us what he considered the essence of filmmaking to be. As the police speed toward the suspect's residence, we see the wheel spinning, the van hurtling through London streets as fast as it can, and police on the radio or driving. The rapid cutting propels this motion even more frenetically, with each shot on average about two or three seconds, and some no longer than one second. The first full montage sequence takes us up to the apprehending of the suspect in his room, with the rapid pace of cutting in place until that point. Two or three shots in this sequence fall in the 10 to 12-second range, and in these Hitchcock shifts the motion to the shots themselves, as in the first one which shows the police ascending the stairs to the suspect's door. Prior to this, shots with motion, such as the police crossing the courtyard of the suspect's building with children playing running games, have been very short, in fact no longer than four or five seconds. Another one of the longer shots, a full nine seconds, shows the suspect in a close-up sitting in bed with his newspaper, slowly looking to his side table with a gun on it. Hitchcock follows this with a series of rapid cuts between the suspect, who intends to grab his gun, and still shots of the police watching him, shots again of no more than two or three seconds in length. His hand starts to move slowly toward the gun and then darts, at which point the police pounce, and this shot takes only three seconds. They struggle, hands seen between the officers from the back, and even this takes only five seconds. The police subdue him, and here ends this montage sequence; the police now talk to him, although we hear no voices, and as they talk and get him out of bed, the shot lasts a full 36 seconds, no longer part of the montage.

This montage lasts almost three minutes, and takes the action to a clear point of climax, the apprehending of the suspect. The climax lacks surprise since we fully expect the police will succeed in their mission, and with this type of climax no acceleration is required to reach it, unlike the accelerating montage that happens in the final train scene of *Shadow of a Doubt*. The montage used here melds together various ones of the types described above, certainly involving variance, and also blending motion with stasis, especially while the police wait for the suspect to make his move for the gun. It also combines shots that contain varying degrees of motion within the shots themselves, or uses motion in a shot in place of motion in cutting. These various approaches to cutting have basic types of musical models underlying them, but in this case, since the entire sequence has a musical accompaniment, with a score provided by Campbell and Connelly, compiled and arranged for the film by Hubert Bath and Harry Stafford, we will make our musical connection with the music we actually hear. The rhythm of the montage will not always correspond directly with the rhythm of the heard music, and in this respect Hitchcock occasionally followed the Russian theorists in the application of counterpoint.

For the most part the tempo of the cutting and the tempo of the music at the beginning correspond directly, with the driving music heard during the titles giving more or less the same motion of both the shots and their cutting. When the police arrive at their destination and pile out of the tailgate of the van, the music slows. During the standoff between the police and the suspect the music remains slow and pensive, but when the suspect's hand darts for the gun, the music accompanies this with a new burst of activity. Just as the montage does not build to the climax, neither does the music. Amid this general coordination, one interesting point of counterpoint occurs, when the police mount the stairs to reach the suspect's room. As they go up, the music goes down, the descending pattern evident in at least two motivic layers in the music. This appears to be strategic, since stairways often represent an emotional ascent for Hitchcock, as they had in *The Lodger*. In this case the ascent may work for the police as they move in on their quarry, about to succeed in bringing him in, but for the suspect a fall looms, and the criminal world of the suspect points decidedly downward. In this counterpoint of sound and image, the image has an underlying basis in sound, allowing an implied or virtual ascent to occur against the audible descent. Another less well-defined montage occurs as the police take the suspect to their headquarters, question him, run him through the prisoner parade, charge him, and secure him in a cell. If one wishes to think of this as montage, variance characterizes it much more than the defined montage immediately preceding it, with shots that range from one second to half a minute, and the shutting of the cell door provides not much of a climax.

One expects montage in the assault scene, and of course some remains in the scenes that lack music, but we now have a balance of montage and diegetic music in the sound version of the film. While Alice removes the costume, Crewe plays the piano, continuing the song "Miss up to date," and he ends it with a rude chord; he then throws her dress into the room before getting up from the piano and taking her roughly in his arms. This shot lasts almost one minute, and because of some dialogue and the music, montage would not have worked. After a short shot of the street below and a policeman walking by, a very lengthy shot follows, lasting over two minutes, which shows the struggle, the death of Crewe, and Alice emerging from behind the curtain. This scene has neither dialogue nor music, and if Hitchcock had wished to use montage leading to the climax of Crewe's arm falling out from behind the curtain, he could have. Clearly he did not, choosing instead to use *mise en scène*. The shot has all the ingredients of a Murnau shot and more, achieving motion through unique means. We first see their struggle only in shadows, and then the struggle continues behind the curtain, with arms or the curtain itself providing the motion. Alice's arm flails about and finds the knife, and with the disappearance of her arm the curtain rustles frenetically to their struggle. Tempo now becomes a factor as the motion of the curtain gets slower, finally stopping altogether, at which point his arm falls through the opening. Even here the shot does not end, as Alice emerges, knife in hand; finally she puts the knife back on the table, and stands still looking distressed. As with the glass floor in *The Lodger*, Hitchcock opted to find rhythm here in an unusual and visually interesting way.

After this exceptionally long shot, and another fairly long one (30 seconds) following it, with Alice looking vulnerable if not shattered, the pace of the cutting picks up sharply, leading into a montage of her departure from the studio. Just before this begins, non-diegetic music enters, with a distorted version of "Miss up to date,"[17] and that music continues for the remainder of the montage. Again we find little acceleration in the cutting, but instead variance that heightens suspense, the suspense resulting from whether or not Alice can leave without being discovered. The cutting of quick shots of her retrieving her dress from the painting of the jester, close-ups of her looking at the jester and slashing the painting, and removal of her name from the sketch of a nude girl made by herself and Crewe, contrast with long shots, such

3.1 *Blackmail* (Anny Ondra with Cyril Ritchard) (Crewe plays for Alice)

as the one with the motion of her dressing, which takes a full minute. As she leaves we get the best staircase scene in any Hitchcock film to date, shot from above and spiralling downward through many flights to the abyss below, a hell into which Alice must descend. She does this gingerly and tiptoes out the door, only to be observed by a man, whose shadow ominously engulfs the front door. Through this final sequence, starting with Alice dressing, we do have an accelerating montage.

Perhaps the most carefully constructed montage in the entire film comes in the London walking sequence, progressing from Alice's departure from Crewe's studio to the scream of the landlady on discovering the body. The double scream of Alice and the landlady has been disparaged by some as a cheap trick on Hitchcock's part, but this overlooks what has actually happened in the way he uses montage to arrive at this climax. The entire sequence lasts almost three minutes and consists of four parts, each one with an accelerating montage leading to a climax, and each part driving toward the final climax of the scream. The first part picks up with Alice walking away from Crewe's studio and ends when the policeman's arm and hand become Crewe's arm and hand; the acceleration in the cutting clearly occurs in the length of the shots. The second accelerating part begins with Alice walking past a theater through a throng of patrons and ends when she sees the neon images of moving gin bottles (the name Gordon's White Purity has been noted by others, Alice's last name being White, and her purity now in tatters) turning into a hand stabbing with a knife. She continues walking, while the camera gives us Big Ben at 11:45 and an aerial shot of London that dissolves into the motion of her feet, with extreme contrast of a long shot followed by a close-up. Finally she walks through Trafalgar Square, haunted by the image of Crewe's arm, and when she sees a similar arm and hand of a sleeping street person, her scream evokes the actual arm of Crewe and the landlady looking at it; the climax has been achieved by way of acceleration (see Appendix 5). An orchestral distortion of "Miss up to date," with only very small lulls, accompanies the entire montage, along with occasional motifs from the opening driving music, of course associated with the apprehending of a criminal. While the montage flows in waves that each build to a climax through acceleration, the music remains fairly constant throughout, allowing the montage to work independently of it.

The last 17 minutes of the film, with their constant building of tension, work as a series of montages, each one with shifting emotional emphasis, but through the intercutting keeping the primary emphasis on Alice and the burden of her guilt, a burden accentuated by Frank's silencing of her at every possible step. The first of these montages starts in a side room at Alice's home, when Frank asks her to close the door and then attempts to shift the blame onto Tracy, knowing full well Alice had been at the murder scene. This roughly five-minute montage ends when Tracy sees the police from the squad car coming toward the room, and he bolts, smashing the rear window to make his escape; this small breaking of the window climax anticipates the much larger one to come, when he falls to his death through the glass dome of the British Museum's reading room. Throughout this sequence the camera gives fairly equal treatment to the three characters, including use of close-ups on them individually; Frank, in a miscarriage of justice, falsely puts the blame on Tracy, Tracy feels the heat knowing his criminal record will work against him, and Alice is distraught because of the false accusation. Tracy and Alice share the climax here, he providing the motion by breaking through the window, and she providing the substance, with the final shot of her alone looking overwrought.

Hitchcock said that he enjoyed a good chase in a film, and he had already proved that in his own films, as in *The Lodger*, where the final chase offers some of the most spectacular and complex shots of the film. Like the London walking montage, the final chase (or chases) in *Blackmail* work as a combination of four connected montages, each one having a small climax leading up to the large one on the dome of the British Museum. While Tracy's attempted escape may be the focus of the action, certainly providing the motion, Hitchcock through intercutting shifts the real emphasis to Alice, allowing us to experience the racing tension of her troubled mind through the action of the chase. Throughout this five minutes of film Hitchcock generates extremely rapid motion through the intercutting of shots that typically last no more than two seconds; when anything longer occurs, such as a 20-second shot in the British Museum, rapid motion in the shot itself takes over, in this case with Tracy climbing down a rope past the large head of an Egyptian sphinx.

The main line of demarcation for these smaller montages becomes Alice, her presence intensifying as the sequence proceeds, and Hitchcock also allows the music to play a critical role. The chase starts with a black screen which after a second illuminates the same spinning squad van wheel from the opening of the film, accompanied by the same driving music which now makes its return. A certain amount of acceleration occurs here, but it hardly seems like acceleration with the number of two-second shots that alternate between the police van and the car in which Tracy rides. Hitchcock marks this sequence off with a four-second shot of Alice at home, motionless as she stares ahead with an intense look of anxiety on her face. We may enjoy the chase, but she certainly does not, as it becomes the image of her state of mind. The next short sequence belongs to the one just seen, the chase continuing until a traffic cop stops Tracy's car, forcing him to run for it on foot. The cutting here works very much as the previous sequence had, with Alice giving us a look identical to the previous one. In this case the music also sustains the shift of emphasis to Alice, since the driving motif grinds to a halt with the stopping of the car, and it temporarily shifts to the distorted orchestral version of "Miss up to date."

A short interconnecting sequence gets Tracy from Great Russell Street into the British Museum, and for this one-minute scene motion remains in force, with a total of 20 shots, some no longer than one second each. For the moment Alice drops out of view, both in the intercutting and also in the music, which returns to the driving motif. That will change in the final montage, lasting almost three minutes, which follows Tracy in his dash through the British Museum with the police in pursuit to the dome above the reading room, but in this sequence of most frenetic motion, Hitchcock cuts to views of Alice eight times. After Tracy's fall, the emphasis shifts entirely to Alice. Throughout this sequence the cutting happens so rapidly that the notion of acceleration almost becomes irrelevant, but since Hitchcock desired an intense building to the final climax on the dome, he allowed the music in conjunction with the cutting to achieve it. The first shots in the British Museum's exhibition rooms tend to be fairly long, and during these shots Tracy spends as much time looking about as he does running. The music, still using the driving motif, moves at a much slower pace than it had, ramping up to a fast tempo when the police spot Tracy and the chase resumes. Now the music incorporates the occasional new motif, and keeps accelerating until Tracy mounts the final ladder to the top of the dome, dropping out at this point after the sound of a gong. For the final seconds of the sequence Hitchcock wanted *musique concrète*, or sound effects, in this case the sound of breaking glass, with a gap of about three seconds for Tracy's fall to a glass cabinet in the reading room below. Alice has looked more or less the same in all of the intercutting of her, staring ahead grimly and intently, still except for some fidgeting of her hands, but in the final shot of her, which ends this montage, she first looks down before resuming her familiar pose. Her eyes seem to fall with Tracy, and when they look ahead this time, they do so with a new desperation, as though she intuits the worst.

The end of the film belongs to Alice and her need to come clean about what actually happened in Crewe's studio, and it appears that once again she has been silenced, first in Inspector Wall's office, and then mocked at the very end by Frank and the attendant, laughing at the prospect of women detectives at Scotland Yard putting the likes of them out of work. Alice finds no humor in their jokes, and through intercutting and montage, Hitchcock gives substance in this film to Alice unlike any other character. Of the two male characters that command most of our attention in the film, Frank and Tracy, one is a blackmailer with no moral values, and the other does not come off much better, more interested in expediency than truth. Only Alice has moral fiber, and Hitchcock emphasizes that strikingly through the intercutting. In the end, Alice stands as the one character the viewer genuinely cares about, and because of her we even care about Tracy's fate. Her emotional depth becomes the heart of the film, and through montage that depth gains a type of musical essence, bringing it home all the more convincingly. In later films that musical essence would become even more pronounced, sometimes derived from specific musical works, engaging the audience in the strongest possible way.

4

Waltzes and the dance of death

Aside from Hitchcock's own cameo appearances, a number of images appear with fairly great consistency in his films, such as his persistent use of visually striking staircases. As often happens with these types of images, a staircase is not just a staircase. Almost every film indulges in at least one staircase, and it can carry psychological depth or prompt us in other ways, through a sense of motion it generates on its own, through camera movement, or the movement of a character up or down. In the Mission tower in *Vertigo*, Scottie's aspirations disintegrate near the top of the stairs, and he sinks to the depths of an abyss of despair as he looks down. Glimmers of this type of treatment already appeared in *The Lodger*. The waltz turns out to be another one of the persistently repeated images, in this case both visually and/or audibly, and if not the waltz specifically, then dance more generally; this can be found in at least a third of Hitchcock's feature films. That makes it a little less ubiquitous than staircases or cameos, but between *The Lodger* in 1927 and *Torn Curtain* in 1966, it emerges often enough to give it a noteworthy status.

One could perhaps argue that the recurrence of this type of dance offers nothing more than an insider joke or private quip, as the cameo appearances quickly became. Hitchcock, after all, went to waltz lessons in his youth,[1] in some respects an unlikely activity for the pudgy young man, and this could simply be the transference of an autobiographical jest into the films. At least one film, *Waltzes from Vienna*, actually focuses on waltzes, and treats the subject lightly, as Shani, the son of Johann Strauss Sr, must make a career choice between baking confections and waltz composition. In most of the films, though, the waltz seems more like staircases than cameos, since it can carry deeper meaning for individual characters or the film itself. One notices without too much probing, for example, that troubling things sometimes happen during or immediately after dancing, the worst of course being death itself. In one of the first films to use a dance visually, *The Lodger*, we discover the tragic background of the Lodger in a flashback—a coming-out celebration for his debutante sister, struck down by the Avenger as she dances in a sophisticated setting. Similar circumstances, if not necessarily quite as dire, occur in *Suspicion*, *Shadow of a Doubt*, *Saboteur*, *Notorious*, *Under Capricorn*, and *Dial M for Murder*.[2]

In many ways *The Lodger* sets the tone for the use of dance in subsequent films in that it becomes a dance of death, or a type of plunging vortex into the evil or chaotic forces that grip many of Hitchcock's films. The fact that this happens in one of his earliest films—certainly the one that best defines his arrival as an extraordinary filmmaker, and remains persistently in his films for four decades, suggests something special about the waltz as a force with unusual potency. If he had simply employed the music of the waltz as background music, that would not necessarily thrust it into a position of special prominence, but in all but two or three of the films that use it, we not only hear it but see it as well, often as a central visual image. He of course establishes that visual centrality in his silent films, prominently in *The Lodger*, and also others; by continuing to use the waltz in sound films, the impetus can clearly be seen to come from the visual quality of the dance in silent films, now with the potential of visual and sound images working together. For a director who thought in visual and sound terms, this combination gave him the potential for something exceptionally compelling, and he embraced it to the fullest. In fact, as we will see in a film such as *Shadow of a Doubt*, he could intensify the effectiveness of the image, following the thinking of the Russians Pudovkin and Kuleshov, by having sound and visual aspects working in an antagonistic counterpoint as well as in harmony.

The waltz: stability vs disorder

The waltz proved to be ideal for Hitchcock to use because of the ways in which it was perceived since its origins in the nineteenth century—as embodying both stability and disorder. One finds evidence of this in any number of ways, including the descriptions of dance masters and moralists, in artworks, the roles it plays in works of literature, and most importantly for Hitchcock, in its treatment in film, especially during the silent era. Aside from his personal interest in the waltz as one who took lessons and practiced it, Hitchcock became the heir to a well-established tradition, evident especially in Germany with the likes of Lang, Murnau, Papst, Ruttmann, Wegener, Wiene, and Lubitsch, but in other countries as well. The fact that German filmmakers would be most inclined to use it should not be surprising, considering that the waltz originated in Vienna, and the craze that soon took hold of the Austrian capital did not take long to spread to Germany as well as other countries in Europe and North America. It did not hurt that one of the pioneers of the film industry in Germany, Fritz Lang, happened to be from Austria, and brought not only a familiarity with the waltz with him but also an awareness of how writers perceived the waltz. While in Germany in the mid-1920s, Hitchcock no doubt became much more aware of the significance of the waltz, and he could certainly observe it being used by Murnau, with whom he shared studio space at Ufa. The German directors, and Lang in particular, knew exactly how the perception of the waltz had allowed it to become a contradictory image in literature, first in Vienna in the works of Arthur Schnitzler and Karl Kraus, then by German writers such as Frank Wedekind, Georg Hauptmann, Georg Kaiser, and others, and soon by writers from other countries as well, including ones as prominent as Hendrik Ibsen and Oscar Wilde.

The waltz came by its character as an agent of order with little difficulty, both in its musical traits and the physical nature of the dance. To allow it to be danced it must be constructed musically in balanced and symmetrical phrases, giving gestures that move away from a starting point followed by a return, and these occur at the smallest level of the individual steps and the largest level of overall motion. More importantly, in contrast to the rustic Ländler with its stomping and hopping gestures from which it evolved, the waltz moved to the sophistication of the ballroom, and its steps became decidedly more graceful, generating motion that seemed to be gliding. In these elegant settings the tempo could increase, and a different type of rhythmic accentuation became possible, giving a lightness of step which, in contrast to the heavy emphasis on each beat in the Ländler, prompted a lighter accentuation on the first beat and a lift on the second and third beats of this dance in triple time. As a result of the gracefulness of the dance, it became closely associated with women.[3]

Despite the best efforts of dance masters to define decorum and gentility in the waltz with an extensive set of rules, indicating among other things where hands should be placed, the positioning of the dancers facing each other and the inevitable physical contact resulted in something else, in fact placing women in a somewhat compromising position as men physically led them. It has been argued that not only contact promoted sensuality, but so did the impulse of the music, since, as Francesca Draughon notes, the "rhythmic gestures of an exaggerated accent on the first beat and the slight shift of accent on the second beat could be understood as a metaphor for a psychological and physiological increase of suspense and a heightened sensation of pleasure."[4] Moralists reacted against what they perceived as an erotic display normally not permitted in polite society, lamenting its subversion and licentiousness, for example Adolph Glassbrenner, who complained about the degenerate waltz craze in Vienna: "One no longer sees dances there, only Bacchantes. The women feverishly thrill as soon as they are touched by the arm of the man, then they press their breast close to his, their head on his shoulder, and now they let themselves be swept about, imbibing in this voluptuous posture with every movement of the man and that lascivious music."[5]

For some male writers this image of the woman invoked a degeneracy that they associated with prostitutes, although for some Viennese writers this was not necessarily a negative attribute. For the most extreme misogynists, such as Otto Weininger, writing in his extraordinarily popular *Geschlecht und Charakter* (*Sex and Character*), which went through 26 printings between 1903 and 1925, prostitutes preoccupy themselves with the pleasures of the world, of which dancing stands first among these, in what he calls a victorious march for their alluring bodies.[6] Other writers, most notably the highly influential Karl Kraus (well known to Fritz Lang) and the eccentric Peter Altenberg, construed elaborate theories of the positive characteristics of prostitutes, arguing that they exemplified the best qualities of women in their freedom from domestic drudgery and marital responsibilities, and they took this to the level of a *Frauenkult* (cult of women) in which these women could ennoble the soul. Generally in solidarity with these writers stood Vienna's premier novelist, Arthur Schnitzler, who included scenes of dancing in his play *Reigen* (*Merry-go-Round*), a work which traces in a fairly matter-of-fact way the sex lives of different persons through ten scenes, each scene connected through a common character to the previous scene. The second of these has a soldier, who had been with a prostitute in the first scene, now with a chambermaid, the two of them leaving the dance floor at the Prater amusement park in Vienna, with the confused sounds of a vulgar dance still in the background. She objects to leaving, since "I'm so crazy about dancing," to which he replies, "We aren't dancing now, you know. Why do you hold me so tight?" Darkness has fallen, causing her to be afraid, and he assures her she needn't be as long as she's with him, all the while leading her to a secluded spot where they can have sex. He compliments her body, and she wonders if he tried "them all out this way?" "Just what you notice dancing," he replies. "You notice a lot, dancing, you know! Huh!" She complains that "you danced more often with the blonde ... than with me, really."[7] Clearly he uses dancing for subversive purposes, but the chambermaid, a "Süsse Mädl" (a girl from the lower classes having a fling with an upper-class man before she marries in her own class), familiar in Schnitzler's works, seems not to mind.

For others the waltz became the most central image defining Vienna at the turn of the century, and specifically the way the waltz allowed the Viennese to avoid dealing with reality. The waltzes of Johann Strauss Jr gripped the city and spread quickly around the world, and in the Austrian capital the gaiety of the waltz gave the impression of a city possessed by merriment and frivolity, masking that the bourgeoisie seemed oblivious to the war they just lost in 1918, or the increasing discontent and misery of ethnic groups and the working masses.[8] The oblivion went much further, affecting even the justice system, as Vienna's most acerbic critic Karl Kraus documented with bitter satire. In some cases satire did not go far enough, so instead he used poetry, as in "Tod und Tango" (Death and tango), in unmasking the case of a young bank executive from a good family, who, together with his wife, stood out for his dancing prowess in elegant society. When his wife filed for divorce because she wished to leave him for another man, the junior banker murdered her, and unsuccessfully attempted suicide. The case came to trial, and with all charges dropped, he resumed his bank position with a promotion. Kraus concluded that those in authority could not bear to see an able dancer removed from society,[9] and incidents such as this prompted the famous remark that the situation in Vienna was desperate but not serious. For one historian, "Vienna was never more vital than when it was dying."[10] The identification of the waltz (or some other type of dance) as a dance of death is put forward time and again, certainly by Kraus in the case of the banker, and much more poignantly in his monumental work *Die letzten Tage der Menschheit* (*The Last Days of Mankind*), where hyenas dance around corpses on a battlefield to the rhythm of the tango.[11]

Some writers had much more specific remarks concerning the waltz, such as Henry Schnitzler, in tackling the myths of Vienna's nostalgia about the good old days. He noted that the waltz first took hold during the Congress of Vienna in 1815, conquering the Continent as a new type of force, which may have shocked old-fashioned people by its immorality, especially the physical contact which prompted the poet Byron to censure it as "this lewd grasp and lawless contact." Even the composer Richard Wagner, not one to shy away from unbridled ecstasy, described a scene which Johann Strauss Sr conducted in this way: "This Demon of the Viennese musical folk spirit trembled at the beginning of a new waltz like Pythia on her tripod and a veritable scream of lust on the part of the audience, intoxicated by his music rather than by the alcohol they had consumed;" this "drove the trance of the magical violinist to heights which to me seemed almost frightening." Another visitor to Vienna, Heinrich Laube, compared the effect of the new waltzes to the bite of a tarantula, and Strauss particularly he thought African in his hot-blooded, crazy, restless, and passionate gestures, exorcising "the wicked devils from our bodies and he does it with waltzes … The devil is abroad." And, most damning, Laube believed "a dangerous power has been given into the hands of this dark man; he may call it his good fortune that to music one may think all kinds of thoughts, that no censorship can have anything to do with waltzes, that music stimulates our emotions directly, and not through the channel of thought ... he is a man who could do a great deal of harm if he were to fiddle Rousseau's ideas; in one single night, the Viennese went with him through the entire *Contrat Social* ... Bacchantically the couples waltz ... lust let loose; no God inhibits them."[12]

For us in the twenty-first century, able to look back on the much wilder dance gestures of the twentieth century, it may be a little difficult to believe these observers from the nineteenth century that the waltz could be anything but the epitome of stability. Even in cinema we have confirmation of that: when Stanley Kubrick wished to represent something completely conventional in *2001: A Space Odyssey*, he used Johann Strauss's *The Blue Danube* waltz for that purpose, setting it in contrast to the modern and discomforting sounds of works by Gyorgi Ligeti to probe the sense of the unknown and mysterious. In fact, these ambivalent notions of the waltz still existed at the end of the First World War, and this made the waltz the ideal vehicle for Maurice Ravel when he wished to represent musically the collapse of social order, as he does in his work written immediate after the war, *La Valse*. Originally naming the work *Wien*, he described it as "a sort of apotheosis of the Viennese waltz which I saw combined with an impression of a fantastic whirling motion leading to death. The scene is set in an Imperial palace around 1855."[13]

Always modest in his descriptions, Ravel clearly saw it as much more than the collapse of the waltz, but in fact as a symbol for a collapsing society, which in the minds of so many people the waltz had come to embody, and the musical progression to complete chaos in his work supports the notion of a much broader social and political commentary. In his highly influential *Fin-de-siècle Vienna: Politics and Culture*, Carl Schorske aptly starts his first chapter with a description of Ravel's work as a chronicle of the violent death of the nineteenth-century world, a "grotesque memorial" in which the illusion of a gay Vienna transforms to "a frantic *danse macabre*."[14] Schorske even describes the musical character of the work to illustrate how it achieves its ends. A more precise musical description of *La Valse* will be provided in the next chapter, since this work has special significance for some of Hitchcock's works—especially *Shadow of a Doubt*, but also *Suspicion* and *Strangers on a Train*. Hitchcock appeared to embrace fully the capacity of the waltz, as it does in Ravel's work, to represent chaos and disorder.

Dance in film

It seems unlikely that Hitchcock would have known any of the literature that generated these attitudes about the waltz or other dances, although he may have been aware of some other works where dancing plays a crucial role, such as Ibsen's *A Doll's House* or Wilde's *Salome*. The comments made by Laube, though, seem entirely in tune with Hitchcock's own notions, not only the potential for the waltz to function in an almost demonic way, but the power of music or dance to get directly to the emotions, circumventing thought, and even subverting it. Hitchcock certainly did know the wealth of cinema that used dancing in this way—especially German films from the silent era that borrowed ideas from literature; even without spending time in Germany he would have been exposed to these major films of the 1920s. Dance in silent films functions in ways that may be different than in literature, but with its direct appeal to the senses visually, it can and does evoke similar responses to literature. Frequently there will be an association with moral decay and collapse or societal disorder, and that can also point to dance as a harbinger of death.

Since Fritz Lang had the closest association with Vienna as a native son, and in fact idolized the foremost Viennese intellectuals such as Karl Kraus,[15] he may be the most useful starting point for a discussion of this type of influence on Hitchcock, who had nothing but admiration for Lang. Hitchcock described his own arrival in Berlin in 1924 with these words of praise, noted in Chapter 1: "Those were the great days of German pictures. Ernst Lubitsch was directing Pola Negri, Fritz Lang was making films like *Metropolis*, and F. W. Murnau was making his classic films … For a version of *Siegfried* they built the whole forest of the *Nieblungenlied*."[16] In fact, that extraordinary set at Ufa's Neubabelsberg lot had to be demolished to make way for a scene in *The Blackguard*, on which Hitchcock worked as scenarist, art director, and assistant director. Aside from these Lang films, he knew and admired others, including *Der müde Tod* and *Doktor Mabuse, der Spieler.*

Hitchcock rightly singled out *Metropolis* (1927) in his comments, this most influential and controversial of German expressionist cinema. Along with all its other extraordinary attributes, it also uses dance in very significant and central ways, carrying forward the way dance had been portrayed in German literature. In this allegory about the division and clash of the ruling and working classes, the focus falls on one character, Maria (Brigitte Helm), an almost saintly figure of innocence and purity, who attempts to find the way of bringing the classes together, separated by their upper and nether worlds of privilege for one and servitude for the other. The manipulative industrialist, Fredersen, having observed Maria preach her message, instructs the mad inventor Rotwang to make his man-machine in the image of Maria to subvert the plan, prompting the workers to outright rebellion so they can be ruthlessly stopped by force. With his Frankenstein-like creature he spawns an evil Maria to coexist with the good Maria, although the inventor, with his own grudge against Fredersen, allows his creation to subvert not only the workers but the ruling class as well, thereby not only killing the workers' peaceful objectives but also bringing down privileged society.

For her first act of subversion, the evil Maria works her powers not on the workers but their bosses, men in black ties at a sophisticated club, and she does this as an erotic dancer, rising elaborately from a cistern to the gasping pleasure of these men, and then performs a Salome-like dance with few veils to remove. They are hopelessly entranced by her alluring dance, and Lang collects their ogling eyes into shots of erotic desire. The industrialist's rebellious son, Freder, has been invited to the dance, and he remains in a state of mental collapse after seeing Maria with his father, unaware that two Marias now exist; scriptural passages which reinforce her maliciously seductive powers pass through his mind—that in fact she embodies all seven deadly sins. Lang backs this up visually with all seven in porticos, flanking death himself, who plays a flute in the shape of a human bone, animating the seven sins. The shot jumps to Freder in complete mental distress, and then quickly to the evil Maria, in her almost naked elegance, rising atop a dragon-like throne, to the delirious ecstasy of the men surrounding her. Death raises his scythe, and the intertitle proclaims "Death descends upon the city," before he cuts his swath. The dance here, not only one of seductive subversion, becomes a dance of death, portending the most dire consequences, which of course will ensue.

When this Maria returns to the depths to speak to the workers, she now carries something of the demeanor of the dancer, with clothes unlike the real Maria's, open at the neck, and as she speaks she moves her body seductively, gestures alluringly with her eyes, and pulls at the opening of her blouse. She seduces the workers as easily as she had their bosses, setting them on their course of destructive rebellion. As for the men of the elite class, their order can be seen immediately to break down, as leers immediately transform to the violence of fist fights and duels, resulting in death. As destruction and death overwhelm the city, both workers and the elite carry on dancing, with the workers in a type of chain dance rapidly circling the machines they have destroyed, repelling the lone foreman on the steps of the Moloch-like structure; he exhorts them to stop, and succeeds only with a desperate reminder that their destruction has caused the city to flood and will result in the death of their children. The jump cut to the elite reveals them dancing as well, with the evil Maria still clad as the good Maria elevated above the others, and the masses on a large ballroom floor swirling in what could very well be a waltz. With exaggerated gestures she shouts to them: "Let's all watch as the world goes to the devil"; as the wild dancing continues, they appear already to be there, swept up in a vortex of motion. Dance, it turns out, plays a surprisingly large role in this film, providing a vivid visual picture of disintegration, chaos, and even death, an image of decadence that German audiences and others in the mid-1920s would readily recognize. That association with the good life, and perhaps even decadence, can also be seen in Walther Ruttmann's *Berlin, die Symphonie der Grossstadt* (*Berlin, Symphony of a Great City*, 1927), in which Ruttmann intersperses shots of dancing couples in close embrace with shots of gambling at roulette wheels or with cards.

The German director with whom Hitchcock no doubt most closely identified himself, Murnau, used dancing in similar ways in a number of his films, and even in *Der letzte Mann* (1924), where dancing occurs at the wedding party of the old hotel doorman's daughter. Dancing under these circumstances may seem fairly innocent, but the manner of presenting it suggests something different. The doorman has just returned home from his humiliating demotion to a lavatory attendant, and we only see the dancing as silhouettes or shadows, first from the outside courtyard looking in, and then inside as shadows instead of direct shots of the people dancing. We have just seen the doorman retrieving his uniform to avoid the embarrassment of his loss of position, followed by his struggle to climb the stairs to his apartment, and dancing as a dark image from the outside may provide yet another comment on his unhappy situation. His attempts to be merry provide a counterpoint to his actual state of mind.

In other films Murnau uses the association of dance with chaos and death much more directly, for example in *Faust* (1926), where near the beginning a silly carnival dance precedes the enveloping black wings of death in the form of the plague. The fear of death drives some to religion, and the preachers of repentance and doom have a ready audience; in the face of this, others dance wildly and give in to decadence, shouting with disdain to the heralds of doom, as the face of the devil fills the sky, that "We still live, we still love! We shall die dancing in each other's arms!" When Faust sets out on his adventures with Mephistopheles, they come upon the wedding feast of the Duchess of Parma, the most beautiful woman in Italy. The dancing of young women sets the background for Faust's seduction of the Duchess and Mephistopheles's murder of the groom. Similarly in *Phantom* (1922), a tale of the moral downfall of an upright young man (Lorenz), we find his demise associated with decadent clubs that have wild dancing, especially by his already fallen sister, who dances on the tables. Late in the film Lorenz has taken up with a woman who likes the decadent lifestyle, and shots of them waltzing at the club are intercut with a velodrome in which a bicycle is caught in a descending vortex; similarly as Lorenz and his partner sit together, the camera shows them sinking into a cavernous hole. As all the motion appears to represent sinking into an abyss, the waltz becomes engulfed in the same descent, suggesting not only decadence, but something much more menacing.

Papst also stood high on Hitchcock's list of favorites, whose well-known *Die Büchse der Pandora* (*Pandora's Box*, 1929) cultivated the closest tie with literature of any of the films from the time, based on the two plays *Erdgeist* (*Earth Spirit*) and *Die Büchse der Pandora* by Frank Wedekind. One of the foremost operas of the twentieth century, Alban Berg's *Lulu*, used the same two plays as its source material, and Berg, an avid cinemagoer, in all probability also took some ideas from Pabst's film.[17] On the surface the plays seem an extreme indulgence in decadence and morbidity, but in fact they have a level of complexity that connects them to as major a literary giant as Goethe. This includes some of the nicknames given to Lulu as well as the title *Erdgeist*, taken directly from the apparition at the opening of *Faust*, Part 1, who dislodges Faust from his musty intellectual world and opens the door of nature to him. Wedekind built dancing into the plays with some frequency, and Pabst followed the spirit of this in his film, allowing it to work in ways similar to some of the other films already noted. At one point Lulu's future husband, the influential publisher Dr Schön, secures a role for her to dance in a revue, but she refuses to dance until she has put Schön in a compromising position. After the revue people waltz at Schön's place too, and Lulu will dance only with Countess Geschwitz, a woman who clearly desires her. At the conclusion of this party Schön, appalled by Lulu's decadent behavior, attempts to forces her to shoot herself, but as they struggle for the gun, the shot hits Schön, and like everyone who gets close to her, he dies. At the end of the work Jack the Ripper, a figure of considerable interest to Hitchcock, brutally murders Lulu in this sordid dance of death.

Numerous other films by the directors already noted or others, from Germany or elsewhere, include scenes of dance which could have been known to Hitchcock, both during the 1920s and later. One of the best known of all silent films, the American *Phantom of the Opera* (1925), has a lavish dance scene, in all probability the waltz, at the masked ball at the opera house, where the figure of death enters appropriately masked, colored in red, and rebukes all for their merriment. Dancing resumes after he, presumably the Phantom, leaves, but not before the chill of death has been left in

4.1 *Phantom of the Opera* (1925, directed by Rupert Julian) (The Phantom interrupts the dance)

the air. Numerous films in Germany make use of dance to the extent that the title of the film has the word "dance" in it, although clearly in not all of these does the dance have sinister connotations, any more than Hitchcock's own *Waltzes from Vienna*. These include the following: Otto Rippert's *Totentanz* (*Dance of Death*, 1919) with Fritz Lang as screenwriter, Murnau's *Der Bucklige und die Tänzerin* (*The Hunchback and the Dancing Girl*, 1920), Paul Wegener's *Der Golem und die Tänzerin* (1917), Robert Wiene's *Die drei Tänze der Mary Wilford* (*The Three Dances of Mary Wilford*, 1920), *Salome* (1922) and *Die berühmte Frau* (*The Dancer of Barcelona*, 1927), Ernst Lubitsch's *Das Mädel vom Ballet* (*The Girl from the Ballet*), Erich Charell's *Der Kongress tanzt* (*The Congress Dances*, 1931), and Geza von Bolvary's *Zwei Herzen im dreiviertel Takt* (*Two Hearts in Waltz Time*, 1930). Prints for some of these films no longer exist, but reviews have left information, for example in the case of *Die Drei Tänze der Mary Wilford*. Apparently intended as a sequel to Leo Lasko's *Die Sünderin* (*The Sinners*, 1919), a few scenes were censored because of their wild dancing. According to a surviving review, the stages of the main character's adult life are marked by three central dances, with the final one a dance of death; her death appears to come at the hands of her criminal lover.[18] The themes of disorder and death in relation to dancing remain central to many of these films.

Dance in Hitchcock's silent films

With *The Lodger* (1926) a number of the traits materialized that would identify Hitchcock as a major filmmaker, and having just returned from Germany, he could draw heavily on his experience there and his familiarity with some of the most important advances in the field. The visual representation of dance turns out to have been one of these traits, and the way he used it put him in very good company among his German mentors and colleagues. Dance plays a deceptively important role in *The Lodger*, not showing up until late in the film, but with its appearance comes the ambivalence that typifies the use of dance, offering both the clarification of the Lodger's identity and the context for the murder that gives the narrative its substance. We learn in the flashback of his sister's coming-out ball, visually presenting what he tells Daisy, that he hails from a good family and now has a responsibility to his dead sister and mother to find and bring to justice the murderer of his sister—the Avenger. More importantly, the murder occurs during the dance, given the visual highlighting described in Chapter 2. In the prominence of its display, the dance here clearly becomes a dance of death, as the murder is woven into the dance scene itself, and that death becomes the driving force of the disorder that propels the film. In this case we do not discover the link with dance until near the end, so when we do see the dance, it becomes a culmination of what has gone on before it. Murder and dance here become almost synonymous, and of course the Lodger himself becomes part of the equation, first as a dance participant, and then as the prime murder suspect throughout most of the film. The viewer knows he did not do it when seeing his flashback, although probably earlier on we prefer to take Daisy's benevolent view of him instead of sharing the suspicion of her detective fiancé—who of course has other reasons for wanting him put away as he observes Daisy's affection for him. For the police the Lodger remains their suspect until they actually catch the Avenger red-handed.

In this early film with dance, Hitchcock sets up the image to pull in two extreme directions. In one sense the dance represents the best of the past, the commemoration of a happy event which one should be able to look back on with pleasure and nostalgia, not unlike the way the waltz represented Vienna of a bygone era. Hitchcock could have simply let it serve an ironic function, as part of the nostalgia that dissipates, but instead he makes the dance scene an actual participant with the darkest possible turn, as a type of accomplice to the murder with its devastating consequences for one family and the basis for the terror that grips an entire metropolis. Here the dance does not signify decadence and disorder as it does in the films of Lang and Murnau, but it fuses something wholesome with the most horrible possible event.

Just one year later Hitchcock would again use dancing very effectively in a silent film, *The Ring*, and this time the dancing comes much closer to decadence, in fact becoming a central part of the dramatic tension. Jack, a fairground boxer, rises in the boxing world, and marries Nelly the ticket seller at the fairground, but Nelly's attention becomes diverted to Bob, the champion—the only person to knock out Jack at the fairground. At a party where Jack signs the contract for his next fight, two exotic dancers perform wildly as Nelly and Bob watch locked in an embrace; Jack can see them through a mirror as he negotiates his contract in another room. The dancers collapse from exhaustion, and guests pour champagne down their throats. They resume dancing, as wildly as before, and now others join them, except Nelly and Bob who remain sitting together. Nelly and Jack have risen in the world, and Nelly embraces the decadent life, highlighted by the dancing and drinking, preferring in fact to be with another man. Hitchcock takes the visual impression of this a step further, by making the dancers fade into a blur, as if to underline the sense of disintegration.

The inevitable confrontation between the two men in both the ring and over Nelly happens just after Jack has won a fight that brings him closer to a match with Bob. Celebrating with his old fairground

4.2 *The Ring* (dancers) (Dancers dissolve into a distorted mass)

cronies in his new plush flat, they wait for Nelly, but she does not arrive until the others have left. They quarrel, and when she mentions the club where she wishes she had stayed, Jack goes there in search of Bob. He enters the club, and his back blacks out everything, until he moves sufficiently far from the camera for it to reveal dancing on the far side, perhaps waltzing. People congratulate him on his win, and a seductive young flapper persuades him to dance with her, which he does. As they dance, he soon finds himself positioned back to back with Bob, also on the dance floor, and when they come face to face, each one holding a dance partner, they scowl at each other, and cross against each other as the dance continues to swirl. When no longer dancing, the confrontation comes to a head; Jack gives Bob a jab that knocks him down, and this becomes an extension of the dance, which continues as they fight. Here the dance underlies the tension and fight, and one can therefore think of the match between them in the ring as a continuation of the dance. While not a dance of death in this case, we certainly have a dance of disorder and conflict, central to the primary focus on marital tension in the film.

In most of Hitchcock's other silent films dancing also emerges with a significant role, and this started as early as his first film, *The Pleasure Garden* (1925). The two leading female characters belong to a dance troupe at the Pleasure Garden Theater, which attracts male patrons in evening dress who come primarily to ogle, but the association with dancing and sin goes further. Dancing takes place at a post-production party for the troupe, and at this event the new star of the show, Jill (Carmelita Geraghty), begins her life of promiscuity, which sets her apart from her steadfast friend Patsy (Virginia Valli). In the film immediately following *The Lodger*, *Downhill* (1927), dancing becomes a dominant force throughout, and runs very much parallel to the general descending progression of what happens to Roddy (Ivor Novello), a student from a privileged background who is expelled from school after being falsely accused of behaving inappropriately (in fact while dancing) toward a young woman. As his life spins out of control in a downward spiral, he can be seen with some frequency at dances, at cabarets and also on a ship, where the dance appears to be a waltz. While on the ship, the dancing becomes delirious, as he sinks into total degradation, and to be even more emphatic about the direction of the motion, we often see people descending on escalators and stairways. Not only does dancing receive prominence in *Downhill* but even the dance musicians become part of the scene.

The type of treatment in *Downhill* continues in the next film as well, *Easy Virtue* (1927), and as the title suggests, dancing will be an ideal vehicle for underlying the theme of the film. Because of her susceptibility to the advances of her portrait painter, Larita Filton (Isabel Jeans) ends up in divorce court, and leaves England as a notorious and disgraced woman. She remarries and returns to England with her new husband to his country estate, and immediately encounters suspicion from his relatives. The family announces a dance at their estate, and at exactly this time the crisis of her disreputable past comes to a head. At the event the musicians arrive and the dancing begins, and contrary to the expectation of her mother-in-law that she will stay in her room, Larita enters, descending a stairway as the belle of the ball, and even dances with the barrister who oversaw her divorce. At the dance her past identity ceases to be a secret, and with marriage in respectable society no longer an option, the barrister finds himself once again with a divorce case involving her. In *Champagne* a year later, dancing again became prominent as it had been in *Downhill*, in this case underlying the downward shift in lifestyle of the Girl (Betty Balfour), whose millionaire father feigns bankruptcy when he assumes her fiancé wants nothing but her fortune. After her life of ease, she gets employment, as a flower girl at a cabaret, where dancing continues almost non-stop, as a backdrop for seduction; exotic dancing easily brings matters to a boil. In all of these films dancing runs parallel to decline, degradation, and sometimes death, even when practiced by members of polite society; the balance makes it very much a dual force that can pull in either direction.

Waltz as subject

With the advent of sound in cinema there seemed no reason not to go much further with the use of the waltz, adding the sound to the visuals, or using the sounds only, as happens in a significant number of his subsequent films. In some of the cases in which we hear waltzes but do not see them, such as in the hotel lobby in Paris in *Rich and Strange* (1932), the dance serves a fairly minor purpose, although at least one notable exception to this occurs (however obliquely) in *Strangers on a Train*. Just one year after *Rich and Strange*, Hitchcock's one film with the waltz as its primary subject was released, *Waltzes from Vienna*, and most observers have dismissed it, including Hitchcock himself, as one of his weakest films. In response to François Truffaut's quip that he could not believe this to be the director's own choice, Hitchcock distanced himself by referring to this "very bad" film as the "low ebb of my career."[19] With this direct engagement with the waltz, in the light of his potent use of dance in his silent films, one would undoubtedly expect something more substantial, and certainly not a film that three decades later would only embarrass him. Truffaut got it right that Hitchcock himself did not choose the subject, since the stage impresario Tom Arnold, looking for an opening into motion pictures, engaged him to direct it. The film appears not to have stood the test of time; only recently has it been made available as a DVD, although previously it could be found in a not readily accessible version dubbed in French.[20]

Most commentators, with one or two exceptions, have dismissed it as readily as Hitchcock did, and typical of these are Eric Rohmer and Claude Chabrol, who called it a "real disaster"; one wonders, "and he himself has no idea," why he made it. They also recount the story of him yelling at the cast that "I hate this film, I hate this kind of film, and I have no feeling for it. What I need is drama, adventures!"[21] According to Esmond Knight, who starred in the film as Schani, the younger Strauss, he actually said, "I hate this sort of stuff. Melodrama is the only thing I can do."[22] These dismissals may have been somewhat premature, and taking Hitchcock's comments about such things as the truth must always be done with some care. When he took the project on, he did so with enthusiasm, as he confirmed in his interview with Stephen Watts quoted in the Introduction, which gives us some of his clearest thoughts about the use of music in films. According to Watts, "the step from that [the approach from Arnold] to actually directing it was taken because the subject interested Hitchcock so much."[23] Connections between the treatment of music in this film and *Rear Window* have been made more than once, and in both cases he had regrets, in the later film about the song composed by Franz Waxman, and in this one more generally what he called a "musical without music." In both cases the composition of a song or waltz underlies the structure of the film, and whether or not that failed in *Rear Window* will be explored in Chapter 6. In this instance, unlike *Rear Window*, the film received miserable reviews, and Hitchcock may have gone with the flow, preferring not to flog a dead horse, especially considering its differences from the rest of his output. Still, the discrepancy between his initial enthusiasm for the idea and his later disparagement of the end product needs to be reconciled, just as it does for *Rear Window*.

In the interview with Watts, Hitchcock outlines some of the basic functions of film music, but he also probes certain ideas which go well beyond that. He compares, for example, music to cutting, and points out that in building to a climax both can do it very effectively. That of course is obvious, and in fact he prefers the possibility of counterpoint, where tension can be generated through music not supporting talking or visual aspects but adding a contrary dimension, in the manner described by the Russians Kuleshov and Pudovkin. To illustrate what he meant, he gave this example to Watts about the possibility of music expressing the unspoken: "two people may be saying one thing and thinking something very different. Their looks match their words, not their thoughts. They may be talking politely and quietly, but there may be a storm coming. You cannot express the mood of that situation by word and photograph. But I think you could get at the underlying idea with the right background music." He may have hoped he could use the waltz to serve that type of purpose in this film, but that would have to wait a few more years, when he discovered the full potential of having a waltz distorted in the manner that Ravel does it in *La Valse*. Near the end of the interview he associates cutting, and by extension music serving a contrapuntal function, with the Russians propensity for violence, and notes that with "quieter subjects, concerned with agriculture, etc., their montage has not been so noticeable or effective." Discussion of a five-year plan cannot be made very dramatic, but at best, "you might express the mood and tone of our conversation with music that would illuminate or even subtly comment on it."[24]

Waltzes from Vienna turned out to be too much like the conversation about a five-year plan, lacking the dramatic possibilities that *Suspicion* or *Shadow of a Doubt* would have, and no amount of music—a waltz or anything else—would change that. The narrative does not lack tension, especially between the Strauss father and son, and also between the younger Strauss's fiancée Rasi and the wily Countess, for whom Schani becomes a disposable love interest. The nature of the comedy, often crossing over into slapstick, does not allow the tension to be taken seriously, and the contention that *The Blue Danube* waltz carries between father and son has little chance of illustrating the tension in any musical way. Part of the problem lay in the fact that the waltz in question, probably the best known of all waltzes, will likely be associated by most viewers with something pleasant. Even the process of composition, running parallel to the structure of the film, has little tension built into it, as inspiration comes in fits and starts from Rasi, the Countess, the rhythm of a baker throwing sticks of bread into another's apron, or the tempo of the dough-mixing machine; in the end this may be cute but certainly not filled with tension. Only one scene of the process, of Schani playing the as yet not fully formed waltz badly at the piano in front of his father and orchestra, and drawing an excoriating review from his father, heightens the tension, but even that accomplishes little. The process of composition also runs parallel to Hitchcock's favorite notion of building a film like developing orchestration, in this case going through whistling, humming, singing, groping at the piano, and finally the fully orchestrated piece, but the film itself had little growth to compare to the music. He undoubtedly learned lessons from this experience, and no doubt one of these was that gradually building toward a familiar tune, from a murky beginning to the melody known to everyone, will have little dramatic impact. The only real potential for this lay in having an original composition in progress, as happens in *Rear Window*, although in that case he had to rely on the composer (Waxman) to create a composition with tension instead of a sugary piece of confection. This experience did not discourage Hitchcock from using the waltz as an image of tension, but clearly it would have to move in a very different direction than it had in *Waltzes from Vienna*.

Finding the waltz's missteps

As if to compensate for the failure of the waltz in *Waltzes from Vienna*, Hitchcock returned to the dance in his next film, *The Man Who Knew Too Much* (1934), and allowed it to function in a way similar to that of *The Lodger*. In what appears to be a pleasant holiday in Hitchcock's own favorite St Moritz, with scenes of ski jumping and skeet shooting, Louis Bernard (Pierre Fresnay) invites the Lawrence family to join him for dinner, and he and Jill (Edna Best) dance flirtatiously on the ballroom floor, teasing Jill's husband Bob (Leslie Banks) with mock affection as they do. Jill has been knitting something, for Louis she facetiously claims, and Bob ties the end of the yarn to Louis's tailcoat as his little revenge. As they continue to dance, all the other dancing couples become entangled in the yarn, much to the delight of onlookers, especially Bob and his daughter Betty (Nova Philbeam). The cheerfulness suddenly changes when a shot rings out, and Louis slumps to the floor, giving Jill a key and information before he dies.

The stage is now set for the dark events which follow, drawing the family into a spiral of intrigue that includes the kidnapping of Betty, and all the subsequent steps they must take into the frightening unknown. Disorder and death have been released, in a dance, and the ambiguity of the image becomes even more poignant because of the yarn prank, drawing everyone on the dance floor together into a web of possible conspiracy. Even the light seductiveness of Louis and Jill becomes part of the complexity, adding a dimension completely lacking in the 1956 version of Hitchcock's only sequel.

With this scene he got back on track with the waltz, and during the rest of the 1930s other experiments would develop similar possibilities. The next one came in 1937, with *Young and Innocent*, in which a young man falsely accused of murder must clear his name. Following a good lead, the search takes Robert (Derrick de Marney) and his new friend Erica (Nova Philbeam) along with the homeless Old Will (Edward Rigby) to the Grand Hotel, where people are dancing in the dining room. When the drummer in the band recognizes Old Will dancing with Erica, and sees police moving in, he loses the beat of the dance, creating his own disordered counterpoint to the stable beat of the band. Rhythmic breakdown leads to a telltale eye twitch, which reveals his identity as the murderer. This time the music becomes directly involved, with the musicians providing it playing a role central to the discovery of the murderer, and Hitchcock achieves his goal by adding an element of disorder into the music, both aurally and visually. In *The Lady Vanishes* one year later, dancing again becomes an element of disorder, although humorously in this case. Near the opening the gentle singing of a street musician (in fact providing a code in song for Miss Froy, played by Dame May Whitty) is rudely disrupted by the clarinet playing inflicted by the inconsiderate ethnomusicologist Gilbert (Michael Redgrave) and folk dancing from a room upstairs. For a few moments the song and the heavily rustic folk dance collide, setting the scene for the unlikely relationship between Gilbert and the young English woman Iris (Margaret Lockwood), who complains. The disorder here is zany, not ominous; menace comes the next time we see the street singer, as an assailant strangles him while he sings.

In these films from the 1930s, dancing proved to be a useful way to highlight the main element of tension or disorder in the film. Early in the 1940s, Hitchcock took this a large step forward, and for this he needed the collaboration of an able composer, along with the cooperation of his screenwriters. These elements came together strikingly in *Suspicion* (1941), with the script provided by Samson Raphaelson, Joan Harrison (Hitchcock's trusted assistant who until that time worked on almost all the scripts), and his wife Alma; Franz Waxman, who had collaborated with him on his first American film, *Rebecca*, wrote the score. A waltz, specifically a very familiar one, *Wiener Blut*, plays a central role in the film, as "our dance" for Johnnie (Cary Grant) and Lina (Joan Fontaine). Lina has fallen in love with Johnnie after a few unusual meetings, and when he unexpectedly arrives at the Hunt Ball and dodges the fact that he lacks an invitation, he completely sweeps her off her feet to the strains of the waltz *Wiener Blut*. Before he arrived she dances with someone else, unenthusiastically, to a dance in 4/4 time; now she dances passionately to the 3/4 meter of the waltz. They escape the ball, and kiss in her family car; when they kiss again at her home, the waltz swells in the background, and after he facetiously asks her father's portrait for permission to marry her, they spontaneously hear their waltz, and dance to it. In its unadulterated form the waltz will be heard later in the film as well, whistled by Johnnie or played on a recording, and when it does it provides a symbol of their love, full of sexual energy and irrational pleasure.

Disorder lurks beneath the surface as a constant factor in this film, shattering the calm of Lina's happiness. While brimming with passion, she has conventional ideas of what marriage should be and how her spouse should behave, and Johnnie makes a pretense of these for her benefit, but in reality lives the life of a scoundrel. This should come as no surprise to her since she knows of his reputation, and he made no secret of it before marriage, but suspicion and knowledge of the truth unnerve her every time they come to the surface. The pattern of his deceptions gets progressively more serious, along with her suspicions which may or may not be true. He allows her to think he still holds gainful employment, when in fact he has been sacked for embezzling from his employer and actually spends his time betting at the racetrack. Things become deadly serious when authorities find their friend Beaky, with whom Johnnie has entered into a business arrangement which gives him access to Beaky's money, dead in Paris, and the police consider Johnnie to be their prime suspect since he has a motive and knows that strong drink causes seizures to his friend. The climax arrives when Lina believes Johnnie intends to murder her for her insurance money, and that he will use a poisoning method which has been the topic of conversation with a crime novelist friend and her physician brother.

The potential for the waltz to play a central role in the breakdown of order in this film occurred to Hitchcock and his writers at an early stage in the development of the script. In its unaltered form *Wiener Blut* underlies love and happiness, but if the waltz were to be distorted, it could represent the opposite, getting at Lina's suspicion, even the disintegration of her love, and progressing all the way to fear for her own safety. The model for this type of distortion existed, and Hitchcock knew it well: Ravel's *La Valse*. Like his other films, the script for this one went through numerous rewrites over a number of months in the development stages, with Raphaelson, Harrison, and Alma working collaboratively with Hitchcock. In a version of the script dated 28 December 1940 with all three writers credited, still using the title "Before the Fact" (the title of the novel by Francis Iles [Anthony Berkeley] on which the script is based), a specific reference occurs on page 168. Just before Inspector Hodgson arrives to make inquiries about Johnnie's possible connection with the death of Beaky in Paris, we see Lina in the Aysgarth sitting room "playing the piano—the tune is their own waltz tune and she is picking out the notes rather in the manner of Ravel's 'La Valse.' She breaks off as Ethel enters."[25] This scene did not make it to the final shooting script, but it indicates the writers and Hitchcock had *La Valse* on their minds not long before shooting began, and that for Hitchcock this particular work had the potential to take a conventional waltz and skew it in a way that could summon dark associations.

Even though Hitchcock did not use this Ravel scene, he clearly wanted to include something like it, and in fact he decided to save that for a more climactic moment and for Waxman to integrate it into his score. The climactic moment, a stunning one for this or any film, occurs when Johnnie, appearing to be the good husband, brings the ailing Lina a glass of milk after she has slept all day, a glass she believes contains the poison that will end her life. Before he brings it, Lina chats with their novelist friend Isobel about the undetectable poison idea, which Isobel fears Johnnie may be stealing from her as a plot for a novel he intends to write. The camera gives a close-up of Lina, whose concerned face reveals her suspicion that this idea will not go into fiction; she asks if it will be painful, and Isobel assures her the death could even be pleasant. A jump cut takes us abruptly from Lina's look of concern to the bottom of the stairway, where a shaft of light reveals a shadow of Johnnie carrying the glass on a small tray. He turns out the light, and walks through the darkened area framed by cage-like shadows, and then ascends the stairs with these shadows now even more prominent. As his own shadow passes through these shapes on the wall, the camera projects a nightmarish image, as menacing as Murnau's Nosferatu approaching the sleeping Nina; instead of bony, threatening fingers he has the glass of milk, illuminated with a light inside of it to focus attention on it.

Waxman accompanies this scene of visual disfigurement with a subdued distortion of *Wiener Blut*, the waltz now evoking evil and menace, having lost its innocent association just as a glass of milk

4.3 *Suspicion* (Cary Grant) (The potentially fatal glass of milk)

has. The German expressionist mindscape merges the tormented visions so common in Murnau, Wiene, Lang, and others, bringing to bear the full potential of the waltz to twist the impression this should have. Before the camera returns to a close-up of Lina, it gives an extreme close-up of the illuminated glass; by this point the waltz has faded out, and gives way to an additional eerie distortion. In reverting to the techniques of silent film here, Hitchcock has released cinematic demons most powerfully, combining the best of visual treatment with the most effective possible musical accompaniment. The visual treatment becomes a form of Ravel's disjointed waltz, and the building to a climax continues as Johnnie drives recklessly along the cliff's edge in what Lina takes to be yet another attempt on her life. The ending of the film, with Johnnie turning the car around to drive home while putting his arm around an adoring Lina, of course does not ring true, considering his admissions about himself and what they have been through. The ending is as much a ruse as the last notes of *La Valse*; this will be described in the next chapter about *Shadow of a Doubt*, which takes the *La Valse* image much further, even using quotations from it in the score by Dmitri Tiomkin. Quotation of this work occurs again in the early 1950s, in *Strangers on a Train*, also scored by Tiomkin. In fact, the quotation here also happens with a very tense scene, this time on a stairway. Guy (Farley Grainger) has come to Bruno's (played by Robert Walker) home to warn Bruno's father about his murderous son, but instead he encounters Bruno in his father's bed. As he attempts to leave, descending the stairs, Bruno points a gun at him, and halfway down the stairs we hear the Ravel quotation.

Aside from *Suspicion* and *Shadow of a Doubt* the waltz or related dances continued to be a factor in Hitchcock's films in the 1940s, in scenes that capture some of the highest drama of these films. In *Saboteur* (1942), Barry (Robert Cummings) and Pat (Priscilla Lane) find themselves prisoners of the saboteurs at a stately mansion in New York, and make their escape to a dance floor where they join in the dance. These seem to be respectable people, but perhaps in looks only, and the ballroom floor and dancing accentuate the ambiguity. Similarly in *Notorious* (1946), an even more elaborately staged dance, in this case a waltz, takes place in a similar type of mansion, where Nazis do their plotting amid apparently respectable society in Rio. The political intrigue is heightened by the role of Alicia (Ingrid Bergman) as an agent with a peculiar love relationship with Devlin (Gary Grant), but married for the purposes of espionage to Sebastien (Claude Rains), the owner of the mansion and perpetrator of the schemes. The tension comes to a head as the dancing continues, with Devlin trying to discover the secrets of the house, and walking the fine line between the personal tensions and political plots. One of Hitchcock's most famous shots occurs during the dancing, with the long zoom of the camera down the stairs to the dance floor and then to the key in Alicia's hand, a key that will allow Devlin to gain access to the wine cellar which stores more than wine. The stairway features prominently in both of these dance scenes.

In *Under Capricorn* (1949) the waltz again becomes a focus of tension, as the dysfunctional Hattie (Ingrid Bergman) makes an attempted return to polite society at the Governor's ball, where she shines. This comes to a rude end when her husband, Sam (Joseph Cotton), storms uninvited into the ball and drags her away, making her feel disgraced. Like the two films just noted, the waltz in this case becomes the event for the high drama; here it could have been a coming out for Hattie, after all the degradation she has experienced, but instead things come to the worst possible conclusion. In this costume drama set in Australia in the nineteenth century, the waltz proved an ideal backdrop for these events, and captures something of the ambiguity of how the new world perceived waltzing. Films that use dancing after *Under Capricorn*, most often visually as well as aurally, do not do so as substantially as earlier ones; these include *Dial M for Murder*, *Rear Window*, *To Catch a Thief*, *The Wrong Man*, and *Torn Curtain*. Even in these the ambiguity of the dance often comes through, adding to the dimension of the struggle between the forces of order and disorder in these films.

5

Shadow of a waltz

When Hitchcock started working on a new film, he had a non-verbal conception of the film in his mind, although his discussions with his collaborating scriptwriters and later the actors seldom revealed what he actually envisaged. Because of the nature of his initial conception, he had to coax it out in a manner that would take a verbal form, and for this he needed help, from his scriptwriter and of course from Alma. With *Shadow of a Doubt* the pieces fell into place with relative ease. The idea came from a six-page story outline by the novelist Gordon McDonell, initially titled "Uncle Charlie," written specifically for Hitchcock and dated 5 May 1942.[1] Something in this outline captured Hitchcock's interest immediately, although not necessarily the details of the plot or even the impressions of small-town America, some of which he dismissed in his critique of the outline written on 11 May.

The most crucial period for Hitchcock in forming his impulse for the film fell between 5 May and 11 May; in writing his three-page critique on 11 May he knew he had something that could work its way through the entire process that ultimately results in a completed film, but at this point the shape of the narrative proved the least important of the various considerations.[2] Some of the characters proposed by McDonell would surely be expendable, the girl's boyfriend for example, but three of them remained central and could not be removed: the girl in her late adolescence, her uncle (the brother of her mother), and her mother. The relationship among all three would be complex, and should have larger social implications in the most striking possible way. It needed to cover everything from the purest and most trusting naiveté to the most degraded and heinous actions and cynicism, and would have to be understood by someone about to embark on her own life as an adult. All of this must happen within the same family, but would project something beyond, with national and even international implications. Horror encroaches on an idyllic town, destroying the peace and lack of guile that reside there, but in getting to that horrific point, humor was essential. The town itself should not be a conventional small town already familiar on the screen but should have a modern edge, with "movies, radio, jukeboxes ... lit by neon signs."[3] With these words written on 11 May Hitchcock started to get at his notion of the film, its dualities and images, its progression through the world we love to the point of collapse, and the point at which we must deceive ourselves into believing that the beautiful world still exists. The images that will help the process should evoke responses from the eye and ear—a radio from which the flick of the dial can get rid of words and envelop us with musical sounds, a jukebox for music only, neon signs with their vivid visual stimuli, and the fusion of all of these in one medium: a film.

In these comments in the second part of his critique, titled "Some notes about the small town atmosphere," although seeming fairly innocuous, we see the essence of the director's mind stirring, not toward a storyline, but in formulating the conception that he cares about most: the combination of sight and sound. He gave much thought at this time to a possible remake of the visually provocative film *The Lodger*, now of course with the possibilities of sound; instead, he created in his own mind an abstract notion of the fusion of sight and sound for his new film, of a visual aura underpinned by an emanation of sound, and of course he needed a composer to formulate the right audible impression. For the script he required a writer who could intuit his underlying conception, and McDonell himself seemed an excellent prospect, considering how his short outline had set the imagination in motion. Things fell into place to get the project started immediately, with a new contract to work again with Jack Skirball, although inevitably and unfortunately with David O. Selznick still pulling the strings,[4] but McDonell, in the midst of writing a novel, could not afford the time. In the search for an

American writer of the highest standard, a suggestion from Miriam Howell, Sam Goldwyn's New York literary agent, turned out to be inspired: Thornton Wilder. He accepted, despite finding the outline "corny," and quickly started the intensive collaboration that Hitchcock expected with any of his writers, producing a 141-page script by 10 June 1942. He had to leave the project to take up a war-related assignment in Washington, and the script had not yet reached Hitchcock's liking when he left on 24 June, still lacking the necessary humor; Sally Benson came on board to complete it, and she added the final touches it needed. As usual, Alma worked on it at every step along the way, from the crucial days of assessing the initial outline to the drafting of the final script, and it can be very difficult to distinguish the differences between her ideas and Hitchcock's.

Titles music and visuals

In this film, as with most others by Hitchcock, the script needed to be driven by his fusion of visual and auditory effects, not the other way round, and in this case he gives us his strongest possible impression of what these may be at the beginning of the film—the very first things we see and hear. In fact, in this film the sound precedes the visual images, starting with a blank screen with titles, giving the name of the producer, and the two leading actors: Theresa Wright and Joseph Cotten. At the instant "Alfred Hitchcock's *Shadow of a Doubt*" comes up we also see, now replacing the blank background, dancers swirling in a waltz, in both foreground and background. A split second before even the first title appears, "Skirball Productions Presents," the music hits us, a familiar waltz, "The Merry Widow Waltz" from Franz Lehar's operetta, and the music continues throughout the titles. The music therefore appears to present itself as the stronger force of the two, and almost immediately even the most unschooled listener will detect something badly amiss with this music. When the dancing couples appear on screen they dance as anyone would a waltz, yet the music does not connect with their dancing; in fact, in the way we hear this music, it would be impossible to dance to it. The waltz, with its triple meter, must be in periodic phrases for the dance steps to be executed, clearly divided into groups of four bars that combine into eight-bar and 16-bar units, and the phrasing pattern of the melody itself will make that design clear. Almost immediately here, certainly before we first see the dancers, that phrasing pattern becomes distorted, lacking the phrasing continuity necessary for a waltz to be danced properly, so when we actually see the dancers, we perceive a disconnection since these people do not actually dance to the music we hear. Aside from wondering what a waltz has to do with the title, Hitchcock immediately forces us to question why the two primary means of cinema, sight and sound, do not connect. This tension extends throughout the first seven minutes of the film, as the puzzling visuals, along with the continuing distortion of the waltz, give no clues about the subject matter of the film.

By 1943 the moviegoer experiencing a new Hitchcock film would not necessarily be surprised to see a waltz or perhaps some other type of dance with a key role in one of his films. American audiences would probably not know his silent films, but if they did, they would recall the key dance scene in *The Lodger*, where the all-important event that motivates the Lodger, the murder of his sister, occurs at

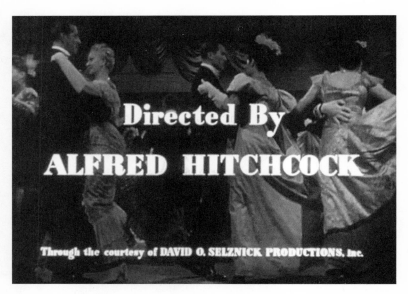

5.1 *Shadow of a Doubt* (opening credits) (The mismatch of music and waltz)

her coming-out celebration amid dancing. Other silent films have dance scenes as well, including *The Pleasure Garden, Downhill, Easy Virtue, The Ring*, and *Champagne*. Of the sound films, seven of them by this time had waltz scenes in them, including *Number Seventeen, Rich and Strange, Waltzes from Vienna, Young and Innocent, The Lady Vanishes*, and *Rebecca*. The one they would know best, though, came only two years earlier, *Suspicion* (1941), where the waltz does not play a minor role, but gains central importance as "their tune" for Johnnie and Lina (Cary Grant and Joan Fontaine), the familiar "*Wiener Blut*," as described in the previous chapter. Most notably, we hear it both in its true form and distorted by composer Franz Waxman, underlying the points of stability and tension—including Lina's realizations not only of Johnnie's dishonesty but the possibility that he may be a murderer with her as the intended victim. With waltzes in this many films, making the most prominent possible impression, we must surely see it as something special for Hitchcock, even taking on structural significance in *Suspicion*. Hitchcock related to the waltz from his lessons in his late adolescence, but of much greater importance, the waltz had become a prominent cultural symbol, both in Europe and the United States, although a very different one on the two sides of the Atlantic (as noted in the previous chapter).

Warping the waltz

When we hear and see the waltz at the beginning of *Shadow of a Doubt*, not only will our curiosity be piqued, but so will our puzzlement. As important as the waltz was to *Suspicion*, now Hitchcock appears to be taking it much further, bombarding us with it as the first things we hear and see, leading us to suspect that it may be at the heart of his own formative approach to the film. We eventually discover through attempts of whistlers to identify the tune—and Uncle Charlie spilling his milk (with a possible link to the milk-glass scene in *Suspicion*) to thwart the identification, that he has been dubbed the murderer of merry widows, and the tune therefore has special meaning for him and the police on his trail. As central as that realization may be, it appears to be only part of the picture. The importance lies not in this obvious identification, but in the problem we hear in the first few seconds, a problem that continues off and on for the next seven minutes. For the composer who should create the twisted waltz, Hitchcock made a selection every bit as inspired as his choice of a scriptwriter, finding Dimitri Tiomkin, a Ukrainian by birth who had a career in his homeland and Paris before coming to the United States. Not only did Tiomkin distort the waltz, but he drew on a specific musical source to accomplish that.

In an article published in the *American Cinematographer* in 1993, George Turner more or less figured it out:

> There is also a unifying visual and musical motif which first appears under the titles: dancers in turn-of-the-century costumes spinning to Franz Lehar's "Merry Widow Waltz," which has been distorted by composer Dimitri Tiomkin into a sinister tone poem much in the style of Maurice Ravel's "La Valse." Image and theme dissolve in and out at several dramatic moments, including that of Uncle Charlie's fatal accident.[5]

Turner could have taken this further: during the first seven minutes, the music goes beyond being in the style of Ravel's *La Valse*: it actually quotes *La Valse*, so fleetingly that someone not very familiar with the work will probably miss the quotes, but amply evident to anyone who knows the work well. With these terse quotations he provides us with a type of musical cameo, in this case possibly even alerting us to something about Hitchcock's conception of the film.

Whether or not these quotations were simply Tiomkin's doing, without input from Hitchcock, we cannot say. Tiomkin, though, in his autobiography, recounted what Hitchcock expected of him for this film, his memory somewhat faded 15 years after the fact:

> I worked with him on a melodrama of suspense, *Shadow of a Doubt*, in which one musical task was to rewrite "The Merry Widow." Somehow or other—I don't remember—the graceful waltz played a sinister part in the picture, and at one place it appeared with horror harmonies and orchestration. I gave "the Merry Widow" the atonal treatment and worse.

At a preview of the film in Long Beach, some of the studio executives fell asleep, one of them actually snoring in two notes: "Even my ear-torturing version of 'The Merry Widow Waltz' didn't wake him up." He expected a full-scale flop when the audience "giggled through my sinister waltz harmonies and laughed loudly in moments of terror." Hitchcock consoled the distraught composer, assuring him that tension causes American audiences to break into nervous laughter; the film of course succeeded wonderfully.[6] In his description of the "horror harmonies" Tiomkin does not mention Ravel, but instead invokes Arnold Schoenberg with "the atonal treatment." The omission may have been intentional: during his years in Paris Tiomkin became friendly with Ravel, and later as a concert pianist he often played Ravel's music, including his own piano transcription of La Valse.[7] No one knows the details of a work better than a performer and transcriber, and Tiomkin could easily have slipped the quotations into his score, finding the right effect and with no one, including the director, any the wiser.

Considering what had happened in the planning of Suspicion, that option does not seem likely. In that case the waltz Weiner Blut needed to be wrenched out of shape to underlie the suspicion about Johnny's misdeeds and possible crimes, and in doing this it provided the ideal model for Shadow of a Doubt only two years later. Hitchcock did not work with Tiomkin on Suspicion, instead using Waxman, a composer with no association with or special interest in Ravel. While some of the distortions to the waltz in that film may be Ravel-like, the specific linkage with Ravel comes through as clearly in the script as it does in the music, as the previous chapter noted, with a scene from an earlier script version that placed Lina at the piano "picking out the notes rather in the manner of Ravel's 'La Valse'," a scene that did not make it to the final shooting script. Shadow of a Doubt was Tiomkin's first collaboration with Hitchcock, and unlike certain other composers later—especially Bernard Herrmann—who may have been engaged to work on the film at a fairly early stage, Tiomkin did not start until much of the editing had been completed. After watching the rushes, and being told by Hitchcock of the importance of the treatment of the waltz, he appears to have noticed something beyond the waltz itself that prompted the association with Ravel's piece, a work he of course knew well.

Thornton Wilder

What Tiomkin recognized in the work, along with the rhythmic aspects generated by the shots and constructive montage, surely included the overall structure, and for the realization of this Hitchcock needed the close collaboration of his writers. In drafting their script the writers had to be directed in ways that would keep the idea of the misshapen waltz central, and in the shortness of time available to Wilder, led by Hitchcock's obtuse and often cryptic prodding, this in fact happened, although not down to the final details of tone. Unlike some Wilder biographers, who saw this collaboration as a blotch on the playwright's career—as literary slumming with predictable results, Wilder took it very seriously and plunged into it with all his energy, thoroughly enjoying the collaboration, as he confided to Alexander Woollcott in a letter dated 23 May 1942: "I am deeply interested in the movie we're doing ... Mr. Hitchcock and I get on fine together. In long story conferences we think up new twists to

5.2 Hitchcock with Thornton Wilder

the plot and gaze at one another in appalled silence: as much as to say 'Do you think an audience can bear it?'"[8]

Typically they met every morning for these story conferences, where Hitchcock encouraged Wilder to develop the narrative as he saw fit, altering the original scenario wherever necessary, and Wilder would then spend his afternoons writing. Before they started on their regular meetings, Hitchcock showed Wilder his film *Suspicion*, according to Martin Blank, to familiarize Wilder with some technical aspects of movies,[9] and while that may have been true, Hitchcock probably had more specific reasons as well. Both films centered on waltzes, and both involved disfiguring the waltz; Hitchcock undoubtedly wanted Wilder to have both a visual and audible sense of that before starting his work.

Film structure and *La Valse*

In familiarizing himself with the rough cuts of the film, Tiomkin could not have missed what anyone who knows Ravel's *La Valse* well would notice: the two works not only have remarkably similar structures, but also parallels in the construction of pace and aura. Whether or not these parallels occurred by happenstance or design, Hitchcock's familiarity with this piece and awareness of what the music does provokes consideration of whether or not the connection is purely coincidental. Ravel wrote his *"poème chorégraphique"* with a programmatic narrative intended for the impresario Sergei Diaghilev, to be performed by his Ballet Russe—the troupe of Russian dancers based in Paris that included the great Njinsky as a member.[10] Overall *La Valse* has a two-part form (see Appendix 6), the first half representing pre-1914 Vienna with its fairly orderly society symbolized by the waltz, presented in such a way that it can more or less be danced as a waltz. The second half sees the disintegration of the waltz, no longer possible to dance in any conventional way, becoming disorderly to the point of chaos, reaching an apotheosis at the end marked by total collapse and destruction. The waltz and its disintegration represent an entire society, with a fatal sense of nostalgia for its past and traditions, and the result of what happens when that vision becomes clouded by forces of evil—forces prepared to sacrifice an entire generation for the personal gain of those in control. Ravel does not give us the waltz at the beginning of the work, but instead lets fragments of its melody emerge gradually as if from a murky abyss; we finally hear the waltz in its four-bar phrasing structure about three minutes into the 12-and-a-half-minute piece. At the beginning we encounter nothing but a musical blur, initially only a muted tremolo in the string basses low in their register. The tremolos spread gradually to the rest of the strings, and as this happens, fragments of the waltz melody pop up here and there, indicating that a waltz will emerge, but at the moment lacking any type of phrasing pattern to define the dance. As the waltz attempts to get started, other sound fragments encroach as part of Ravel's rich orchestration, such as occasional *glissandi* in the harp, a run in the clarinet, and a chromatic run in the flute with flutter-tonguing, all creating a musical haze that prevents any attempt at finding order. The material that divides parts one and two reverts back to the opening blur, using the same low tremolo in the strings and also the disconnected fragments of the melody; the opening and middle therefore play their own structural role, as a disturbing introduction and an indefinite, nebulous, and disorienting separation of the two parts. In contrast to the beginning and middle, the end takes a stab at order, in the last two bars giving a cadence in the key of D, the key of the waltz at the beginning of part one. After the many bars of chaos that precede this ending, no one will be convinced by this as closure, and in fact it seems to be something of a ruse, certainly not capable in its raw unison of lurching out and disarming the overwhelming forces of destruction just experienced. The attentive listener will probably respond to this final cadence with something like "You must be kidding!"

This larger design, unique in the way that the distorted material at the beginning and middle modifies its two-part form, fits remarkably with *Shadow of a Doubt*, which also has two parts, a blurred introduction, a foggy section dividing the two parts, and even a similar type of ruse as a conclusion. In the first seven minutes of the film the camera presents us with images that make little sense—views of urban decay that raise questions and give no answers. William Rothman describes the mystery these disjointed visual impressions invoke with this:

This camera movement does not disclose the thoughts on which Cotten is dwelling. Why is this man, rolling in money, lying in bed in broad daylight in a seedy rooming house? Where has all the money come from, and why is he so indifferent to it? In introducing him in this manner—rather, in withholding a proper introduction, in presenting him to us as unknown—the camera's autonomy is asserted, its enigma declared.[11]

One could expand on Rothman's list to include the bridge and the street scenes, the strange conversation Joseph Cotten has with his landlady about men he has never met, and the overhead shots as he gives these men the slip. The urban blight corresponds with Ravel's opening nebulous sounds, or musical disarray, and the glimmers of information work like the fragments of the waltz theme. Ravel's orchestration includes other unrelated material, *glissandi*, scales, and chromatic runs, and Hitchcock's camera also gives us apparently unrelated details, of a bridge or children playing. During these seven minutes Tiomkin provides the only audible identification of *La Valse* with fragments from it.

The film's first part begins in Santa Rosa, an archetypal American town, with ordinary people and the fixtures of an orderly town, including a courthouse, a library, a bank, churches, a soda fountain, a policeman at a main intersection who keeps things running smoothly, and simple yet attractive houses. In a town such as this, small enough that everyone knows everyone else, things run as they should, typified by the life of Joe Newton (Henry Travers), a bank employee with a wife, three children, a house, and car, who attends church, reads the newspaper, and believes nothing can be more important than his job. His life is ordinary to the point of boredom, which he does not really mind, although even he needs to liven it up a little by playing murder games with his neighbor Herb (Hume Cronyn). His wife Emma (Patricia Collinge) does not notice her life because of being too overwhelmed by household duties, but their oldest daughter, Charlie (Theresa Wright), notices everything—the state of the family, the state of the town, and she even has a sense of the larger world out there, which she believes cannot possibly be as tedious as their existence. Convinced of their unfortunate rut, she believes they need something to give their lives a spark; nothing could do that better, she imagines, than a visit from her mother's brother, Charles (Joseph Cotten), a man of the world who could bring them everything their tedious existence appears to be lacking. Part one establishes the family and the town, and gives us the pleasant aspects of Uncle Charlie's visit. For the most part life continues to be orderly and now enjoyable as well, festive with the uncle's arrival, like the pleasurable aspects of the waltz—sufficiently orderly and phrased so it can be danced.

The second part begins after young Charlie's trip to the library, where she discovers the horrible truth about her uncle, as she reads the article in the newspaper he had destroyed from the family newspaper, establishing his identity as the "Merry Widow" murderer, one of whose victim's initials appear on the ring he gave her as a gift. Her relationship with him now takes a turn in the opposite direction as she finds him repugnant and wants him to leave as soon as possible; he quickly learns that she knows the truth, and he makes little or no attempt to conceal it. For him it will not do to have anyone know the truth, and since she knows, even as his favorite niece, she must be expunged. He makes three attempts to kill her, although the first one, the broken step on the outside stairway, could have been a maintenance problem with the stairs. The second attempt, the running car in the garage with no key and a closing garage door that traps her, no longer leaves much doubt about his intentions. The third try, on the train, brings everything into the open. Not only a repugnant person who kills women he describes as useless, Uncle Charlie has now crossed the last line into the realm of heinousness, prepared to destroy the person that we as viewers most love and respect, the beautiful and intelligent young Charlie. Like the black smoke of the train that brings him to Santa Rosa, Uncle Charlie's evil has contaminated the beautiful surroundings of this town, although for the moment only young Charlie grasps that. He gets killed in the act of attempting to take her life, but we have now seen the human condition at its worst, an individual representing the lowest form of existence and the most degraded state of humanity. The sweet town of Santa Rosa has lost its innocence and order, at least in young Charlie's mind; the apotheosis of chaos and destruction has come to her town (to *Our Town*), and in fact the America of goodness and decency cannot fend off the encroaching horror. Few will recognize the evil, and certainly not the naive and blinkered residents of Santa Rosa.

At various points in the first part young Charlie sees her uncle behave strangely, make odd comments, and even hurt her physically, but the clincher comes when she correctly identifies Jack Graham (MacDonald Carey) as a detective looking for her uncle. She tries to locate the missing article in the newspaper, and unable to, she goes to the library to find it, on the advice of her little bookworm sister. The library will close soon, but she cannot wait, wishing to prove her uncle innocent but fearful of what she will find. The issue now racks her brain to distraction, and she rushes to the library as though in a fog; this trip to the library marks the end of the first part and parallels the blurred dividing section in *La Valse*. The directions for the scene confirm the blur:

CAMERA MOVING with her, she approaches the shopping district—lights flash across her face. She looks up at the clock: It is four minutes to nine. She runs faster and faster—her hair flying behind her.

CAMERA MOVING with her as she almost races along … suddenly she is pulled up sharply by a voice:

MR. MORTON: Just a moment, Charlie. What do you think I'm here for?

At a street crossing she was about to dash across against the policeman's signal. She steps back onto the sidewalk, breathless.

She almost races again along the street near the library—her eyes ahead—her lips moving but with no sound we can almost feel her saying to herself "It can't be—it can't be …"

She arrives at the foot of the library steps—breathing heavily.[12]

Now obsessed with finding the answer, she has lost her usual sense of decorum, violating the order that policeman Morton represents. As she hurries along, lights flash across her face, the neon lights that Hitchcock explained to Wilder he required to give things an edge—lights that will dominate at other points of tension, along with penetrating sounds. After she learns the truth from the newspaper, "The 'Merry Widow Waltz' slowly swells to a fortissimo … As she slowly begins to drag herself across the room, the dancing

Edwardian figures DISSOLVE IN until they completely obliterate her" (p. 97). Not only in a fog, the image of the waltz, as disjointed as its appearance as the first visual impression in the film, now completely overwhelms her. The second part begins with the waltz still heard, and young Charlie warning her mother not to hum the tune in Uncle Charlie's presence.

At the climactic moment of Uncle Charlie's death in the path of an oncoming train, which by luck was not young Charlie's death, we have a LAP DISSOLVE, and "there is a crash of noise and lights. The 'Merry Widow Waltz' tune rises to a discordant note, then slowly dies away and there is perfect quiet ..." The next picture gives us the town square and the funeral. In the background we hear organ music and the voice of Dr MacCurdy: "Santa Rosa has gained and lost a son, a son that she can be proud of. Brave. Generous.—(His voice fades out)."[13] The viewer knows better of course, but even Charlie and Jack, standing together talking, contribute to the ruse. She comments that "he thought the world was a horrible place. He couldn't have been very happy ... He didn't trust people. He hated them. He hated the whole world." Jack concedes that "sometimes the world needs a lot of watching. Seems to go crazy every now and then. Like your Uncle Charlie." This seems enough to snap her out of her funk: "The worried look goes from her face and she smiles up at him. They turn and walk away from CAMERA, hands clasped. The organ music swells. FADE OUT: THE END." Do Hitchcock and Wilder think they have fooled anyone with this ending? The happy ending at this point will not erase from the mind of anyone what has just happened—that Charlie's view of the world has forever been contaminated, and that the sleepy townsfolk of Santa Rosa did not get it. Charlie looking up to Jack and smiling will not convince us of hope for the future any more than Ravel's cadence in D at the end of *La Valse*.

Actors

Having coaxed a script suitable for his purposes out of Wilder and Benson, Hitchcock had to bring his actors to a similar point of understanding, especially his two Charlies—Joseph Cotten and Theresa

Wright. With these two he had immensely talented but still fairly inexperienced actors, ideal for his purposes since they would have few preconceived notions of screen acting to get in the way. Cotten had worked with Orson Welles two years earlier on *Citizen Kane*, and that experience was not likely to prejudice his thoughts about any new film since Welles's own inexperience and experimentation at the time did not fit into any type of Hollywood mold. Wright, approaching her mid-twenties, had worked with an outstanding and seasoned director prior to this, playing a supporting role in William Wyler's *The Little Foxes* (1941). Now she had a starring role, and Hitchcock made a great effort to acquaint her with what he wanted. When he met her in mid-June he put his unique mode of familiarizing her with the role to work, not analyzing the character, but telling her the story of the film at great length, and watching her reaction very closely. Wright described their session in this way: "To have a master storyteller like Mr. Hitchcock tell you a story is a marvelous experience. He told me everything, including the sounds and the music." He did this so vividly that when she saw the screening of the completed film months later, she reacted that "I've seen this film before. I saw it in his office that day."[14] With Cotten, he took a somewhat different tack, telling him as they drove home after lunch of his plan to use a fragment from Franz Lehar's "The Merry Widow Waltz" as a leitmotif in the film. He followed this with a final piece of serious advice: "I think our secret is to achieve an effect of contrapuntal emotion. Forget trying to intellectualize about Uncle Charlie. Just be yourself. Let's say the key to our story is emotive counterpoint; that sounds terribly intellectual. See you on the set, old bean."[15]

In both cases he used music when introducing the roles to the actors, borrowing one of the techniques of his idol D. W. Griffith, who, according to Lillian Gish, would actually sing arias to his actors to establish the emotions he wanted. Hitchcock's invocation of music went far beyond the individual roles, as he tried to capture something with his musical images about the aura of the entire film. That undoubtedly included the waltz for Wright as well as Cotten, and although she does not say it, that may also have included the notion of counterpoint for her. She must play a role in which she progresses from a fairly typical young woman, endowed to be sure with a healthy sense of skepticism and ability to see through things, to someone capable of comprehending the most horrible and dark recesses of the soul. Cotten had to play the pleasant uncle who brings a generous spirit and vitality to a family stuck in the mud, and while continuing that spirit to the end, he must also reveal his evil nature, directly to his niece and indirectly to others not alert enough to catch the signals. Of course counterpoint underlies how the role must be played.

Counterpoint: foreground and background

Counterpoint, though, exists at a deeper level, not just involving the roles but in fact the entire impression that the film should leave, and this works in distinctly different ways in the two parts of the film, in a type of counterpoint that one could describe as a relationship between foreground and background. In the first part, the foreground consists of the stability of family life, the stability of the town of Santa Rosa, and the pleasure and the good spirit derived from the visit of the favorite uncle; all of this has clarity to which we can respond in a direct way. The background lacks this clarity and transports us into the realm of mystery, derived from the little we know about Uncle Charlie from the opening seven minutes of the film. Amid the foreground of family and town life, fragments of the background encroach, sometimes having little or no impact but at other times more painfully apparent, leaving us mystified about these little eruptions. The first of these comes with the belching black smoke from the train that brings Uncle Charlie, polluting the entire sky over Santa Rosa, certainly an ominous portent but possible to write off as a locomotive that needs some maintenance. Others come bit by bit. Young Charlie imagines her uncle to have a secret which she will discover, and the initials on the ring he gives her offer the first hint of that, although still innocently at this point. The recognition that the tune stuck in young Charlie's head is not by Victor Herbert or the "Blue Danube" results in Uncle Charlie spilling his milk, and his reaction to an article in the newspaper also prompts strange behavior. When young Charlie finds the paper in his room, he takes it from her roughly, hurting her with his grip.

His suspicion about the government men conducting a survey, his refusal to be photographed, and his deprecating remarks about women do not belong in the ambience of this town, and neither does his joking at the bank about Joe as an embezzler. These background elements continue to pop up in the first part, but they remain in the background, not altering our view of the family, the town, or young Charlie's adoration of her uncle.

In the second part, after young Charlie returns from the library, a different relationship between background and foreground begins to take hold, and eventually a complete reversal sets in, where background has become foreground and vice versa. Scenes at the dinner table quickly become unpleasant, as neither of the younger children want to sit beside their uncle, young Charlie relates a nightmare she has had about her uncle, and Uncle Charlie goes into an insulting rant about wealthy widows. Young Charlie flees the table with her own rant, tired of the murder games her father plays with Herb, and her uncle pursues her and drags her into a bar, the sort of place she would never go on her own, with garish lights and loud jukebox music. His reference to them as twins repulses her as she now knows the horrible truth about him. Some shots of the previous foreground continue, such as the end of a church service or the reception for the adored uncle after his lecture to the ladies' group, but all of these become clouded by the background, as the detectives use the church scene to speak with young Charlie, and a chill runs through the reception when young Charlie descends the stairs and reveals that she has the ring. The background decidedly becomes the foreground as he describes the entire world as a hell, and makes attempts on his niece's life; these scenes become the focus of the final quarter of the film. Even the romantic scene between young Charlie and the detective occurs not in a park with cherry blossoms but in the visually squalid family garage, the location for one of the upcoming murder attempts. The climax takes place on the train, and the movement of the train runs parallel to the build-up of the music and frantic heightening of tension as he roughly drags her to the open door, and holds her as the train builds up speed; they struggle, and he plunges into the path of an oncoming train. Even in this final scene a reversal of the prior foreground and background occurs as the train with the children on it shows normalcy, but that changes completely as the train in fact becomes a murder weapon.

This interplay of foreground and background represents a highly sophisticated usage of counterpoint, and here too one is struck by the similarity to *La Valse*. In his mastery of orchestration (of course one of Hitchcock's favorite images: "there is a bursting impact of images, like a change in orchestration"[16]), Ravel uses the same type of relationship between foreground and background that Hitchcock realizes in this film. The waltz itself provides the primary foreground material of part one of *La Valse*, given at first with a phrasing regularity that makes it possible to dance. The strings carry the waltz melody and its accompaniment, but in the richness of his orchestration, Ravel allows other things to happen, such as short runs in the clarinets and double bass that seem to have a life of their own, disconnected from the waltz. Also in the second cello part a rumbling tremolo underlies the waltz, a barely audible but certainly reflective reminder of the introductory blurred section. As the first part proceeds, more strange little outbursts occur, such as *glissandi* in the harps, more runs in the woodwinds, and role reversals as the woodwinds occasionally take the waltz melody while the strings have runs or staccato chords. Brass instruments enter the fray as well, with loud rhythmic interruptions, but at no point in part one do these interjections completely overwhelm the waltz, although they do at times dislodge it from its danceable phrasing pattern. While the background can become very intense and disruptive, it remains a background in part one, although as the music approaches the middle of part one, the foreground has much more difficulty holding its own.

In the second part that changes completely, as the previously disruptive background material gains ascendancy and eventually takes over altogether, and in fact becomes the foreground. Before the final apotheosis this can happen in a number of ways, such as fragmentation of the dance melody to the point that the fragments become completely detached from any recognizable phrase pattern, or the dance melody can pile up on itself, with three separate dances running independently of each other, not unlike the fourth movement of Charles Ives's Fourth Symphony, which actually requires three conductors. The most interesting illustration of background becoming foreground comes at a point where we initially hear a pattern of short descending chromatic scales. Following this the waltz melody makes its entry, in both cellos and clarinets, taking a forceful stand as the foreground material, although with the chromatic figure still in the background. Very soon a new type of background material enters, almost unnoticeable as it starts quietly in the lowest strings and woodwinds, with a gradual rising pattern of notes moving chromatically upward. Eventually a crescendo makes it more noticeable, but it still does not interfere with the waltz melody. As the chromatic line moves upward other voices of the orchestra join in, and when the brass instruments do, it becomes very audible, running now at equal strength with the melody.

Throughout the rise more instruments take up the one-bar chromatic passage heard earlier, finally making it all but impossible for the melody to compete with the two levels of chromaticism. As the extended chromatic line gets progressively louder, it also accelerates, instead of one note per bar now with three per bar. As it builds to a fortissimo climax, the waltz melody gets pushed out entirely; at the end of this sequence the melody instruments do nothing but play a tremolo figure, transporting the low tremolo from the murky introduction into the upper register. The waltz recedes into the background and then suffers complete defeat, reduced to a blurry tremolo, while the background rising chromatic material has become the foreground through its acceleration, loudness, and permeation of brass, woodwinds, and strings. In its last gasp the waltz becomes metrically dislodged as well, losing its phrase pattern. After this major assault of the background, few traces of the waltz melody remain, and Ravel proceeds into what can only be described as musical chaos, with the ear-wrenching and violent background material now having taken over completely. All of this is relatively easy to hear, even for inexperienced listeners.

Rhythm in music and montage

Aside from the reversal of background and foreground, the extended rising chromatic passage just described bears another striking similarity to the procedures of the film, related to what Hitchcock and Pudovkin call rhythm, although in fact a very particular kind of rhythm, having more to do with pace. Like the type of harmonic rhythm noted in Chapter 3, where the rate of harmonic change accelerates to a point of climax, that type of acceleration to a climax can happen in other ways as well. In the Ravel passage in question, the rate of the chromatic change drives the pace. That principle of acceleration to a climax had been the crux of Hitchcock's formula for editing or montage in silent films, and of course it worked just as well in sound films. Throughout *Shadow of a Doubt* a progression of climaxes occurs, building to the final climax of the attempted murder of young Charlie by her uncle on the train, and each one of these follows some variant of acceleration to a climax in the editing. These do not always necessarily work as a straightforward acceleration, but can vary the pace erratically, in fact destabilizing things even more that way. A small one happens in part one at the dinner table, as young Charlie hums the waltz tune and the family tries to identify it. The sequence lasts exactly one and a half minutes (the breakdown of shots is shown in Appendix 7[17]), and while it may seem to be varied, in fact a type of acceleration does occur leading up to the spilled glass, preventing the name of the correct waltz from being uttered.

In this case no music accompanies the building up to a climax since the waltz tune provides the subject of the sequence, and young Charlie's humming gives all the music we need. The climax here in any event is slight, nothing like a murder attempt or the discovery of the painful truth, and in those scenes music plays a significant role. For young Charlie's trip to the library we have climaxes within climaxes, first of all getting to the library (only Hitchcock could turn something as mundane as a walk to the library into a momentous event), and then the discovery of the truth. The first sequence starts with her in her sister Ann's bedroom looking at the rumpled news clippings retrieved from her uncle's wastebasket. Here a very significant acceleration in the length of shots occurs as she nears the library in the dark with lights flashing; the final acceleration happens as she breaks through townsfolk on the curb into the street—where a car almost hits her—returns to the curb, and looks anxiously at the clock tower.

Tiomkin's music also plays a significant role in this building up, and in fact carries through to the next climaxes. While in her sister's bedroom we hear gentle music in the background, "our town" music, for the most part undisturbed. As she hurries down the back outside stairway (the first locale for the death attempts of part two), the music intensifies. As she rushes through the streets, at one point straight at the camera, Tiomkin adds a piano to the score, creating music with new intensification that sounds very much like a piano concerto by Sergei Rachmaninov. The next climax comes as she bolts to the door of the library with a clear acceleration of shots; the Rachmaninov-like concerto peaks as she runs past other people and up the library steps. Now we hear the bell in the clock tower strike nine times, and as this becomes the music, we may very well think of the clock striking 12 in Berlioz's *Symphonie Fantastique* (part 5), just before the witch's sabbath, and the final grotesque return of the *idée fixe*. In the final climax of this scene, Hitchcock does not use editing in a significant way, but hands the job over to Tiomkin, who again intensifies his music as she searches for and finds the newspaper. With the close-up of the title, "Where is the Merry Widow Murderer?," and young Charlie's grasp of the situation, Tiomkin gives a piercing stinger chord followed immediately by the waltz itself, loud and very much in the foreground. She checks the inscription on her ring, leaves in a fog, and that fog deepens with the double image of the waltz superimposed over her, followed by an exterior shot of her home the next morning with Uncle Charlie holding a newspaper. Similar climactic sequences occur elsewhere, such as the attempt by Uncle Charlie to murder young Charlie by asphyxiation in the garage. As usual the editing pace, while accelerating overall, does not do so in a consistent way.

The attempt to murder young Charlie on the train brings the final and most pronounced climax of the film, and now Hitchcock's montage gives the strongest possible acceleration to a climax, not unlike the chromatic section near the end of *La Valse*. Here he uses Pudovkin's type of constructive editing in a classic way, with the breakdown of shots giving a clear acceleration (see Appendix 8). Their actions parallel the editing as they struggle, she attempting to free herself, made all the more vulnerable by his hand over her mouth, and the pace also intensifies with the blur of the ground visible from the open door.

Here too the music plays a classic role, not entering until the other children have disembarked and young Charlie remains alone with her uncle. For Hitchcock concrete sounds can sometimes achieve the same results as music, and that happens at the start of this sequence, when the clanging of the train's bell gives the most prominent background sound as the train pulls into the station and stops. At this point the bell may very well take us back to the library sequence, where its ringing had an ominous urgency for young Charlie. When the music proper now starts, young Charlie clearly apprehensive to be on the train without her siblings, Tiomkin starts quietly with a distinctive film noir musical tone—a background shuddering without any distinctive melodic character. As the situation becomes more ominous with the train moving and her uncle's refusal to let her off, Tiomkin builds to a crescendo, paralleling the emotions she experiences during her entrapment. When they reach the coach door and he opens it, his intentions now entirely clear, the music becomes louder and more chaotic, finally bringing in fragments of the familiar waltz, again in a *La Valse*-like style, but without actual quotations. The music reaches its dynamic and disruptive climax when the editing and action reach theirs, and because of the chaos it must fade out and be replaced by something closer to the actual waltz as the visual waltz dissolves in. Few films will reveal the potential connection between montage and music as spectacularly as this one.

Dualities

While *La Valse* has notable parallels to the film's structure, it also has a parallel to the content, not only Ravel's version of the dance but the waltz in general. A number of features of the film strike us forcefully, but none more directly than the relationship of the two Charlies, members of the same family, twins as they both on occasions claim, and their relationship with the glue between them—young Charlie's mother and Uncle Charlie's sister—Emma. While they enjoy their twin-like relationship, starting with the telepathic urge by each one to contact the other, the relationship has the potential to be too close for comfort. When it crumbles, because of what young Charlie knows about her uncle, once again Emma plays a key role, since her fragile stability would be shattered by this knowledge, and her world of respectability would collapse if her own brother were to be arrested for murder. We have a powerful pairing in the film, the twin Charlies, but a triangle as well, contained within a single family, governing the dynamics of their actions and interactions. Young Charlie resists doing what she knows to be right because of what it would do to her mother.

When making this film Hitchcock had been in America for only three years, and despite having made five films while on American soil, with two of them set in the US, this would in many respects be his first American film, or in any event his first film to capture an essence of American life. To make this plausible he had one of the finest American writers as a colleague, Thornton Wilder, but Hitchcock himself had formed opinions of the country by this point and apparently wished to say something about it. Clearly he felt some tension living in California during the war years, regarded by some in Britain as having abandoned his homeland, and for some time his life and his films would continue to have a transatlantic nature, full of dualities and contradictions. The America he observed similarly had contradictions, and to some degree the industry in which he worked reflected this, with films on the one hand that portrayed the country as good in every possible respect—morally upright, clean, decent, with strong family values, and wholesome in the extreme. On the other hand a darker vision of America existed in film noir,[18] full of crime and corruption, with moral decay reflected in urban blight, where things happen in darkness instead of daylight. Both Americas existed, and in *Shadow of a Doubt* he took the bold step of putting both genres in a single film, taking the consequences for what might happen when the two become mixed together. The worst aspects of the physically and morally decaying East infiltrate the America of goodness and apple pie, Santa Rosa, and this raises the question of how one will respond to the other. Santa Rosa has its head in the sand, trying to remain oblivious to the horrors that exist around it; its inhabitants live insulated lives, bolstered by institutions such as church and school, and murder for them seems no more real than the games that Joe and Herb play after dinner. When an actual murderer comes among them, they do not notice a thing;

only the perceptive young Charlie does, and at the end we must consider the consequences of this for her life and the America she has known to this point. All of this works within the dynamics of a single family, the bedrock of all American institutions. The evil does not encroach from foreigners or other alien forces but comes from within, and part of the family, Emma, keeps her eyes firmly closed to the evil. That vision of family looks very much like the whole country, which did not need the likes of Hitler to acquaint it with evil, having plenty of its own to go round, and much of the country preferred to remain oblivious to the decay. An interloper from England may not strike us as the ideal person to attempt to show this to Americans in their medium of mass culture, but Hitchcock, to be fair, had never hesitated to reveal to the British their own shortcomings and worse.

For a film that deals with fundamental dualities within persons, families, and larger societies, the waltz proved to be an inspired choice as an image against which these dualities can unfold. The waltz itself churned with contradictions, on both sides of the Atlantic, playing an extraordinarily important role as a type of social institution in its own right. The consistency with which waltzes turn up in Hitchcock's films can be seen as a preoccupation tantamount to some of his other enduring images, such as staircases or actresses' hair. With some of these favorite images he created the context himself, but in the case of the waltz it already existed, in part because of the widespread popularity of waltzing, but also because of what it came to represent. In Vienna, its home, the waltz became much more than a dance craze, ultimately standing as a symbol of society itself. The music had charm without being overly complex, with a lilt that gave it verve, and richness in the hands of the Strausses, Lehar, or the other waltz kings. To be danced it required musical stability, and that stability, along with the charm, came to represent the Viennese themselves in the nineteenth century, with their obsession with order balanced by the charming eccentricity of their world. Those who could dance well could gain social advantages not available to poor dancers, and Vienna's severest critic, Karl Kraus, could use this as an instrument of satire, as noted in the previous chapter, showing how a bank employee guilty of murdering his wife could be forgiven (and have his case dismissed in court) by the Viennese because of his prowess as a dancer.[19]

When the waltz came to America in the nineteenth century it quickly became extremely popular, threatening the formality of other types of dancing. Unlike Europe, where everyone danced it and persons in the highest positions of authority saw it as healthy, the more moralistic Americans of the time took a very different view, in part because the waltz, unlike the other family group dances, put couples together, even allowing them to touch. Europeans had gotten over that in the eighteenth century, ignoring dance masters of the time who objected to the lasciviousness of the *contradanse* in their moral treatises. A century later Americans fought the same battles, such as the writer for *The New Englander* who protested in 1867, comparing the traditional dances and the waltz, that "in the former, the sexes meet with perfect propriety; in the latter, they publicly embrace. The former are modest—the latter immodest, and still worse ... There can be no doubt that the round dances now in practice in society are essentially wrong. The waltzes ... and all that variety are a moral abomination."[20] The moralists had a serious problem on their hands: thousands of young people loved to waltz, and refused to give in to this type of censure.

The waltz itself works well for the film, combining stability and moral degradation, an image for the two Americas also represented by the Charlie duo, but if Ravel's *La Valse* can be added to the mix, another rich dimension becomes possible. As a pantomime intended to be danced by a ballet company, it has, despite Ravel's comments to the contrary, striking social implications, moving from the stability of the waltz in part one with its nostalgia for a bygone past to a *danse macabre* in the second crescendo (part two), destroying that wonderful vision of the past. Shortly after its composition it provoked through what Roger Nichols calls its "ambiguity, stridency and disturbing lack of restraint" assumptions that it had socio-political implications, such as the decline and fall of the Habsburg Empire, or something more broadly applicable to all of Europe following the First World War. In a letter to his friend Maurice Emmanuel, Ravel tried to quell all such speculation:

Some people discovered in it an intention of parody, even of caricature, others plainly saw a tragic allusion—end of the second Empire, state of Vienna after the war etc. ... Tragic, yes it can be that like any expression—pleasure, happiness—which is pushed to extremes. You should see in it only what comes from the music: a mounting volume of sound, which in the stage performance will be complemented by lighting and movement.[21]

Ravel apparently shared Hitchcock's dislike of exegesis, saying about as much about it as Hitchcock says about his film, even sounding like Hitchcock with his references to expression, lighting, and movement. He could trust Emmanuel to make this opinion known, and in a Europe (especially Austria) not in the mood for pondering its social collapse, he had no interest in rubbing salt in the wound. Hitchcock too would be perfectly happy to have the film regarded as the trailer presented it, as his latest suspenseful entertainment, and not as something that should force the audience into deep introspection. For those prepared to take this step, as young Charlie in the film must, nothing need stop them. When Uncle Charlie greets his sister on arriving in Santa Rosa, he gives her portraits of their parents, and comments on the wonderful world that existed then, not like now. Everything that happens in the remainder of the film reinforces the nostalgia for a bygone time, a world that Santa Rosa tries to hold in its grasp, but a world no longer possible because of a member of their family. The downward spiral comes from within, just like the internal process generating the distortion of the waltz—not the result of an outside invasion, and the apotheosis this results in looks and sounds remarkably like the one in *La Valse*.

Of all the films he made, *Shadow of a Doubt* stood out for Hitchcock, although during the interviews with François Truffaut he tried to play that down. When Truffaut commented "I take it that of all the pictures you've made, *Shadow of a Doubt* is the one you prefer," Hitchcock replied "I wouldn't say that *Shadow of a Doubt* is my favorite picture; if I've given that impression [which he certainly had], it's probably because I feel that here is something that our friends, the plausibles and logicians, cannot complain about."[22] Of course that feeble response does not wash; talking in the early 1960s about his whole body of films and carefully shaping the view the world should have of them, he did not find it useful to stick to this preference. Pat Hitchcock O'Connell, Hitchcock's daughter, once asked her mother "'which one is your favorite of Daddy's films?' Without hesitating one bit, she replied, *Shadow of a Doubt*. It was Hitch's favorite, too."[23] On this Pat gets the last word, and we can assume Hitchcock liked it as he did for reasons that go far beyond its plausibility and logic. Here we have a spectacular piece of entertainment that resonated with a large audience, and at the same time a complex work of the highest artistry, not only challenging us with its psychological, social, and cultural urges, but hanging together as an extraordinary example of a combination of cinematography and sound. When Gordon McDonell saw it, having played a small but crucial role with his original scenario, he wrote to Hitchcock on 10 January 1943 with his unrestrained praise and great perception:

> Dear Hitch:
> I saw it on Friday ... I shook like a jelly for a full two hours afterwards ...
> Everything about it was absolutely right. Scripts, dialogue, acting, casting—and as for the music and the way you handled the camera:—that was everything ...
> And the tremendous, shattering impact of the music in conjunction with the newspaper headline, in the library ... And that wonderful shot, downwards, macabre, of her leaving the library ...
> Very rarely have I seen a picture where it ceases to be a picture and you are sitting there in the theatre not realising you are, transported completely into the life which is there upon the screen ...
> I do think it is a masterpiece which you have created.
> Please give my regards to your wife,
> Yours
> Gordon McDonell[24]

6

Through a rear window darkly

Rear Window may very well be the most perfectly designed of all Hitchcock's films. While he normally had everything under control, leaving very little to chance, in this case he took that even further, working on a set designed entirely for the film, constructed in a Paramount Studio storage building with meticulousness that made it the envy of the film world. Now at a point in his career that he could surround himself with the best in the business, and not have to deal with studio brass looking over his shoulder, he worked with people he knew he could trust who would give the best possible results. These included previous collaborators such as director of photography Robert Burks and costume designer Edith Head, and new ones who would be with him for the long term, including editor George Tomasini and assistant director Herbert Coleman. He could not have hoped for better actors than James Stewart as Jeff, whom he knew well from *Rope*, and Grace Kelly as Lisa, with whom he had worked much more recently on *Dial M for Murder*. Both were good personal friends, and exemplified the best features of acting that he preferred.

Yet, all was not well. Finding a screenplay writer to suit his purposes always proved difficult, and over the years he had let a number of them go unceremoniously before they completed their jobs. In this case he opted for the radio writer John Michael Hayes, and he liked him well enough not only to keep him throughout the making of the film but to engage him for his next three films. In the end, though, in response to a comment by François Truffaut, who called this "your very best screenplay," Hitchcock, in a not unusual way of belittling the credit to those around him, said nothing more about Hayes than that he "is a radio writer and he wrote the dialogue."[1] Even about Kelly, in many respects his favorite of the blondes who populate his films, who exemplified the notion of passion burning beneath a cool exterior, he also managed to find some fault. In prompting Hayes for his work on the film, Hitchcock told him that Kelly "has a lot of charm and talent, but she goes through the motions as if she is in acting school. She does everything properly and pleasantly, nothing comes out of her. You've got to bring something out of her, bring her to life. Would you spend some time with her?"[2] Here Hitchcock may of course have been pulling one of his favorite tricks, simply looking for better results from Hayes; or, it may, as Steven DeRosa speculates, have been designed to see if "his leading lady would make a conquest of another lowly screenwriter."[3]

His most excoriating put-down, though, he reserved for his composer, Franz Waxman, another veteran of his films, who had previously scored *Rebecca, Suspicion,* and *The Paradine Case.* Most of the music for *Rear Window* comes from a wide array of popular and classical music,[4] creating the most elaborate musical collage to be found in any of his films, but Hitchcock needed one original piece, and not just any piece. He described to Truffaut in some detail what he wanted: "You remember that one of the characters in the yard was a musician. Well, I wanted to show how a popular song is composed by gradually developing it throughout the film until, in the final scene, it is played on a recording with a full orchestral accompaniment." Here lay an idea both unusual and groundbreaking (despite the unfortunate attempt in *Waltzes from Vienna*), with the development of the composition of a song running parallel to the unfolding of the film, with music having the possibility of taking on an essence that can be the underlying urge behind the structure of the film, and also prompt the tone of the film.

The music in this case could not have had a more important role in shaping the film in its most critical respects, and Hitchcock had to rely on the skills of a composer to make it work. In the end,

Hitchcock complained that "it didn't work out the way I wanted it to, and I was quite disappointed."[5] Not one to press such matters very far, Hitchcock never really explained what dissatisfied him, but he did add that "I was a little disappointed at the lack of a structure in the title song. I had a motion picture songwriter when I should have chosen a popular songwriter."[6] These comments have generally baffled those who have discussed the music in detail, with Elisabeth Weis wondering about the actual structure of the song or that he may have wanted something more popular. Jack Sullivan, who interviewed Waxman's son John and heard about disputes on the set between his father and the director, quoted John as saying that "Hitchcock knew what he wanted—he always did—and he wasn't getting it from my father." Sullivan thinks Hitchcock missed the boat on this one, in fact that he "sounds a bit like Jeff, a man who doesn't know what a good thing he has."[7]

Script

John Waxman's comment about Hitchcock's expectation for the song he hoped he would receive from Franz Waxman seems to come to the heart of the matter. Many admire what the composer did with the song "Lisa" and how it weaves into the narrative, even rescuing Miss Lonelyhearts from suicide, but a case can certainly be made that by not giving what Hitchcock wanted, it ultimately weakened the film, depriving a vehicle of such centrality from having the desired effect. Hitchcock seemed unable to explain the deficiency of the song, but in examining the process of the film's development, along with other comments by Hitchcock, the case can be made. The starting point can be the script and the director's collaboration with Hayes. The song is woven into the fabric of the film from beginning to end, and its conception arose not as an inspiration from Waxman, but as something Hitchcock himself saw as essential to the film. A songwriter in one of the windows viewed from Jeff's apartment certainly did not exist in the source short story "It had to be Murder" by Cornell Woolrich, and Hitchcock gave even more importance to the song by making his cameo appearance in that apartment, setting the

6.1 *Rear Window* (Hitchcock's cameo, with Ross Bagdasarian) (Hitchcock prompts the composer)

composer's clock on the mantle, and then speaking to the composer while he works at the piano. This song, in short, needed to have a significant role in the film, carrying structural importance in providing a type of glue for the film; it was not intended to be sentimental, or nicely resolved with all the loose ends tied together.

As to how the film took shape, we have some widely divergent views, with Hayes' version of events bearing little resemblance to that of others who observed it at first hand. In a short documentary accompanying the DVD of the restored *Rear Window* entitled "A conversation with screenwriter John Michael Hayes," Hayes spoke of the independence Hitchcock gave him as a writer, leaving it to him to design the work and flesh out the dialogue.[8] He leaves the impression that Hitchcock handed him the short story and told him to go away and write a film scenario, and that he did this with little or no supervision—certainly not with Hitchcock looking over his shoulder.

With this description, he takes most of the credit for the scenario, the characters and their relationships, and the script itself.

Why, then, would Hitchcock call him a radio writer who provided the dialogue? We know, of course, than Hitchcock never simply turned his writers loose, but worked with them on an almost daily basis, and only after their regular detailed discussions did he send them off to shape the ideas and develop the dialogue. Steven DeRosa, in his book about the collaboration between Hitchcock and Hayes, made this clear in his first paragraph of the Introduction, quoting Hitchcock on how he worked with writers: "The most enjoyable part of making a picture is in that little office, with the writer, when we are discussing the story-lines and what we're going to put on the screen. The big difference is that I do not let the writer go off on his own and just write a script that I will interpret. I stay involved with him and get him involved in the direction of the picture. So he becomes more than a writer; he becomes part maker of the picture." DeRosa then expands on this: "From selection of the basic material, to the hiring (and firing) of every writer, to the final revision of the final shooting script, Hitchcock involved himself in nearly every aspect of developing the screenplays for his films. Although he rarely did any actual 'writing,' especially on his Hollywood productions, Hitchcock supervised and guided his writers through every draft, insisting on a strict attention to detail and a preference for telling the story through visual rather than verbal means."[9]

If one imagines that Hayes had a different type of relationship with Hitchcock than all the other writers had, Herbert Coleman, who sat in on some of their sessions, quickly makes it clear he did not. As assistant director, Coleman played a central role in this his first production with Hitchcock, at times to the annoyance of Hayes. Coleman remembered Hayes arriving at the studio in June, and the three of them went through the same routine day after day, although it consisted more of gossip sessions than work on the script. When they did get down to work, as Coleman describes it, they "went into Hitchcock's office. He indicated the typewriter and chair I'd had the office service provide for Hayes. After another dirty look at me, Hayes sat down, ran a sheet of paper into the typewriter, and typed the opening scene as Hitchcock dictated." What followed amazed Coleman, as Hitchcock, "pacing slowly around his office, described in detail the opening scenes. The camera movement through the window of Jimmy's apartment to the apartments across the courtyard. A half-dressed ballet dancer, seen through her open window. And action in other apartments. Then to Jimmy's leg in a cast. He stopped for a moment and turned toward Hayes. A smile replaced his usual somber expression: 'I've decided to have Jimmy asleep when Grace makes her first appearance in our film.'" He proceeded to describe all the other characters and their apartments, "who they were and how their lives affected the thinking and actions of Jimmy." This was not an infrequent activity, but "the routine of Hitch dictating and Hayes typing continued for many days. Schooldays for me and maybe for John Michael Hayes, also. We were receiving a graduate school course in screenplay development. The day he dictated the final scene, Hitch told Hayes to take a copy of the script and add the dialogue." On 12 September 1953, "Hayes gave me what he called his screenplay. But it was more like the treatment I'd heard Hitch dictate, with dialogue added. Some good. Some very good."[10]

Whose version of these events should we believe? One can think of no reason that Coleman might have to distort things; his eyewitness account certainly appears to be accurate. Hayes, on the other hand, had a nasty falling-out with Hitchcock a couple of years later over Hitchcock's insistence on giving his old friend Angus MacPhail billing as one of the screenwriters for *The Man Who Knew Too Much*, and the rift became permanent. He may have been inclined to stress his independence as a writer, and distance himself from the director who probably bruised his ego.

Perhaps the key point in all of this is that Hitchcock wanted his writers to think in visual rather than verbal terms, a tall order for someone who makes a profession of putting words together. Whether or not his writers could achieve this, it seems fair to assume that Hitchcock himself thought this way, in fact taking this to an extreme that "dialogue should simply be a sound among other sounds, just something that comes out of the mouths of people whose eyes tell the story in visual terms."[11] The words, to be sure, are important, but they do not generate the essence of the film; at their best they will give hints about those stronger underlying forces, the ones Hitchcock held as his own central goal. As for Hitchcock's expectation about what Hayes should accomplish, Coleman once again clarifies that: "Hitch told everything, every camera move, everything but the dialogue. When it came to the dialogue, he'd say, 'Now, Mr. Hayes, the dialogue must convey this meaning.'"[12]

The narrative of this film, embodied in Hayes dialogue, aside from the grisly aspects of the murder of Anna Thorwald, gives us comedy, and even the murder becomes part of the comedy, when the nurse Stella (Thelma Ritter) describes how Thorwald (Raymond Burr) did it, how much of a body can be buried in a flowerbed, or how Thorwald spread the body parts around the East River. The central part of the narrative concerns the relationship of Jeff and Lisa, and the impact of the events unfolding in the line of vision from Jeff's apartment on their relationship. If we take the narrative as the most important part of the film, we can follow the downs and ups of this relationship, and arrive at the end with the assumption that all is well. Even though Lisa puts down the sleeping Jeff's book on the Himalayas in the final scene in favor of her own *Harper's Bazaar*, this does not evoke more than a smile, about two people who appear to have resolved their main differences, and will become a loving couple with nothing but small points of irritation between them. Perhaps we can leave the theater confident that a wedding will take place and happiness will ensue.

This narrative, though, does not get much support from the camera. Our first visual introduction to Lisa comes not as a camera shot of her, with all the extraordinary beauty that Grace Kelly has, but as a shadow, which crosses the face of the sleeping Jeff, erasing him, as it were, certainly casting her long shadow as a dominant force, but more specifically throwing Jeff into darkness that proves to be dislocating for him. She appears only briefly before the shadow continues to engulf his entire head; words have no place as she leans forward to give him a kiss, and no male member of the audience can imagine why he would not be madly in love with her. During and after the kiss the light hits her face at an angle that continues to throw a shadow on him. As she gives her facetious introduction, she also provides illumination, turning on a light with each of "Lisa," "Carol," "Freemont," but light proves to be a tenuous force. The shadows, or outright darkness, will play prominent roles as the film proceeds, with the dark wall of the opposite side of the courtyard at night separating the inhabitants of the various apartments, and darkness looming at key menacing points from Thorwald's windows. The darkness in the hallway outside Jeff's door and the darkness of his apartment become even more unnerving as Thorwald comes toward him. Jeff attempts to fight him off with light—the extreme light of flash bulbs, but to no avail, as these only delay the inevitable physical confrontation. The dark aspects of the film cannot to be minimized, as the discussion later in this chapter clarifies.

In the scenario so carefully prompted by Hitchcock, the song "Lisa" receives, as one would expect, detailed treatment, and some of the divergences between this and the film as we know it may also help to explain Hitchcock's dissatisfaction. After the 12 September screenplay referred to by Coleman, additional work on the script moved fairly swiftly over the next few months. Paramount used a color coding for the scripts, with a yellow script as the first shooting script, and Hayes finished his first draft of this on 20 October. Filming started on 27 November, and at this point Hayes had not yet completed the final white script, or the final shooting script, which dates from 1 December. Aside from final retakes, shooting ended on 13 January, and clearly the final shooting script went through some changes. That script, in the possession of the Margaret Herrick Library, outlines very specific treatments of the song which were not followed. We hear the song for the first time when Jeff talks on the phone with his editor, as we hear the songwriter picking out notes at the piano. In the script this music clashes abruptly with the music from Miss Torso's apartment, but in the sound balance actually used, that clash can barely be discerned. The prompting for Jeff to look in the direction of the composer in an irritated manner has been entirely removed, as well as his line of text in which he complains of the clash being worse than a form of torture.[13]

As that scene in the script continues, the composer, a short, balding man (entirely unlike Ross Bagdasarian, who played the role), struggles against the interference of the ballet music from the dancer's record player, forcing him finally to give up because of the collision of sounds. When he tries to continue, he inadvertently picks out the notes of the ballet music, and again Jeff scowls at the double sound. This is missing from the film, but the description of him appearing drunk and sweeping his manuscript paper off the piano comes very close to the actual scene. In the script, he looks at the piano in a disgusted way, and his action of dislodging the music is "vicious" (p. 47). Prior to the party at his apartment he continues to poke at the notes of the song, and only when an attractive young woman comments favorably does he play it more fully. Once again his music runs into stark interference from the orchestral ballet music in a modern style, and Jeff now turns his head in the direction of the new music. As the party continues, the composer plays the song for his guests, and while the beauty of the song becomes apparent, it remains by no means fully formed, as he improvises different variants of the melody. Later, for the session with other musicians and the final playing of the completed recording, we have a fairly close correlation between the script and film.

Altering perception

The narrative of the script follows a fairly linear course, but the camera seems to tell a very different story. In his conversation with Truffaut, Hitchcock explained how this can work, calling *Rear Window* a "purely cinematic film" based on what can be achieved with montage. He proceeds by suggesting three ways of thinking about the film, starting with "an immobilized man looking out … The second part shows what he sees and the third part shows how he reacts." To explain this "purest expression of a cinematic idea," he invokes Pudovkin, who, "in one of his books on the art of montage, describes an experiment by his teacher, Kuleshov. You see a close-up of the Russian actor Ivan Mosjoukine. This is immediately followed by the shot of the dead baby. Back to Mosjoukine again and you read compassion on his face. Then you take away the dead baby and you show a plate of soup, and now, when you go back to Mosjoukine, he looks hungry. Yet, in both cases, they used the same shot of the actor; his face was exactly the same." This could be done, with the greatest of ease, in *Rear Window*: "in the same way, let's take a close-up of Stewart looking out the window at the little dog that's being lowered in a basket. Back to Stewart, who has a kindly smile. But if in the place of the little dog you show a half-naked girl exercising in the front of her open window, and you go back to a smiling Stewart again, this time he's seen as a dirty old man!"[14]

Here more than anywhere Hitchcock confirms his expectation about acting, and why he had relatively little use for alumni of the Actors Studio, such as Paul Newman in the 1960s. Actors may use facial expressions to attempt to convey specific emotions, but depending on cutting, those expressions can be entirely misread, construed to mean something entirely different than one's first impression. The cutting itself will tell us how we should respond, and that may take us in an entirely different direction from the narrative. In his example, Hitchcock raises the possibility of voyeurism, of Jeff being "a real Peeping Tom," something the reviewers picked up immediately and has been much discussed since. One critic in London saw this as demeaning the entire film, but Hitchcock wondered, "what's so horrible about that? Sure, he's a snooper, but aren't we all … I'll bet you nine out of ten people, if they see a woman across the courtyard undressing for bed, or even a man puttering around in his room, will stay and look; no one turns away and says, 'It's none of my business.' They could pull down their blinds, but they never do; they stand there and look out." Truffaut agreed that "we're all voyeurs to some extent … And James Stewart is exactly in the position of a spectator looking at the movie."[15]

The issue of rear window ethics gets full treatment in the script as well, with Stella badgering about how the crime of being a peeping Tom may be punished, and Lisa dropping the blind when Jeff shows too much interest in Miss Torso. Something similar comes up in the conversation with Truffaut about *Vertigo*, when Hitchcock described the re-creation of Judy into Madeleine as building toward sexual fulfillment, once again with James Stewart as the viewer, but that seemed more a simile (unsuspected by Truffaut) than actual sexual deviance. Voyeurism runs throughout *Rear Window* as a constant motif, so much so that Lisa says at one point she will need to get an apartment across the way and do the dance of the seven veils every hour to keep Jeff's eyes off Miss Torso. Is this simply an innocent bit of sport for the incapacitated photographer, or should we find something more ethically troubling at stake? The persistence of Miss Torso seems to suggest something closer to the latter, and the descriptions of her in the script seem to bear this out. Page 2 of the final white script describes the extent of her exposure, and everyone knew full well that this would not get past the censors. We first see her fully naked above the waist, and only a shadow hides what should not be seen; she picks up a coffeemaker, and swinging her body around she moves with such skill that she avoids her breasts being exposed. Concessions had to be made to the censor, but not to the extent that the imagination could not add what the picture did not show, and by the 1950s' standards Hitchcock managed to get more than expected past the censor. One of the first tenants we see as the camera pans the apartment windows after the opening titles is a disrobed Miss Torso, in her bathroom combing her hair.

Exposure of skin is not limited to Miss Torso. Near the opening of the script we have the description of the two bathing beauties on an adjoining rooftop, who do not merely sun themselves, but intentionally position themselves to be noticed; Jeff sees them, and he seems disappointed when they lie down out of sight. In the film the

6.2 *Rear Window* (Miss Torso)

power of suggestion must add what cannot be shown, since we can see that they have removed their robes, but Jeff and the audience receive no additional view. Curiously, at the moment they lie down, a helicopter flies overhead, for no apparent reason other than for the pilots to see what Jeff and we cannot.

Hitchcock appears to be speaking hypothetically about the cutting between the dog, Jeff, and Miss Torso since no such sequence actually occurs. We do, though, get some variants on this; just before the dog comes down in his basket for the first time, the sculptress identifies her work as "Hunger," and the camera immediately moves to Miss Torso dancing. After the dog's descent the camera turns in on Jeff getting a massage from Stella, and the only expression on his face is a mild grimace. As Stella works the camera gives a fairly rapid back shot to Miss Torso, and Jeff clearly has her on his mind, to Stella's annoyance. That evening, after the owners reel the dog back up, the camera moves to Miss Torso, again combing her hair in her bathroom, continues to the sculptress working on hunger, then to the newlyweds' closed shade, and finally to Lisa and Jeff embracing. Lisa expresses concern that she does not have Jeff's full attention, and considering the sequence of the camera, Jeff's failure to be attentive appears to be provoked at this point by something other than a possible murder plot. Lisa gives up on her long embrace as Jeff talks about Thorwald, and as she lights a cigarette, the camera strays to Miss Torso, this time with her lying in bed reading, and eating an apple; she brushes food crumbs off her chest. Jeff talks seriously about the difficulty of murdering someone, but the camera makes it considerably less clear what may be on his mind. He sees Miss Torso in bed, with an apple no less, and is distracted by her breasts which have been one of his main preoccupations—none of this seems coincidental. The narrative appears not accurately to reflect his state of mind.

The motion of the camera suggests the notion of a purely cinematic film that Hitchcock had in mind. With this he could generate levels of meaning that may or may not be apparent in the dialogue, which too should find the underlying meaning, but of course could not always. We know from the dialogue of the troubled relationship between Jeff and Lisa, but the script leads us to believe that the problems resolve. Not only does the narrative steer in that direction but so do some shots, such as the prolonged embraces, or the unfolding of events in the latter part of the film, as Jeff's admiration for Lisa increases in direct relation to her brave acts of putting herself in danger to find evidence of a murder. The camera, though, seems to imply that Jeff's difficulty with marriage has less to do with career incompatibility or his refusal to be domesticated. His visual interest in Miss Torso, and the camera's intercutting of her into his stream of (sub)consciousness, seem to suggest something darker; despite his age, he remains unprepared or unable to spend his life with one woman, or in Hitchcock's own words, he's too much of a dirty old man. To resist the charms of the character that Grace Kelly embodies, there must be something seriously wrong. He enters the film sleeping, perhaps a sweating satyr in the heat of the day, awash in erotic reveries, and he exits the film again sleeping, never perhaps having recovered from his state of reduced consciousness.

Hitchcock achieved what he set out to in the visual treatment of the film, and here, of course, he had full control. With actors he did not need a level of acting that would convince the audience of a certain emotional depth since with the use of the camera he could not only redirect those emotions but he could completely redefine character. Music turned out to be the element he could not control in that way, although there were aspects of the music he could have controlled, but curiously did not. One of the notable uses of the camera was to generate a type infiltration, as has just been described, prompting a redirection of impressions with motion or montage. The musical treatment described in the final white script could have worked in a similar way. Just as visual images of Miss Torso encroach on the Lisa/Jeff relationship, similarly the music from Miss Torso's apartment could encroach on the composition of "Lisa," making its progress all but impossible, as its volume could blur the song, even, apparently, forcing the composer to pick out the notes of that music instead of his song. Very simply, this did not for the most part happen, although it seems possible that with the right mixing it could have been done. The problem in the end was not a technical one, but probably had more to do with the nature of the song Waxman composed and the speed with which the song comes together.

The two rear windows

A number of shots, including the first one after the titles, start with a pan of courtyard windows and balconies which reveals, although not necessarily all of them, the owners of the dog, the balcony sleepers, the sculptress, the unseen singer, Miss Lonelyhearts, Miss Torso, the Thorwalds, the composer, and the newlyweds, showing, in Hitchcock's words, "every kind of human behavior—a real index of individual behavior. The picture would have been very dull if we hadn't done that. What you see across the way is a group of little stories that, as you say, mirror a small universe." Most importantly, though, these tie directly to Jeff and Lisa: "The symmetry is the same as in *Shadow of a Doubt*. On one side of the yard you have the Stewart-Kelly couple, with him immobilized by his leg in a cast, while she can move about freely. And on the other side there is a sick woman who's confined to her bed, while the husband comes and goes."[16] The camera gives the confirmation of this symmetry, as in the first shot and others, panning from the yard windows directly into Jeff's window, making that small universe his universe, sometimes overtly but also unconsciously, as the end point of the pan may be a sleeping Jeff, who takes in that universe through the conduit of the camera.

Much happens in these windows that will bemuse us, but clearly not all. Jeff's apparent obsession with Miss Torso can work as comedy, but not always, as the camera appears to make something else of it. Miss Lonelyhearts may at times seem pathetic in a gently laughable way, but not when she dissolves into tears after toasting her imaginary suitor, when having to fight off an aggressive young man with only one thing on his mind, and certainly not when she comes within a few bars of a song from committing suicide. When the owners of the dog find their pet dead, we care, along with almost the entire neighborhood, because we have enjoying the slightly comical view of the dog descending and ascending in the basket. Even the Thorwalds appear somewhat comical at the beginning, as we see them quarrelling while Jeff explains that wives in his neighborhood do not discuss but nag, and this sets the tone for Jeff's views on marriage. This leads to something much darker, with the symmetry of Jeff dealing with his own misapprehensions about marriage superimposed on the grisly events in the Thorwald apartment;[17] perhaps the most notable part of this symmetry is the conversion of Lisa to Jeff's point of view on what has happened there. Initially she resists, objecting to his preoccupation as ghoulish, but she then comes round, by which point the two of them no longer discuss marriage. Here Hayes succeeded with the dialogue in finding the symmetry, or the underlying meaning that Hitchcock wanted him to reveal.

Looking at the way the dark aspects of this film permeate the lighter side of course is not new: Robin Wood for one did it very early on, looking at Jeff as having "been confronted by the darkness that Hitchcock sees as underlying—or as surrounding—all human existence: the chaos of our unknown, unrecognized 'Under-nature'." He seems somewhat reluctant to apply this terminology more appropriate to Shakespearean tragedy to "a light comedy-thriller," but continues with the broader observation that "the Hitchcock hero typically lives in a small, enclosed world of his own fabrication, at once a protection and a prison, artificial and unrealistic, into which the 'real' chaos erupts, demanding to be faced." Other stark examples occur in *The Wrong Man* and *North by Northwest*. Wood looks at the ending of *Rear Window* as having too neatly tied together the loose ends, "and we are left with the feeling of the precariousness of it all." He concludes his discussion of this film with these words: "Order is restored, within and without—in the microcosm of Jefferies's personality, and in the external world which is on one level an extension or reflection of it; but we are left with the feeling that the sweetness-and-light merely covers up that chaos-world that underlies the superficial order."[18]

Wood has accurately described the central dichotomy in this and other films, and the camera supports this position even more vigorously than the script. Windows provide the gateways to almost all that happens in *Rear Window*, and what we do not see in these windows can be just as important as what we do see. Normally the windows open the small worlds that connect to Jeff's own world, as we receive a view of what happens inside the apartments of Miss Torso, Miss Lonelyhearts, or the composer. Sometimes the view can be obscured, with shades partly or fully drawn, including Jeff's own shade when Lisa pulls his with the comments that the show's over for tonight. Action obscured in this way becomes much murkier, feeding suppositions of what may be going on, or it may become ominous, as happens when we see Thorwald's dark silhouette looming through a closed blind. With the removal of all light, something even more menacing takes over, as the sense of the unknown assumes the worst possible character, implying a lurking feeling of horror. The first such blackout occurs when Jeff and Lisa argue about the impossibility of marriage, and Lisa says goodbye instead of goodnight, leaving with tension lurking in the air. As they talk about the impossibility of their lives intersecting, the shots of Jeff show his windows in the background, now completely dark, with no light from across the yard. After she leaves, the camera frames Jeff's head against his large open window, now with the windows across the way barely visible as dark blue spots, even as he looks at them. When his attention becomes more focused on the windows, the camera pans the usual windows, now with no views inside, with some of them (Miss Lonelyheart's and the composer's) completely

6.3 *Rear Window* (Grace Kelly with James Stewart) (Love problems and dark windows)

black, and the shades drawn at Thorwald's with only a dim light inside. As the camera pans further, just past the composer's window, we hear the scream and a glass crashing that become the markers of the fatal moment for Mrs Thorwald.

The linkage here does not bode well, setting up parallel events as yet undefined but later to become central. The apparent breakdown of marriage and what ultimately proves to be the murder become linked in time and space, with the most prominent image being that of darkness, both in Jeff's apartment looking out and the windows across the way. The concerned look on Jeff's face connects to the unpleasant confrontation with Lisa, but because of the camera's motion, it connects to the as yet unsuspected murder as well. Only with the rain that forces the balcony sleepers to dive through the window does the atmosphere lighten up, as Jeff wakes up and smiles at their difficulties (prompted by a Hitchcock prank) in getting through the window. His look darkens when he sees Thorwald leaving his apartment with his metal display case, at almost 2 a.m. The darkened windows used here become of critical importance at various key points as the film proceeds, usually in relation to Thorwald's apartment, or his in relation to others in the yard. A little later Thorwald sits in his apartment in the dark, and Jeff even comments to Lisa that that's what he's doing. In another pan of the windows, we see the dog descending in its basket past a darkened Thorwald window. When the dog's owner vents her grief after finding the dog dead, the camera's pan reveals light in all windows with one exception, and Jeff notes to Lisa that Thorwald did not come to his window.

With other shots of Thorwald's darkened windows, that darkness becomes a powerful image of the evil and menacing forces referred to by Wood, forces linked all too often with Jeff's apartment and the events unfolding there. Before Lisa drops the blinds to end the show for that night, she leans down to kiss Jeff from behind, and as she does, the camera moves away from lit windows to the darkened windows of Miss Lonelyhearts. Through the closed blind only one window can initially still be seen, Thorwald's, and he appears to be folding clothes and packing. The darkness becomes decidedly menacing when Lisa climbs into Thorwald's apartment through his window; that window now becomes a very different kind of gateway, and Thorwald returns to confront her. He enters a lit apartment, but as they struggle and as she cries out for Jeff, he turns out the light, and may very well have finished her off if the police had not arrived at a most crucial moment; only when they ring the doorbell does he turn the light back on. Jeff squirms in agony at this point, because of his own inability to do anything. As a result of the way Hitchcock links the prospects for marriage with Thorwald, though, there may be something even more sinister happening here, as her bravery looks foolhardy to the point that it could cause her to lose her life.

The darkness taking place in Thorwald's apartment with Lisa of course has its parallel in Jeff's. When Thorwald catches Lisa displaying the wedding ring for Jeff to see, he can now tell who has been spying on him. Jeff immediately tells Stella to turn out his light, which then stays out for the rest of the extended sequence. Thorwald confirms his location with a phone call, and footsteps bring him down Jeff's hallway to the apartment door. Jeff looks across the yard at Thorwald's dark windows just before the phone call, and the slamming of a door in Jeff's building brings the action to his apartment. When he looks to his door he sees only darkness except for a ribbon of light from the hall under his door, and that light goes out when the footsteps halt. Darkness takes over as the looming figure of Thorwald enters, and Jeff arms himself with the only weapon he can think of using, light—extreme light, intended to blind Thorwald and prevent his advance with his camera's flash unit. It slows his attacker's forward progress, as shards of light pierce the darkness, but the darkness—and the force it represents, prove too strong for this counterattack. As Thorwald leans toward Jeff, grabbing him by the throat, casting his enormous shadow with all the darkness and shadows he summons, one may be inclined to remember the shadow cast by Lisa over Jeff on her first appearance. Thorwald gets his way, throwing Jeff to the hard courtyard below, and could very well have killed him had the fall not been broken by Doyle and other policemen.

Jeff's impotence in the face of the darkness spread by Thorwald raises fascinating questions for the end of the film, and this of course brings the composer's song back into the equation as well. Jeff may have solved the murder, but this has not necessarily lifted the darkness that surrounds the film. The film's finale, aside from

Jeff's two broken legs, gives the impression that all ends well. The temperature has cooled down, and Miss Lonelyhearts stands in the composer's apartment; before listening to the completed recording of the song she tells him how much the song has meant to her. A new dog descends in the basket, and Miss Torso's true partner arrives home, a small man in uniform with much more interest in the icebox than her body, unlike most other males in the film. The sculptress snoozes, and "hunger" now becomes more literal as the soldier opens the icebox. The one sign of discord involves the newlyweds, who make a rare appearance from their presumed lovemaking; had she known he lost his job, she would have thought twice about marrying him (it seems not to have occurred to her that he had lots of time to spend in bed).

As has happened many times before, the camera moves from the activities of the courtyard into Jeff's apartment, and now with symmetrical reference to the beginning, we once again find him asleep. Wood warns us to be wary of this ending, and there are good reasons why we should be, not the least of these being the apparently imminent failure of the newlyweds' marriage. The camera throughout the film has not supported the prospect of a good marriage between Lisa and Jeff, giving the upper hand visually to chaotic darkness and disorder. Hitchcock may very well be using both the script and the more cheerful visual images to suggest one possibility while using darker images to prompt the opposite view. In explaining the film to Truffaut, he compared its symmetry with that of *Shadow of a Doubt*, and here the comparison may run deeper, since the ending there, similarly in the face of dark and destructive forces, could only be deceptive, as the eulogy for Uncle Charlie rubs our face in it. In that case the trivial family life of Santa Rosa proved to be a mirage, now forever tainted in the mind of the person capable of understanding what had happened, and marriage itself may come in for similar treatment in *Rear Window*. In fact, it is not so much marriage that receives this treatment, but marriage as a representative of stability and order, and the potential for disorder to assail the institution held dear in the 1950s. In the case of the newlyweds, sex was probably not enough to make it work, while for Miss Torso and her hungry soldier, the apparent lack of interest in sex may be as big a problem. For Jeff and Lisa, the admiration which Jeff finds for Lisa based on her bravery may very well be the Kuleshovian curve that Hitchcock throws us; the camera has not confirmed that this will be enough to get Jeff over the hump.

Along with the rest of the deceptively cheerful ending comes Waxman's "saccharine-sweet inspiration, 'Lisa'."[19] On the recording the composer plays for Miss Lonelyhearts we finally hear the song with its text, and this text, in confirming this to be Lisa's song, may also be throwing us off the track. The Lisa this song describes, from the perspective of its male narrator, bears very little resemblance to the Lisa in Jeff's eyes: "Lisa, full of starry-eyed laughing grace/ Hold me and whisper the sweet words I'm yearning for/ Drown me in kisses, caresses I'm burning for/ Lisa, every touch is new ecstasy/ Lisa, angels dance when you cling to me/ If this is dreaming I hope I never wake/ But dream forever in your arms/ Oh, Lisa ... Lisa."[20] We have seen no evidence of any such yearning from Jeff—certainly not ecstasy, and we have encountered only minimal interest from him for her embrace. The only point at which it becomes more or less accurate concerns dreaming and hoping never to wake, as Jeff remains asleep. Since we have had no prior evidence that the dreams described in the song could be the ones he now dreams, it seems more probable that his sleep has simply made him dead to his surroundings—at least so far as they concern Lisa.

Hitchcock may have enjoyed this kind of ironic use for the song at the end, but considering the major role he intended the song to play in the film, that seems hardly enough to justify the manner of its treatment throughout. He seemed to think the song could be a kind of co-conspirator with the visual images, subverting our view of things as the film unfolded, but it turned out to be much too stable to accomplish that. Making his cameo appearance with the composer seemed intended to be designed to give the composer some prompting on how the song should work, and in fact, John Fawell, who wished to learn what Hitchcock may have been saying to the composer, discovered this from lip-readers: "B, B flat."[21] This could suggest he wished the tone of the song to be darkened, making it less saccharine, perhaps shifting to the minor mode, which B flat would do in the key of G. This prompting seems to have had an effect on the composer, who, only a short time later, while scrubbing his apartment floor, reaches over to the piano and plays a major chord followed by a minor chord. During the previous evening, we see the composer, apparently drunk, angrily knock his music off the piano's music stand, but neither this nor the chords make much sense in relation to Waxman's song, which develops too fluently. What Hitchcock elicited with the directing of Ross Bagdasarian works visually (and audibly with the chords), but it did not connect with his real composer Waxman, whose music seems to be at odds with the visual promptings and certainly with the visual tone of the film. Suggesting that a popular composer instead of a film composer could have solved this problem misses the point, although with his lack of specific musical knowledge he may have thought this would help. In fact, he needed a composer who could grasp what he hoped to achieve with the film, and on this occasion that appeared not to be Waxman. The composed music for the film, "Lisa," supports the notion of a comedy thriller, not a film with the depth that the camera carries.

7

The piano: Instrument of seduction

Not unlike the waltz, pianos turn up in a significant number of Hitchcock's films, close to half of them, certainly often enough to force one to ask if the piano has special status in the way that the waltz does. It could, of course, simply be an object that one would expect to find in the drawing room of any elegantly furnished home, or for that matter in just about any middle-class home, as in real life. If, though, it becomes visually privileged, drawing special attention from the camera, or if we hear it or see it being played at significant points, it may very well be more than an attractive although commonplace furnishing. In the more than two dozen films in which the piano makes an appearance, a few distinctly different categories emerge: it can be seen but not heard, it can be heard and seen, or, most commonly, we will see and hear someone sitting at the piano playing. As a performance vehicle it can play a prominent role in a film, and the points at which we hear these performances may be of special importance to the film. Even when seen but not heard it can be of notable dramatic interest as a backdrop to the events unfolding, or more importantly, it may contribute to a striking visual impact that could only be achieved with it present. It can play both reinforcing and inimical roles.

In order to assess the nature of the role it may play, consideration needs to be given to the ways we perceive pianos, both as visual objects and as musical instruments conveying sound. The sounds—the works that we will hear performed or someone's improvising—add another dimension since the music itself may be of special significance, which can be intensified by becoming part of the diegesis. The instrument has been with us for roughly three centuries, invented in Italy by Bartolomeo Christofori early in the eighteenth century, and it quickly became a serious rival to the other comparable keyboard instruments such as the harpsichord and the clavichord. By the end of the eighteenth century it had become the preferred instrument of composers who wished to use it for virtuoso purposes in concertos, such as Mozart and Beethoven, although for these two it never became the vehicle of pure virtuosity that it was for some other composers, since their works for it always retained a strong element of intimate expression. Perhaps because of its beauty as an object in its own right, it became by the end of the eighteenth century a required furnishing of every elegant home, and not as an object that sat idly in the drawing room. It evolved into the preferred instrument of women, and part of the finishing education of any central European woman included accomplishment at playing the piano. Women had always been active as musicians, but the piano provided advantages that had not previously existed in society which insisted on decorum. Deportment prevented women from playing instruments that involved lifting the arms too high, or worse, opening the legs, as the cello requires. The piano must be played sitting, and arms do not have to be raised very high.

Gender

Composers quickly recognized the new market for music publication, and until well into the nineteenth century they wrote almost all solo piano music for women, as one can see from the dedications of these works. That included piano sonatas and all the miscellaneous types of keyboard music such as rondos, variations, minuets and other dances, fantasies, impromptus, and the full range of character pieces. During most of this time women remained amateur pianists, usually performing for salons or other intimate gatherings, or simply playing for their own enjoyment. Some became highly skilled players, able to perform the most difficult works written by the likes of Haydn and Mozart, but as talented amateurs. Those with professional abilities, such as the sisters of Mozart (Nannerl) and Mendelssohn (Fanny), struggled with social conventions, which more or less barred them from public performance after the age of 18, when society expected them to become submissive wives. Even Robert Schumann's wife, Clara, one of the greatest pianists of the nineteenth century, struggled with this, both as a pianist and a composer. The principle established for solo literature also more or less held for chamber music with piano, which women most often performed. Until the middle of the nineteenth century it remained relatively rare for men to play the piano, with the exception of professionals, who usually wrote piano music for themselves or improvised in public, and that tradition, most famously practiced by Franz Liszt, persisted well into the twentieth century.

The piano, then, became gendered, a woman's instrument, and that association determined how the instrument was perceived and in some respects even how makers made it look. As the instrument evolved, in the hands of the outstanding makers such as Schantz and Bösendorfer in Austria, Errard and Pleyel in France, Broadwood in England, and Steinway in Germany and the United States, it gradually lost its straight lines and took on graceful curves, increasing its physical attractiveness. By the middle of the nineteenth century the grand piano as we know it existed, and the subsequent changes ceased to be structural, simply varying the size or adding ornaments such as elaborate carving to make it even more attractive. With the invention of the upright piano the instrument became much more accessible to middle-class homes, and even here physical attractiveness remained a priority, with shapes or carving that set these pianos apart as objects of beauty, able not only to produce beautiful sounds but to catch the eye as well.

In writing piano literature specifically for women, composers gave this music a distinctive character, in many cases allowing it especially to appeal to the emotions, or to move the player and listener in engaging and even passionate ways. As one would expect, the

other arts also recognized this essence, most notably painting and
the novel; authors such as Samuel Richardson and Henry Fielding
particularly directed their novels toward women. For women writers
an obvious path existed to make the piano a significant image, and
no one achieved this more effectively than Jane Austen, herself an
accomplished and passionate pianist. Male writers also grasped
its potential as an image, as Johann Wolfgang von Goethe did as
early as his *Die Leiden des jungen Werthers* (*The sorrows of young
Werther*, 1774), in which a tale of unrequited love can in part unfold
because of the capability of Lotte's piano playing to move and even
seduce Werther, who in the end commits suicide because he cannot
have her. Decorum prevents the engaged and then married Lotte
from giving him verbal signs of her affection, but she does it by
playing for him, playing which gives him hope, and certainly seduces
him, although not with her full consciousness of how it may be
stirring him. In that sense the piano and her playing of it can be
detached from her, as the piano itself carries the seductiveness. That
image of the piano has lasted to the present, perhaps most strikingly revealed in Jane Campion's *The Piano*, where the playing of the
instrument by Ada (Holly Hunter) arouses Baines (Harvey Keitel), and
only gradually does lust transform itself to love. Campion allows the
camera to penetrate the instrument as though it is a sexual object,
and she reinforces this with Baines lovingly caressing the beautiful
instrument while naked, as he would a woman's body.

For Campion the line blurs between love and subversion, while
for others subversion or something much worse takes full control,
as in Elfriede Jelinek's *Die Klavierspielerin* (*The piano teacher*), transformed into the film *La Pianiste* by Michael Haneke. The long history
of the use of the piano as an image suggests the existence of a dual
or conflicting sense about the instrument, which can represent very
different impulses. On the one hand it engenders something entirely
wholesome, in the best spirit of the nineteenth-century in which
decorum symbolizes a purity about women in their domestic roles. This
held on both sides of the Atlantic, as one sees in this description by
Craig H. Roell about the piano in America, a view shared by the British:

The piano became associated with the virtues attributed to music
as medicine for the soul. Music supposedly could rescue the

distraught from the trials of life. Its moral restorative qualities could counteract the ill effects of money, anxiety, hatred, intrigue, and enterprise. Since this was also seen as the mission of women in Victorian society, music and women were closely associated even into the twentieth century. As the primary musical instrument, the piano not only became symbolic of the virtues attributed to music, but also of home and family life, respectability, and woman's particular place and duty. Indeed, most piano pupils were female, and both music making and music appreciation were distinctly feminized. The glorification of the piano was no mere fad; it was a moral institution. Oppressive and opulent, the piano sat steadfast, massive, and magnificent in the parlors and drawing rooms of middle-class homes, serving as a daily reminder of a sublime way of life.[1]

In marketing a new piano model in 1915, Steinway tried to accentuate these qualities, running an ad with this caption: "To the bride, the Steinway Piano is a most acceptable gift. Its perfect tone, resonant and sweet, lends harmony to happy days, and its superior craftsmanship makes it an enduring possession to be more and more cherished as the years come and go. Style M, the new Steinway Grand, is especially adapted to the modern home or apartment."[2] The illustration shows an elated bride sitting at the piano, with a contented husband leaning against it. Writers and painters such as Edward Samuel Harper (*A Reverie*) or Sir Frank Dicksee (*A Reverie*, 1895) could heighten the subversive aspect of the instrument by starting from the assumption of the association with purity. The sensuality of the instrument could be intensified by some having painted illustrations of naked women on the interior of the lid.[3]

Implied sounds

It did not take long for Hitchcock to use pianos in his films as an image of ambiguity or outright conflict, and by starting this in his silent films in the 1920s, he initially established it purely visually. The most striking early use comes in *The Ring* (1927), where the piano features prominently in the love triangle that develops among Jack the fairground boxer (Carl Brisson), his new bride Nelly (Lillian Hall-Davies), who sold the tickets for his impromptu matches, and the champion, Bob (Ian Hunter), who has already beaten Jack before, in one of these challenges. The two boxers have risen in the world as victories have put money in their pockets. Jack and Nelly now live in a fashionable flat in a much better part of town, and they own a grand piano, which Nelly plays. We first see this piano during the wild dancing scene described in Chapter 4, as the two exotic dancers shimmy to the accompaniment of a piano player, who moves his body in a manner appropriate to the rhythm. During this scene Jack negotiates his next fight contract in a back room, while Nelly flirts with Bob in the living room, almost sitting on his lap. As the dancing continues, Nelly and Bob go well beyond flirtation, and the vision of the dance becomes a swirl to Jack, dissolving into an elongated blur. The camera then jumps to the piano, focusing on the piano player's hands and the keyboard; just as the dance becomes a blur, so does the keyboard, as the black keys dissolve into a similar type of elongated blur, generating a nightmarish visual image which represents the sounds that Jack hears. Visual layers now become superimposed, as the keyboard becomes more distorted through the motion of the player's hands and the addition of a spinning gramophone record. Bob and Nelly kiss amid these disfigured images, and Jack's face now betrays a look of panic. Tension has reached a peak, and the piano provides a powerful catalyst for this as it becomes a visual representation of the sounds of disintegration. The elegant furnishing and instrument of domestic calm has cut a jagged edge of tension and decay.

An equally striking scene with the piano occurs just after this breakdown of Jack's peace of mind, immediately following the departure of all the guests. Jack thinks training away from his wife will lead to a divorce, and the promoter reminds him that Bob wears the champion's belt. Jack enters the empty living room, where Nelly now sits at the piano playing, and the look on his face makes it clear that all his old feelings about her have been aroused; a seductive look emanates from her face, and he walks to her ready for love, standing behind her as she continues to play. As he bends down and reaches forward to caress her, he sees the portrait of Bob on the piano, the

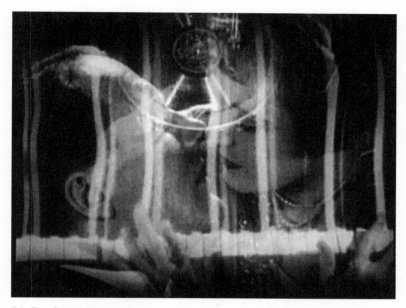

7.1 *The Ring* (Lillian Hall-Davies and Ian Hunter against piano keys) (Piano keys and an unfaithful wife)

object of Nelly's seductive looks, and the arrested motion of his hands leads to a jump cut into a very different view of his hands, now as bare fists swinging violently at a punching bag. The piano here plays the role defined in literature and painting, as something sexually charged with seductiveness and perversity, anything but a symbol of domestic bliss. This treatment of the piano in 1927 put Hitchcock in good company with the other arts, and set the trend for the ways he would use the piano as a duplicitous image for the next half century.

The Ring may hold the earliest vivid use of the piano as a visual and implied sound image, but it had appeared even earlier, in *The Lodger*. Here a large upright piano stands in the family parlor, and despite never being played, it becomes the backdrop for a number of telling scenes. The first of these happens in the parlor just after Joe puts handcuffs on Daisy, and she makes her lack of amusement at his little joke clear, with the piano in the background. They kiss, but with reluctance from Daisy, who rushes out of the parlor up the stairs to the Lodger. Another scene of tension between Joe and

7.2 *The Ring* (Lillian Hall-Davies with Carl Brisson) (She loves Bob in the picture on the piano, not her approaching husband)

Daisy takes place in front of the piano, after Joe gets angry because the Lodger has taken Daisy in his arms when she sees a mouse in his room. Daisy's mother first suspects that the Lodger may be the Avenger as she and her husband talk framed by the piano, and Daisy opens the package with the gift dress from the Lodger, which her father refuses to allow her to accept, with the piano in the background. Here the piano sits passively as just another furnishing, but unlike the domestic scenes in the kitchen, we see it only when scenes of tension unfold.

This type of silent-film approach to the piano, simply showing it as a backdrop for tension, Hitchcock used effectively in sound films as well, for example, in *Suspicion*. The lavish house that Johnnie provides for his new wife Lina of course has a grand piano in the drawing room, but only on a couple of occasions do we see it. One happens when Lina discovers that Johnnie has no money, and admits his hope to make ends meet with her future inheritance. Another happens during the visit of Johnnie's friend Beaky, when Lina discovers that Johnnie has pawned the two chairs that her father gave them as a wedding gift. At no point do we see Lina or anyone else playing the piano, although we know that was part of earlier scripts, such as the one described in Chapter 4, when Lina plays "their" waltz in the manner of Ravel's *La Valse* just before the arrival of the police inspectors who inform Lina of Beaky's death in Paris, and raise questions about Johnnie's possible involvement. The distortion that that scene would have brought appears to have been replaced by an abstract Picasso painting on the wall, which one of the inspectors views uncomprehendingly as he enters and later when he leaves.

In other early adaptations of Francis Iles's novel *Before the Fact*, both Johnnie and Lina play the piano, for example in the draft prepared by Arnaud d'Usseau, dated 9 November 1939, in a scene at Lina's home shortly after she and Johnnie have met. Johnnie sees a piano, and asks who plays, to which Lina replies that she does, badly. Johnnie then sits down and begins to play, telling her that he wrote a melody to commemorate their first Sunday together: "The melody Johnnie plays is an arresting one with a definite haunting quality. Lina listens, falling under its spell, and as her eyes begin to shine, Johnnie starts improvising."[4] After playing, he draws her down to the piano bench and gives her a kiss, which she returns. Later when she opens the box with her engagement ring, Johnnie plays the piano. One scene involving a piano from the early adaptations that does survive to the final shooting involves a description of a murder plot from the latest novel by their friend Isobel, which she describes at her own dinner party. A certain note of a piano is wired to a hidden revolver, and fires when the victim opens the door; Johnnie quibbles that the complexity of this makes it implausible. The discussion then turns to the use of an undetectable poison, which Lina suspects Johnnie will use on her, so the piano as lethal weapon segues directly into her greatest fear, making the piano in a sense the harbinger of something horrible. In the early scripts the piano moves from the instrument of love to one of doom, but in the end the actual film, in dropping the early piano scenes, leaves that to the imagination.

The piano, then, plays a purely visual role in *Suspicion*, as it does in *Shadow of a Doubt* just two years later. After speaking at the Santa Rosa women's club (and making his second attempt to kill young Charlie), a reception in the family parlor features an upright piano, and Mrs Potter, perhaps a potential future victim, sits on the bench, facing away from the piano. The instrument seems to support the domestic niceties of the situation, as all the guests admire Uncle Charlie's skill of oratory, but an icy pall falls over the room when young Charlie descends the stairs and displays to him the ring which prompted her realization that he had murdered the widows in the East. Not long after this he will make his third and final attempt on her life. In other films the piano also appears in a silent role, but in some of these the instrument will play a more active role in the conflict, as happens in *The Man Who Knew Too Much* (1934) and *I Confess* (to be discussed later).

Seduction or femme fatale

The presentation of the piano in *The Ring* sets the tone for the way it would be used in subsequent films, as an agent of disruption, in conjunction with sexually loose behavior, and more often than not associated with women—although it does not necessarily have to be played by a woman. In his first sound film, *Blackmail*, Hitchcock continued what he had started in *The Ring*, here placing the piano at the center of the events that become the dramatic crux of the film. Alice (Anny Ondra), the apparently sweet girl from an honest small-business-owning family, lives, it appears, something of a double life, with a detective boyfriend Frank (John Longden) on the one hand, and a more adventurous spirit on the other. She has a date with Frank to have a bite and take in a movie, but a note in her purse indicates she may be meeting someone else, and for a while she cannot make up her mind if she will go to the movie with Frank or meet up with the other person. When she sees the other man, she changes her mind about the movie, and after Frank pays the restaurant bill and leaves in a huff, she goes off with the artist Crewe (Cyril Ritchard), with their departure observed by Frank. He takes her up long flights of stairs to his flat, which she admires, and while he lights a fire she explores, first finding the painting of the jester, and then the piano, on which she plays a few notes, a scale, and a chord at the end of the scale which she does not get quite right. She has opted to spend the evening with Crewe, not Frank, and she feels seductive, although this develops innocently. Taking the palette and a brush she draws a woman's head at the easel, and he helps her to complete the sketch, in fact of a nude woman; when they complete the breasts she playfully calls him awful, but immediately signs her own name to the picture.

Her next discovery, a costume dress he uses for models, takes her flirtatiousness to the next level, as she speculates on how she would look as one of his models. He suggests she put it on, and when she declines, he sits down at the piano and begins to play, saying he would have liked to sketch her in it but that it probably would not suit her. As he plays what we soon recognize to be the song "Miss Up to Date," she changes her mind, convinced she would look good in it; for the moment she continues to play the more seductively aggressive role. As she takes off her own dress and puts on the costume dress, a screen separates her from him as he plays and now sings; the camera here takes in both giving us a type of visual and aural fusion, with her act of undressing providing a type of extension of the nude sketch from a few moments earlier, while these become transferred to the piano and the song. She emerges from behind the screen and leans on the piano, clearly displaying herself to him as he continues to play and sing. She cannot do up the back zipper and does not object when his attempt also fails. The scene becomes more intimate as he takes the straps off her shoulders and adjusts her hair, and she appears to enjoy all of this until he goes one step too far, embracing and kissing her. The seductive mood has been broken, and only now do we discover the darker possibilities, emphasized by the harsh look on his face and the almost tattoo-like shadow on his cheek. The piano continues to play an active role as she takes off the costume and he grabs her dress and throws it over his shoulder as he sits down at the piano again and plays the song much faster and more aggressively than before, luring her to come out and get the dress. He ends his playing with a crashing disruptive chord, and leaps up to look at her, breaking the barrier of the screen; as he drags her away we see them in shadows only, with the scene of horror taking on a German expressionist manner. The piano in fact has been central to the shift from seductiveness to the menace of attempted rape; not only does the much discussed song[5] back up this action, but the piano itself propels events forward.

The piano turns up in a number of films from the 1930s with various functions that underline conflict, but as a vehicle of seduction and disorder it appears prominently in a trio of successive films released between 1946 and 1948: *Notorious*, *The Paradine Case*, and *Rope*. In each of these the image functions in a much more complex way than it had in earlier films, and in the two later ones it becomes a persistent image, linking parts of the film together or actually providing continuity. Its appearance in *Notorious* may seem slight, but one of the brief appearances and the music heard at that point prove to be exceptionally rich. Alicia Huberman (Ingrid Bergman), the daughter of a disgraced and convicted Nazi spy, like many of Hitchcock's characters, lives a double life, not only branded by her father, but also in her lifestyle of excessive drinking and easy virtue. We see her in this milieu when she and Devlin (Cary Grant) first meet at a party at her house, where she drinks heavily and probably would have been more seductive if she had not been so drunk.

A piano stands in her living room, but unlike the script which describes the early exchanges between Alicia and Devlin taking place beside the piano,[6] in the film we do not see it until the two of them leave the house to go for a drive. A couple of drunken guests lean against it, and the lid serves as a repository for discarded liquor bottles. Since a piano will have a different seductive function later, it may have been decided at this point that it should not serve a similar role for a different character. Devlin, a secret service agent, has come to recruit her for an undercover job involving Nazis in Rio de Janeiro, and he confirms her potential for this by playing a recording in which she disavows Nazi ideology. She agrees to take the assignment, and as she falls in love with Devlin in Rio, her notorious past and attempts to be reputable in the present clash, initially about staying on the wagon, and eventually about her capacity for lovers. The assignment turns out to be the seduction of the head of the Nazi post-war operations in Rio, Alexander Sebastien (Claude Rains), in fact a former flame, from whom she should extract secrets, and she proves to be so successful at enticing him (without really trying) that he marries her. Devlin does not deal with her assignment well, finding her professions of love disingenuous, and at one point believes she has fallen off the wagon.

Seduction, then, plays a complex role in the film. Alicia has fallen in love with one man, but her job requires her to seduce another, which she does exceptionally well; she must live an extreme type of double life, and Devlin doubts she really feels anything for him. The two of them plant the seed with Sebastien, a supposedly accidental meeting while horseback riding, and Sebastien takes the bait, inviting her to dinner, where he expresses his readiness to be seduced. He invites her again, this time to a dinner party at his home, and for this she enhances her seductive allure with stylish clothes and the jewelry rented for the occasion. After being chauffeured to the house, she walks up the front steps, and even before Emil the servant opens the door, we hear the sound of a piano gently playing, so gently that it proves difficult to recognize the music, seeming to be little more than background music. Emil leads her through an elegant hallway to the drawing room door, and upon entering the room, we see an ornately carved piano with the bust of a woman on

7.3 *Notorious* (Ingrid Bergman) (Alicia hears Schumann)

the closed lid, a bust that portrays beauty in a classical manner; Alicia walks by the piano slowly and stops so that the frame captures her looking at the bust on the piano. She has come to seduce, and the piano, along with the bust on it, becomes her visual ally.

Unlike other uses of the piano in Hitchcock's films, this time we see a piano and we also hear it, although with no one actually playing it, as it sits with the keyboard lid open. By now we have heard the music long enough for those familiar with piano literature to recognize it: it is "Chopin" from Robert Schumann's highly complex *Carnaval*. The choice may seem curious, but it becomes even more puzzling when the music segues to another piece, not from *Carnaval* but in fact Schumann's "Warum?" (Why) from the *Phantasiestücke* (Fantasy pieces). Jack Sullivan, who mentions only the first of the two pieces in *Hitchcock's Music*, sensibly suggests that the choice of music denotes the good taste of the Nazis.[7] This may be, but one suspects that with such a peculiar fusion of works there may be more to it, adding a level for those who recognize the music, which in 1946 would have been many more people than now. "Warum" could have a fairly obvious possibility, since we hear it only after Alicia meets Sebastien's mother (Madame Konstantin), who first says she now understands why her son so admires Alicia. She then raises the matter of Alicia's father, noting how unusual she found it that Alicia did not testify at his trial. Alicia points out that her father refused to allow her to testify, which prompts Sebastien's mother to say, "I wonder why." Sebastien arrives to break the ice, but already in this first meeting his mother has doubts about Alicia, doubts that will be confirmed later and will drive her to poison Alicia in the hope that Alicia's death will prevent the other Nazis from discovering the ineptness of her son—who allowed a seduction which can cause their undoing.

Whether or not Hitchcock had anything to do with the choice of this music we cannot say, but he did know Schumann's piano music, especially *Carnaval*. Even if he knew the piece well, he was unlikely to be familiar with the program of the work, with its representation of the loves of the young Schumann's life, and the entourage of carnival-like characters who represent the conflicting sides of Schumann himself. His musical representation of Chopin caused a rift between the two composers since Chopin heard it as a vapid stereotyping of his music and consequently as an insult. No composer of the nineteenth century, though, had feminized the piano and its literature as much as Chopin had,[8] and Schumann may have specifically wished to portray this, not as the genuine Chopin, but as a caricature. That may have made it useful as a representation of Alicia, whose disingenuous feminine seductiveness here would not be well served by an actual piece by Chopin, but works better as a false representation of the master. The way we hear it modifies it as well, since the actual piece should be played *agitato* (agitated) and loud, not in the quiet and gentle manner of its presentation. A number of things about it do not ring true, and neither does Alicia's seduction, which the jealous mother recognizes. "Warum" on the other hand should be gentle and slow, but deceptive tensions dominate it, with numerous suspensions—the holding of melodic notes beyond the entry of chord changes, creating dissonant chords that only resolve when the melodic notes resolve; these give credence to the notion of the question "why" being filled with tension. In *Phantasiestücke* one finds a general progression toward darkness and sadness, and the question "why" focuses attention on this dark descent. A similar focus begins in the film at this point, addressing not only Mother's doubts, but the overall direction in which Alicia's dangerous seduction of Sebastien will lead, eventually to the brink of death which would have actually resulted in death if Devlin had not made his orphic rescue at the end.

Inadvertent seduction

Hitchcock's next film, *The Paradine Case*, did not succeed for a number of reasons, including the weakness of the script[9] and the uninspired performances of some of the actors, but under different circumstances it could perhaps have had a better outcome, and with the treatment of the piano, it almost did. Here the piano plays a much larger role than it did in *Notorious*, and part of the failure of the film resulted from the fact that the use of the piano works at cross-purposes to the script. Hitchcock's own instinct would be to let the piano carry the underlying thrust of the film, but David

O. Selznick's screenplay seems to fight it at every turn, hitting the viewer over the head with verbal notions that get in the way of what should be absorbed audibly and visually. The film centers on inadvertent seduction, coming from Maddelena Paradine (Alida Valli) but completely unintended, of the great barrister Anthony Keane (Gregory Peck), who falls in love with an illusion, not a person, which thereby threatens his marriage and career. If the seduction works it does so because of the piano, not the screenplay, and certainly not the acting of Peck.

Before the film slips into the mediocrity of its text, we have visual and sound images that could have made it work. At the start the camera pans down a fashionable London street to a stately house, and before it enters the house, the sound of the piano wafts gently out to the street. Inside the house the sound becomes more persistent, and sound becomes picture as the butler brings a drink to Mrs Paradine seated at the piano, with her back facing the approaching camera; the sheet music from which she reads sits visible to us on the piano's music stand. The final shooting script from 10 December 1946 describes her as slim and beautiful, dressed in black, with the manner "of a woman who has been through a great deal but is controlling her emotions."[10] This script preceded Franz Waxman's involvement as composer, and states that she plays Schubert at this point. As the butler announces dinner her face comes into full view, and she takes a sip of the drink, continues playing, and looks at the portrait of her recently deceased husband; the butler interrupts her playing with the announcement that police inspectors have come to speak with her. Close-ups of her face reveal a beautiful woman with a somewhat icy look, very conscious of her appearance as she looks in a mirror before the inspectors arrest her for the murder of her husband. She betrays no emotion, seeming very British despite her foreign accent, but her piano playing tells us more about her, as she reads from a score titled "Appassionata;" we hear not a wildly passionate piece but instead gentle music by Waxman, that if anything boils beneath the surface. These opening images should set the tone for the film, and in some ways they do; it will not take long for the script to undermine this.

Keane will be her defense lawyer, but as he interviews her in preparation for his case, he commits the unpardonable sin of his trade by falling in love with her. At the first interview in prison he falls for her as he talks of her blind husband who could not see her as he now does, and the intensity of his look tells us what he sees, with her hair not up as it had been in the opening scene, now accentuating the beauty of her face. Even though he has never seen her at the piano, her playing which started the film seems to become the seductive force that grasps him and will possess him later. At their next meeting he cannot avoid discussing the matter of her character with her, which will surely be used against her at the trial, and he learns about her somewhat sordid past, running off as a mere 16-year-old with a married man, in no way exploited by him but if anything taking advantage of him. She calls herself a woman who has seen a great deal of life, and along the way there have been other men as well. Later questions about her relationship with her husband's valet Latour (Louis Jourdan) force her to recoil, especially when Keane informs her that Latour has said of her that "if ever there was an evil woman, she is one." Her seductive powers seem clear to all, especially Keane who mistakenly imagines them directed toward himself; others also recognize her powers, especially Keane's wife, who sees the effect of this force on her husband. With all the gossipy chatter about her, or the comment by Keane's older colleague Sir Simon that she "brings my pulse up," the script persistently makes nonsense of what Hitchcock establishes with the piano at the beginning.

If we doubt the piano's capacity to achieve this, Hitchcock confirms it in one of the best scenes in the film, in Mrs Paradine's bedroom at her country estate in the Lake District, a scene which lacks dialogue, achieving its effect purely through visual images and sound. Two main objects stand out in the bedroom: her bed, with a portrait of her looking seductive (or with a Mona Lisa smile, according to the script) on the headboard of the bed no less, and a grand piano, with the same score on it that she had played at the beginning, the "Appassionata," by the fictitious composer Francesco Ceruomo, an Italian like herself. The camera zooms with Keane's gaze to the portrait, shows some private articles such as negligees strewn about on the bed, and then moves from the portrait to the piano, which he touches while reading the music's title "Appassionata." His reverie breaks when he hears laughter from outside, from Latour with the carriage driver, Latour being the one who more than anyone will shatter his illusion of love about her. For the moment he comes back to reality, but the illusion persists as he sees her for another interview, at which point she refuses to talk more about her past and especially Latour; he apologizes for his line of questioning, and holds her hands when he vows to do all he can to secure her release. Again he mistakes this hand contact for something other than the gratefulness that she feels. The visual image of the piano makes no further appearances in the film, but Waxman keeps it alive in sound, for example after Keane's wife urges him to win the case and set Mrs Paradine free, knowing she will have a chance against a real woman instead of an illusion. Waxman accompanies her speech with orchestral music, but the instant she leaves, the piano takes over, with the "Appassionata" of course. Piano and orchestra now briefly compete, as though to replay in music the competition Keane's wife knows she must face.

One of the most striking features of the adaptation of Robert Hichens's novel for Hitchcock by Muriel Elwood that did not make it

7.4 *The Paradine Case* (Gregory Peck) (The piano evokes Mrs Paradine for Keane)

to the script involves the fact that Keane has a pianist friend named Arthur Lieberstein, who tells him that he knew Colonel Paradine and that music had a strange and profound effect on him. This pianist made a transcription of the "Blue Danube," which according to Keane and his wife "could cause a terrible ache in anyone who had been a great success and had fallen upon tragedy, as Paradine had done." This would have returned as a factor at the trial, when the prosecutor revealed that after Mrs Paradine poisoned her husband, she "went downstairs and played Lieberstein's transcription of 'Blue Danube' while waiting for the poison to take effect. She insists that she played this piece to soothe her nerves."[11] Here piano and waltz extraordinarily come together as a double dose of the dance of death and the piano as agent of disorder, and one can only speculate on how effective it would have been to include this in the film. Mrs Paradine turns out to be guilty, something that everyone but Keane seemed to know, and the battle in the courtroom pales in comparison to the power of the piano to have an effect on Keane. Dialogue takes over, and leaves a severely weakened piece of cinema in the end.

Piano and murder

In this trio of films from the late 1940s the piano progressively takes on a larger role, moving from an image in the background to one of central and ongoing importance, as happens in *Rope*, in which the persistence of the piano also brings a very high level of complexity. We see the piano vaguely in the darkened living room at the beginning of the film, when Brandon (John Dall) and Phillip (Farley Granger) strangle David Kentley, we see and hear it at the end of the film with the police on their way to arrest the pair of murderers, and we see it almost constantly throughout the film. Certain objects as images for obvious reasons have attracted much interest, including the piece of rope which doubles as a murder weapon and a way to hold books together, and the chest which holds the body of the victim. The chest also serves as the original storage place for first-edition books, becomes a type of altar with candles placed on it, and provides the surface for serving food—as a bizarre kind of communion table. The piano in the course of the film becomes every bit as important as the other two objects, as it assumes a dominating role in the apartment, not only visually privileged but also a hub for action, and not only from being played by Phillip. On a number of critical occasions the camera takes in the chest and piano simultaneously, for example when Rupert (James Stewart) moves to open the chest to discover the corpse, in a sense equating the two objects, suggesting that the piano too holds secrets that need to be revealed.

All commentators agree that Brandon and Phillip are homosexuals, and that a homosexual agenda underlies the narrative—perhaps even that the murder of David stands as symbolic of a homosexual act. Hitchcock never discussed homosexuality on the set, but of course the representation of it hung in the air, and did not need to be verbalized. In part this could happen because of the screenwriter Arthur Laurents, an openly gay writer, whom Hitchcock could trust to get things right without having to spell it out. To add to the layer of homosexuality, Laurent wrote the part of Phillip specifically for

7.5 *Rope* (James Stewart with Farley Granger and John Dall) (The case of death and the piano)

Granger, who happened to be his lover at the time. As was true of many gay or bisexual actors in Hollywood, there may have been rumors, but such matters never came into the open, since this would have brought a career to a screeching halt; only in 2007 did Granger officially come out, with the publication of his autobiography.[12] The film has another significant gay element, and this concerns the only music played by Phillip at the piano: an adaptation of the "Perpetual Movement No. 1" by Francis Poulenc, an openly homosexual French composer. Hitchcock can certainly take responsibility for the choice of this music, as we see from a studio memo from Joseph McLaughlin to Helen Schoen, dated 21 January 1948, in response to the possibility of using some other music, such as pieces by Jacques Ibert or Percy Grainger: "Hitchcock the Producer is putting up a lot of his own dough for this picture and it really wasn't a question of substitution as he was insistent on using the above composition."[13] When Rupert comments to Phillip, "you're very fond of that little tune, aren't you," that remark turns out to be much more loaded than we may suspect. Most descriptions of its use emphasize how it runs parallel to the long shots of the film, but that may be the least of its significance. In all probability Rupert forms part of a gay triangle in the film (perhaps more implied than real), although Stewart may not have had the slightest idea that he could have been playing a gay character.[14]

In the previous two films, the piano has been associated with women, building on the traditional connection with the instrument, but *Rope* makes the association with a man, although to be sure a gay one. Because of this, a level of complexity comes into play, since the piano in fact serves its traditional role here, as a feminine image associated with the appropriate character. All seem to be in agreement that of the two murderers Brandon stands as the dominant character while Phillip plays the submissive one, and at least one commentator, Richard Allen, labels Brandon the "male" partner and Phillip the "female" one, even "hysteric."[15] The two of them see their existence in artistic terms, and Brandon goes so far as to describe a murder as a work of art; Phillip though is the real artist as a concert pianist in training, and he has the more volatile artistic temperament, which includes his susceptibility to guilt. As a pianist, Phillip's future lies literally in his hands, and at one point during the party with David present (in the chest), Mrs Atwater takes his hands in hers and comments that "these hands will bring you great fame." Since the first shot in the apartment shows Phillip's hands pulling the rope that strangles David, we immediately catch the double meaning, even before Phillip looks with distress at his hands—which he clenches in the shape of German expressionist murderous claws. That linkage supports the visual combination of the piano and the chest, as both encase the darkest possible view of humanity, if not outright chaos. Just as the rope serves as a lethal weapon and a binding of intellectual products—the books, now symbolic of the intellectual aberrations first emanating from Rupert that led to the murder, so too does the piano play a not unfamiliar role of being an image of disorder, and a complex gendered one at that.

During the first third of the film the piano remains a visual image, as a backdrop to unfolding events or as an image fused with the chest. Phillip first sits down and plays after Mrs Atwood looks at his hands, and Granger actually does the playing himself. Rupert now makes his entrance, and compliments Phillip on his improved touch, again a comment with double meaning which Phillip appears to catch, making him stop playing to listen as the conversation turns to David, between Rupert and David's father. The next time Phillip plays comes after the maid, Mrs Wilson, tells Rupert about the strange behavior of Brandon and Phillip, sowing the seeds of suspicion in Rupert's mind. As Phillip plays, Rupert leans on the piano to talk with him, asking why everyone appears to be so somber, and more directly, what's going on; Rupert turns on the light sitting atop the piano, and Phillip asks him to turn it off, preferring not to play with light in his eyes. While they discuss what's going on, a police siren from the street cuts into the sounds from the piano. As they talk of Rupert's suspicion, and specifically the whereabouts of David, Rupert turns on a metronome, faster than the pace of Phillip's playing, and this creates a clash as Rupert manipulates the pace. The intensity level rises as Rupert catches Phillip in lies, one that Rupert suspects about David's whereabouts, and the other real, about Phillip's denial that he ever strangled a chicken; Rupert resets the metronome to an even faster pace for the second lie.

Until the dying moments of the film key events leading to the truth play out with the piano prominently framing these, such as

7.6 *Rope* (Farley Granger with James Stewart) (Rupert sets the tempo too fast for Phillip)

when Phillip breaks, literally breaking a glass on the floor in his anxiety. Rupert observes that Brandon has a gun in his pocket, and Brandon tries to make light of it, slapping the gun down on the piano, making it the holder of a weapon that may have been intended for use against Rupert. In a state of panic Phillip takes the gun from the piano, and when he and Rupert struggle for it, the gun goes off, grazing Rupert's hand. Phillip slumps down at the piano, and shortly after this Rupert moves to the chest to open it to confirm his suspicions, with the piano and chest now visually linked. Before this Rupert describes, still somewhat facetiously, how the two would have carried out the murder, pointing out the role Phillip would play before the murder. After opening the chest, Rupert gives his impassioned lecture about the disconnect between theory and practice, thanking them for correcting his own perverse theoretical views of superiority, and asking Brandon if he thought himself to be God; this lecture takes place firmly in front of the piano. He fires the gun through the open window to attract the police, and as they come, sirens blaring, Phillip plays Poulenc one last time, now much slower than before, as though it has become a march to the scaffold.

The linkage of Phillip and the piano with homosexuality and murder takes the piano and the music coming from it to a new level of disarray and imbalance. We can probably add misogyny to the equation since the duplicitous developments unfold tied to an object with traditional feminine associations. If anything redeeming emerges here, it lies in the fact that the "male" character appears to lack a conscience, feeling nothing but the fear of being caught, while the "female" character, who, pushed with some reluctance into the evil deed and certainly with no conviction about intellectual superiority and being above common morality, does have a conscience, and seems to welcome the progression to the gallows. The fact that he can play the piano at the end, knowing his fate, seems to allow the instrument and its music to carry an ambivalent function, on the one hand as a participant in the murder (not unlike Thomas Bauso's view of our complicity in that we laugh at Brandon's macabre jokes[16]), but at the same time it signals the hope that decency has not been killed.

In conflict

The piano makes an appearance in numerous other films, not necessarily in a gendered way or related to seduction, but always as an image central to the conflict of the film, and that may concern the overall conflict or in some cases simply a specific scene. In some instances the piano may be thrust into the midst of the conflict itself, as in *Rope*, while in others it comes in the calm before the storm, usually in these cases played as well as seen. Two films already noted in which a silent piano participates in the action are *The Man Who Knew Too Much* (1934) and *I Confess*, although in the former we do briefly hear the piano. After the attempted assassination at the Royal Albert Hall, the London police track the terrorists led by Peter Lorre to their hideout, and before the shootout begins, the police take their position in a merchant's flat. As they enter the flat we see a large ornately carved upright piano, open, with music also open on the stand, and one of the policemen plays a few notes on the badly out-of-tune instrument. The captain points out that they do not need a concert now, but the jangled notes give him an idea, as he tells the others to move the piano closer to the window, where they can use it as a barricade. With this delightfully bizarre move, one wonders who but Hitchcock would think of a piano as the key prop in open battle, absorbing the shots from the enemy with its soundboard; when gunfire begins, Hitchcock does not take this to the point of giving the sounds the piano would make receiving shots in the back.

In *I Confess* the piano also appears during a shootout scene, near the end when the real murderer Otto (O. E. Hasse) has been tracked to one of the ballrooms of the Chateau Frontenac in Quebec City. The police catch up with Otto running in front of the stage of the ballroom, and on that stage stands a grand piano. As Otto climbs the stairs of the stage he fires a shot, and then goes to the piano, leaning against its side almost as a singer would at a performance. Otto performs, with a war of words against Father Logan (Montgomery Clift) and with his gun, all the while with the piano prominently displayed, as though it has become one of the characters, perhaps as support for the irrational and desperate Otto against the police doing their duty. We do not hear this instrument, but we see close-ups of it, revealing an elaborately decorated side.

Organs and pianos may be very different instruments, but they at least have in common the fact of being keyboard instruments, and both have a longstanding tradition as instruments providing accompaniments for silent films. Something akin to this happens in *The Man Who Knew Too Much* (1934), when the chair-smashing brawl breaks out at the Sun Tabernacle, and one of the conspirators tells the organist to play to drown out the crashing noises. With the stereotypical dowdy female organist playing hymns while all hell breaks loose, the scene seems like something from a Mack Sennett piece of slapstick, the music of course running entirely counter to the action. A much more ominous organ "performance" takes place in *Secret Agent* (1936) at the Langenthal Church in the Swiss Alps, where agent Ashenden (John Gielgud) and "The General" (Peter Lorre) go to meet the double agent organist in this First World War espionage thriller. As they enter the church they hear what at first seems to be a sustained dissonant chord, and when the same chord continues for about two minutes, they finally grasp that this is no minimalist musical work but comes from the dead organist, slumped over the keyboard; dissonance in this case clearly equals death. The film has so many comical touches that minimalism at first seems an option (if it had existed at the time).

Another at times screwball espionage thriller from the 1930s, *The Lady Vanishes* (1938), brings in the piano near the end of the film, when the ethnomusicologist Gilbert (Michael Redgrave) arrives at the Foreign Office in London, expected to be able to hum or whistle the coded musical message which he has memorized on the Continent and has carried through a harrowing trip back. As he enters the office, he commits an unforgivable lapse for his profession—he forgets the tune, but as he enters the Undersecretary's office, he hears the tune played on the piano by Miss Froy (Dame May Whitty), the lady who vanishes, having now reappeared, much to his surprise and relief. She rises from the piano to embrace Gilbert and Iris (Margaret Lockwood), now lovers after a rocky start. The piano here becomes an instrument of espionage as well as the point of binding for the youthful lovers.

The piano plays a much larger role in *Saboteur*, as will be noted in Chapter 8, with the blind man playing Delius's "Summer Night on the River" on the piano in his rustic lodge for Barry (Robert Cummings), now a fugitive from justice and in shackles. Tension hangs in the air as Barry tries to conceal the shackles, but a sense of calm permeates the scene, generated by the blind man, and that calm gives some relief before the storms that will come. Similarly in *Stage Fright* (1950), a film which verges on musical theater with the presence of Marlene Dietrich as performer, the piano plays an unusual role in its association with the forces of good, represented by the detective Wilfred "Ordinary" Smith (Michael Wilding), who plays the piano well enough that Eve (Jane Wyman) introduces him to her mother as a pianist. He comes to tea at Mother's house and she persuades him to play, which he does, with a piece that sounds vaguely Chopinesque, and no doubt convinces Eve that she has been in love with the wrong man (in an early script it was to be a Chopin ballade). An attraction then develops quickly between them, and whether or not he had been trying to seduce her with his playing, it works. One could say that Smith, despite his profession, plays a much gentler person than the man Eve first assumed she loved, Jonathan (Richard Todd), who turns out to be the murderer, and Smith's gentleness shows in his performance at the piano.

The piano plays a central role in two of the most musically striking films of all Hitchcock's, *Rear Window* and the later version of *The Man Who Knew Too Much* (1956), both of which I discuss in other chapters. In *The Wrong Man* the piano stands as a symbol of family stability, played by one of the boys, who practices a Mozart minuet and looks forward to lessons from his father. Jack Sullivan aptly points out that the only member of this family who does not play a musical instrument, the mother, is the one to suffer a mental breakdown as a result of the wrongful conviction of Manny (Henry Fonda), the bass player at the Stork Club.[17] The piano makes appearances in a few later films as well, including *The Birds*, in which Melanie (Tippi Hedren) plays Debussy's Arabesque in E; this may be related to her feelings about Mitch (Rod Taylor). The piano she plays appears later in the film as well, sitting silently before the birds attack the house, again providing some sense of calm before the storm.

In one of the last films, *Topaz*, the piano makes an appearance in the safe house near Washington DC for the Russian defector, who has been whisked out of Europe with his wife and daughter. The daughter, Tamara, like many young Russians, plays the piano, and this she does in a notable scene. In the original planning of this scene much thought went not only into what she should play, which should have a nostalgic Russian feeling about it, but also how the piano itself should be presented. In production notes before the completion of the final script, Tamara asks, when shown her room by the housekeeper, if it will "be possible for me to have a piano." This goes further, to a scene at a department store, where one of the American men responsible for the family's wellbeing says to the other, smiling: "The young lady asks if she can have a piano."[18] These lines did not make it to the final script, but she gets a piano for her bedroom, and as the camera moves toward the house, we hear the music faintly at first, and then louder as we see her from the back playing a small upright. A brief shot of her mother trying on a new dress with the help of two other women gives it a domestic slant, but that quickly changes as the scene shifts to a room with the Russian defector surrounded by American agents at a table interrogating him about NATO documents and other matters he resists addressing, including the question if he recognizes the term "Topaz." The piano continues to be heard softly in the background throughout the entire scene, and it provides a clear counterpoint to the tension of the interrogation. Perhaps it is no coincidence that the name of the Russian defector, Kusenov, has some similarity to Hitchcock's idol of cinematic counterpoint, Kuleshov.

In a delightful publicity shot, we see Hitchcock in a tuxedo pulling the appropriately rigid arm of a corpse from under the lid of a grand piano. Of course he enjoyed these kinds of waggish shots of himself, but considering the number of films in which pianos turn up, this one may be more than simply jocose. The part of the piano we see, the curved side and the slightly open lid, is the place from which sound would emanate, and the arm bursts out not unlike a stinger chord. The corpse will surely remind us of *Rope*, where the piano and chest

7.7 Hitchcock with hand in piano (Hitchcock finds a corpse in the piano)

holding the body merge together, or perhaps the whimsy of using a piano as a barricade for bullets in the first version of *The Man Who Knew Too Much*. In thinking about his frequent use of pianos, one could perhaps substitute the word "piano" for "organ" in his comment to Truffaut about the fascinating game he played with the audience, noted at the beginning of the Introduction: "I was directing the viewers. You might say I was playing them, like an organ."[19]

8

Mozart vs Wagner: Order and ambiguity

Throughout the four and a half decades that Hitchcock made sound films, he frequently used source music by major composers well known to the public. These quotations can be lengthy or brief, and can be as diverse as a selection heard on the radio to a theme whistled by someone or played on a tin flute. Whether substantial or fleeting, these quotations can be highly charged with significance based on generally agreed upon associations that the composers or their works evoke, associations that Hitchcock himself generally understood well, and he often made the selections of the source music. In some films the entire essence of the tone or atmosphere can be defined by these musical associations, while in others the quotes underscore the overall approach taken in the film. As such the music plays a central dramatic function, with the ability to underlie the primary conflict of the drama, especially when that conflict lies in vague urges or notions that may be difficult to put into words.

Of particular importance in Hitchcock's films is a sense of ambiguity that can be variously characterized as disorder, furtiveness, the irrational, mystery, darkness, or dysfunction, all of which defy precise description, and in contrast to that there will usually be a defined order against which the deviance can be measured. One of the prime ways to embody this type of conflict is with music, which itself resists verbal explanation, and provides the best possible complement to the director's visual art. The movement between order and disorder has been a familiar theme in writing on Hitchcock, and some of this has included the role of music, as in Elisabeth Weis's article "Music and Murder: The Association of Source Music with Order in Hitchcock's Films." She starts her article with these words: "Perhaps the most pervasive structural pattern in Hitchcock's film is the descent, on both a personal and social level, from order to chaos and the struggle to regain order."[1] Regaining order does not necessarily always occur, and sometimes when it appears to happen, as at the end of *Shadow of a Doubt*, it turns out to be deceptive.

The way a filmmaker may use music to serve this type of purpose does not necessarily correspond with everyone's notion of what the music in question signifies, and this proves especially true for sophisticated musicians who know the works intimately and recognize the diversity of impressions these works can convey. For the purposes of this chapter I will divide music into two broad categories, signifying order and stability on the one hand, and ambiguity with all its various facets on the other, since Hitchcock routinely makes this separation, most often with contrasting musical forces representing each in the same film. More often than not he draws these musical forces from the classical repertoire, usually but not always placing composers in opposing camps, but he also borrows from other genres, including jazz, popular music, and folk music, sometimes with surprising results, especially for jazz lovers who may not appreciate the way Hitchcock uses their favorite category of music. Undoubtedly his own personal likes and dislikes come into play here, but by no means does he necessarily assign the music he dislikes to represent disorder.

The type of music used to represent order will come as no great surprise; it focuses on the Viennese classics of the late eighteenth and early nineteenth centuries, as well as their followers who wrote in similar styles. Mozart stands as the composer most singularly designated as a representative of order, and this surely corresponds with the impression of the public at large. Most listeners will perceive in the works of Mozart the embodiment of classical balance, in phrasing structures, harmonic and tonal departures and arrivals, and the statement and return of themes. Some works do this more willingly than others, such as *Eine kleine Nachtmusik*, divertimentos, or the numerous small works for piano, such as the minuets. Those who know Mozart's music well, of course, realize that this does not give a fair assessment of his works, with complexity and ambiguity abounding in development sections of sonata form movements such as the first movement of Symphony No. 40 in G minor, or the levels of disorder in just about all of the large ensembles in his late operas, and especially the subversive *Don Giovanni*. Even *Così fan tutte*, which on the surface seems the pinnacle of order, uses that sense of symmetry in the first three-quarters of the opera to set up its breakdown in the final quarter. But these considerations are of little interest to most listeners, who will readily agree with Hitchcock that Mozart provides the ultimate musical exemplification of order. Furthermore, the examples of Mozart's music used in the films will support this notion.

Along with Mozart's music one might expect his colleague Haydn's works to serve a similar purpose, but at no point does Haydn show up on Hitchcock's radar. The composer who does turn up with some consistency is Beethoven, although for reasons somewhat different than Mozart. Popular culture has assigned Beethoven an extraordinary role as the composer who more than any other represents the highest aspirations of humanity, and for good reasons. Beethoven bestowed himself with this mantle, writing in his Heiligenstadt Testament (a letter to his brothers—but perhaps even more to posterity—on how he would cope after the onset of deafness) that from that point on he would strive in his works only for the betterment of humanity. In the first major work to follow this, the "Eroica" Symphony, he set out to do exactly that. The heroic emphasis here comes not so much from an association with Napoleon, but from what the music itself achieves, in the first movement, for example, overcoming severe obstacles with a brilliantly worked out solution. In later symphonies he does similar things, with the ongoing development of the three-note motif in the Fifth, or the colossally uplifting finale of the Ninth. The late string quartets reveal his most intensely personal statements of overcoming hardship, and even the later piano sonatas became works of symphonic grandeur.

Hitchcock's interest lay primarily in the symphonies, especially the Fifth, and in part this resulted from an aura taken on by the Fifth, most decidedly in Britain, but internationally as well. During the Second World War this symphony became one of the most powerful symbols of resistance to the Nazis, in fact rubbing their faces in the irony of a German composer taking on that role. The opening of this symphony became the signature sound of the BBC in London during the war, used as the introduction to broadcasts to the occupied Continent, but similarly used that way for programming in Britain itself, including addresses that Winston Churchill made to the nation. Aside from the association that the work had with the highest achievements of humanity, it also had a more covert purpose, something everyone recognized and no doubt appreciated because of the need for coded messages at the time. The first four notes of the work, the primary motif which permeates not only the first movement but the later movements as well, consists of three short notes followed by a long note; in Morse Code the letter made up of three dots and a dash, "V", provided the pervasive symbol of victory. In public appearances and on newsreels Churchill consist-ently gave the "V" signal with his fingers, and for some this would have evoked Beethoven's Fifth, which they would, in any event, have heard at the start of his broadcasts to the nation.

Hitchcock of course used this symphony symbolically in at least one film well before the Second World War, and while it did not yet have the specific association it would later take on, it nevertheless would have been accepted as a symbol of overcoming obstacles and of striving for truth and justice. Beethoven's contemporary Schubert did not attempt to do in his music what Beethoven had, but by association his music also came to represent order in the public consciousness. Some of Mozart's contemporaries, whose music may in fact achieve an even greater sense of balance and symmetry than Mozart's, could ably be used in connection with order, as happens in Hitchcock's films with Muzio Clementi and J. C. Bach—one of the sons of J. S. Bach, who spent the better part of his career in London, where Mozart in fact met him. Other more recent composers could serve the cause of order as well, not surprisingly Mendelssohn, who carried on aspects of the approaches of Mozart, Schubert, and Beethoven (we hear Mendelssohn's Scherzo from the

Music to a Midsummer Night's Dream strategically placed during an argument in the music shop in *Strangers on a Train*). Even Ravel and Debussy can serve this purpose, depending on the works in question, and also the British composer Frederick Delius (whose parents had emigrated from Germany), whose blindness late in life ties him to the character in *Saboteur* who plays his music; in the same film the accused saboteur, while hitchhiking on the run, whistles the opening of Beethoven's Fifth. Various other genres can support order, most notably liturgical music and folk music.

Identifying the music of ambiguity may be much less straightforward than that of order, since these associations often depend on personal points of view that may require misrepresentation of the music itself. For Hitchcock one composer more than any other takes on this role: Richard Wagner. We may be inclined to connect this side of the equation with negative factors, especially if the ambiguity leans toward darkness, furtiveness, dysfunction, and irrationality, and the composer who represents these things could get that distinction by being one the director especially dislikes. Not so for Hitchcock: John Russell Taylor, Hitchcock's personally sanctioned biographer, recalled an anecdote of Hitchcock visiting the home of John Galsworthy, whose play *The Skin Game* Hitchcock made into a film in 1931. "Mrs. Galsworthy asked him what kind of music he liked. 'Wagner,' replied Hitch; 'he's so melodramatic.' 'Oh, no,' said Mrs. Galsworthy conclusively; '*we* like Bach.'"[2] Here as a young director visiting an aging and famous playwright, Hitchcock did not hesitate to identify Wagner as his favorite, in contrast to the Galsworthy's preferred master of order.

One can only speculate on the nature of Hitchcock's attraction to Wagner, since aside from Taylor's anecdote we know little of his thoughts on the matter. Hitchcock had a vast collection of recordings that he loved to listen to, and according to his daughter Pat he preferred symphonic music.[3] In his youth his family regularly attended the symphony, the Albert Hall on Sundays and the Queen's Hall on weekdays, and when asked about his favorite orchestral pieces, he replied Roussel, Elgar, Wagner, and Dohnanyi's *Variations on a Nursery Suite*.[4] Since Wagner in fact wrote very little orchestral music (and what he did write tends not to be performed), he probably meant the preludes to the operas, which are frequently performed as concert pieces. Since the preludes connect intimately to the operas they accompany, he may have known a fair amount about the operas, whether he actually saw one or not.

As an avid listener, spending, as Pat tells us, much of his spare time in that activity, he could certainly hear the basic differences between the music of Wagner and that of composers from a century earlier. Unlike the phrasing patterns and harmonic or tonal progressions of earlier music, Wagner abandoned virtually all cadence-oriented progressions, and this results in music very much cast adrift according to the old standards, developing through a type of chromaticism that rejects harmonic or tonal stability. With this type of procedure Wagner could develop musical thoughts in extended passages, slowly and gradually building to massive climaxes that frequently achieve a sense of ecstasy in the development—possibly lasting as long as 20 minutes or half an hour. While that thrust toward ecstasy generally can be envisaged in spiritual terms, it frequently has an erotic element as well, and the spiritual and the erotic often can be equated to each other. A long tradition of that equation of course existed, from Dante's Beatrice and Petrarch's Laura in literature through the painters and sculptors from Michelangelo through Raphael, Bernini, and numerous others. Wagner sets up the potential for this in the librettos, for example the nature of the illicit love between Tristan and Isolde, but the erotic ecstasy comes to life through the music, Wagner's most powerful weapon. We get a strong sense of that in the prelude to *Tristan und Isolde*, and the climactic capping off of this in the "Liebestod" at the end of the opera, with Tristan already dead and Isolde about to join him, moving distinctly from the physical to the spiritual world. Such heights can only be achieved with a musical ambiguity that has the potential of developing in any one of a myriad of possibilities, preventing any predictability or premature resolution.

Because of the nature of his musical language, in a sense using traditional harmony and tonality as reference points from which deviation will occur, Wagner emerged in the second half of the nineteenth century as the voice of modern composition, haunting the next generation of composers not only in Germany but around the world. Even Arnold Schoenberg, who defined modernism early in the twentieth century, went out of his way to avoid comparisons with Wagner or being tagged with the dreaded (for him) label of being called a Wagnerian. Modernism abandoned the traditional notions of stability, and the new approaches to ambiguity owed everything to Wagner. With opera Wagner not only wrote the music, but the librettos as well, and even took a strong hand in designing sets, originating the idea of the *Gesamtkunstwerk*, the all-embracing artwork, a notion that would later appeal of some film critics as the *auteur*.

Wagner certainly had a darker side as well, although knowledge of that has emerged slowly, and one can be fairly certain that Hitchcock knew nothing of this. Some recent studies have made much of his anti-Semitism, apparent not only in the tract he published with the title *Das Judentum in die Musik* (*Jewishness in music*) and other essays, but also his placement of characters in his operas with stereotypically negative Jewish features, such as Alberich or Hagan in the Ring cycle or Beckmesser in *Die Meistersinger*.[5] Wagner played an active role in the political arena, especially with his involvement in the peasant revolts of 1848 and his numerous political writings, which later attracted much attention from a wide range of politicians, including Hitler. For Hitler, Wagner became a powerful force, certainly the music, but also the political views and anti-Semitism, as Joachim Köhler has ably demonstrated in *Wagner's Hitler: The Prophet and His Disciple*.[6] The use of Wagner's music at death camps left an indelible mark on survivors, and for many years an unofficial ban on Wagner's music remained in place in Israel. Yet, for many German Jews before the Second World War, Wagner simply stood as one in the great tradition of German composers that could be liked or disliked, along with Schumann, Brahms, or anyone else. Considering that most German Jews before the war did not know of these darker matters, it should hardly surprise us that Hitchcock would not, and he could choose to like him at will. He did, and Wagner's ability to build to climaxes and the ambiguous process of the music no doubt influenced his choice.

Along with Wagner, a few other composers or musical genres can be associated with darker elements in Hitchcock's films, although these do not necessarily belong to a Wagnerian tradition. Ravel has already been noted, although he can go either way, depending on the nature of the music. In some cases the composer for the film can write evoking certain aspects of the style of a particular composer, as

Bernard Herrmann does with Wagner in *Vertigo*, or with Stravinsky and Debussy in *Psycho*. Music can go beyond ambiguity or other dark matters into something decidedly painful, perhaps even as a form of torture, and one can only assume that the director has a strong distaste for a type of music to use it in this way. In Hitchcock's films this happen with jazz, most directly in *Foreign Correspondent*, but less acutely in other films as well; jazz lovers will not be amused. With these contrasting types of music, we have another way to get at the underlying drama of the films, through something that can function as powerfully as visual images as it works in concert with them.

Murder!

The first of Hitchcock's films to use classical source music to heighten the conflict between order and ambiguity, *Murder!* (1930), employs not only Beethoven and Wagner but Clementi as well. Not unlike *Blackmail* which ended ambiguously, *Murder!* also does, but this time deceptively, giving the impression that matters have been resolved when in fact they most certainly have not. During the opening titles we hear an adaptation of Beethoven's Fifth Symphony, first an excerpt from the opening of the first movement, and then jumping quickly to the third movement, not the opening of that movement but instead the passage that emphasizes the rhythm of the work's primary motif. Only after the statement of this does the music segue into material related to the start of the third movement. Until the end of the opening titles we have only the title itself with its exclamation point and Beethoven's symphony to give us clues about the nature of the film, and these provide a stark contradiction. In 1930 audiences knew none of the associations that the Fifth would bring a decade later, but despite that everyone will make the connection with the upward striving of humanity, and those who know the symphony well will enjoy the musical process of taking a short motif and developing it not only in the first movement but the third and fourth as well, a new procedure for Beethoven at this point in his career. The adaptation at the beginning of this film emphasizes that development process which spans the movements, although the music and the titles conclude with a passage that may leave a musical question mark. Still, with Beethoven we expect something to happen which will lead to resolution and triumph, and this set against the title *Murder!* may be somewhat disconcerting. Another association this music has, which may have stuck in the minds of some viewers, is the well-known comment by Beethoven's secretary and confidant Anton Schindler, that the opening motif represents fate knocking at the door. Schindler would like us to believe that better than anyone he had the gift of anamnesis after the composer's death, but his fabrications on so many fronts to aggrandize his hero make the statement highly suspect. In fact, the motif comes directly from the call of the yellowhammer, a bird Beethoven would have heard where he lived on the outskirts of Vienna.

Despite the title, the music leads us to assume that the film will take us in a positive direction, perhaps with the solving of a murder and a criminal being brought to justice. The opening visual images after the clock striking take us immediately in the opposite direction, with a view of houses and a church that could come from Murnau's *Nosferatu* or perhaps even Wiene's *Caligari*, creating an eerie atmosphere quickly augmented by a close-up and a scream, a black cat in an alley, lots of shadows, and a persistently loud knocking sound.[7] That visual atmosphere holds as the camera pans the windows of people wakened by the scream and knocking, with one woman seen dressing in silhouette. The atmosphere changes when the camera reaches the room of the stage manager Markham and his wife Doucie, who lean out of a window that refuses to stay open; Markham mumbles incomprehensibly before he gets his teeth in, and Doucie struggles with little success to put on her undergarments. We can put this down to Hitchcock's classic touch of humor in the face of seriousness, which continues at the murder scene, when the camera pays more attention to the landlady making tea (which the inspector declines) than the investigation. The ambiguity, though, remains throughout the entire film, permeating it at every possible level, and certainly does not disappear at the end.

If we do not know the name of the play from which the film derives, Clemence Dane's *Enter Sir John*, we will not be able to identify the leading character until a full third of the film has elapsed.

A young actress has been murdered, and all the evidence points to the guilt of another actress, Diana Baring (Norah Baring), whom a jury, on which the noted actor Sir John (Herbert Marshall) sits, convicts and sentences to death. Sir John has doubts, and spends the rest of the film sleuthing with the help of the Markhams in an attempt to find the real murderer. They succeed in identifying another actor in the troupe putting on the play *Nothing but the Truth*, Handel Fane (Esme Percy), as the culprit, and Fane, returning to his former aerial circus act, hangs himself in the end. Eventually released from prison, Diana plays a leading role in Sir John's new play, and we may be inclined to believe they are now lovers. Aside from Sir John not emerging until a third of the way through, we have various other reasons for finding him an unlikely leading man. We first meet him during the jury's deliberations, and as one of three dissenting votes, he makes his case last, after the two others have been persuaded to support the majority guilty verdict. Plays within plays feature in this film, and in a sense this starts here, as Sir John stands against the unison chorus trying to dissuade him. The camera separates him from the chorus while he argues, and unifies him with the group when he caves in. Considering the ease with which he does fold, condemning her to death, we can at this point find little to admire. When he searches for the truth, we still have difficulty admiring this upper-class stuffed shirt, who does not mind embarrassing the Markhams in front of his butler when he has them over for cocktails and lunch. He appears to be searching for the truth, but his motives remain much more ambiguous.

In an apparently pivotal scene in the film, we see Sir John standing in his bathroom shaving, and just before that the piano in his drawing room at Berkeley Square receives prominent emphasis. His butler brings a radio into the bathroom, from which we hear a headline about the conviction of Diana Baring, followed by a plea from the police for information about an accident. This leads to an orchestral program, and we now hear the prelude to Wagner's *Tristan und Isolde*, giving us an inner drama as Sir John's voice-over runs through the flawed details of the case along with his contemplation of the fate of Diana, whom he clearly found attractive (we discover later that he knew her, and had arranged her current acting position). Hearing Wagner's *Tristan* at this point can trigger various types of associations, and some writers have picked up on this in considerable detail. Jack Sullivan does, as one would expect in his book *Hitchcock's Music*, and he focuses on the sensual nature of the music and Sir John's attraction to her; the music becomes the underlying eroticism—even guilty passion—that Sir John's stiff demeanor will not reveal.[8] This seems an entirely plausible interpretation, although limiting it in this way misses the complexity and ambiguity of the work. Because of the pivotal placement of this scene, it appears not to be limited to the scene itself. A much less plausible reading comes from Tania Modleski, who finds the use of Wagner here appropriate because, according to Nietzsche, Wagner implies something theatrical and feminine in a pejorative way (in Nietzsche's words, "people, herd, female, pharisee, voting cattle, patron, idiot—Wagner").[9] She neglects to inform her readers that Nietzsche wrote this after his falling out with Wagner over religious matters, and wished to find the ultimate insult for his former friend after their bitter parting of the ways; using aspersions hardly builds a convincing case. Elisabeth Weis rightly notes that this performance on the radio carries the emotions.[10]

The placement of this prelude by Wagner here, which along with its sensuality provides a musical embodiment of ambiguity, seems appropriate to the film in a much more pervasive way, getting at the heart of the enigmatic nature of the film. Temporarily Sir John can be the focus of that, but as the film unfolds, it spreads in every possible way. As we fix upon Sir John as the leading character, we discover him not to be the most interesting character by any means, but simply a foil for that interest to lie elsewhere. The two characters of greatest interest, Diana and Fane, in fact appear on the screen only a small percentage of the time, especially Diana, who gets barely more than a couple of minutes. She seems prepared to go to her death to conceal what she believed to be a horrible secret, in fact protecting Fane from infamy, and the strength of her determination makes her a far stronger character than the weak-kneed Sir John, who, in a moment of conformist pressure, agreed to see his protégée hang.[11] He now desires her, and their meeting at the prison gives him hope, as she explains why she keeps a photo of him, but they remain separated, either by an absurdly long table between them, or a prison guard who later stands between them. Despite the ending of the film, they probably continue to be separated; Sir

John may have the qualities of an older mentor—an icy one at that, but hardly the demeanor of a lover. When they appear to be happily together in the final scene, the camera pulls back to reveal the proscenium for the final play within a play, and this prompts cinema to give way to the more prosaic stage.

As fascinating as the scarcely shown Diana may be, she fades in comparison to the highly complex and certainly ambiguous Fane, who, aside from his brief appearance as a cross-dresser early on while an inspector questions actors with the play in progress, we do not really see until the last quarter of the film. Just before Sir John's prison visit to Diana, he looks at Fane's room, and now the shots become especially expressionist, most notably the entryway to the room with its *Caligari*-like angles and the need to stoop to get through. The secret about him, which Diana inadvertently blurts out at the prison visit, is that he is a "half-caste," a term thankfully no longer in use, but not an uncommon one in 1930 in England. Specifically it means a person of mixed blood, completely unaccep-table to polite society of the time, but we have no reason to believe it implies anything racial in this film.[12] The first shots of Fane show him dressed as a woman, and the inspector asks cast members about the identity of this woman. The answer labels Fane as "100% he-woman," and that "he's our leading man," a comment made twice in short succession. Indirectly he plays the leading man in the film as well, despite his actual time on the screen, since everything in fact revolves around him. The term "half-caste" in the film in contrast to the novel seems to be about his sexual ambiguity instead of race, and Hitchcock leaves it to our imaginations to determine what the nature of that ambiguity may be: obviously terms such as homosexual, bisexual, transvestite, or transsexual do not come up. Whatever the term means, Fane claims to be in love with Diana.

When Sir John sees that Fane murdered the actress Edna, he attempts to lure him into a trap, asking him to come round to his place and read a part for a new play, a *Hamlet* type of ploy of a play within a play, with a plot as close to the actual murder as Sir John can formulate it. The ploy works, as Fane leaves a note (discovered after he hangs himself during his aerial performance) for Sir John which completes the part of the plot Sir John had not been able to reconstruct. At Sir John's rooms, though, instead of feeling repugnance, we probably feel some sympathy because of Fane's wounded demeanor and the goading, bullying role that Sir John plays to out the criminal. The sympathy continues when Fane hangs himself in full public view, clearly racked with emotional pain as he sees visions of Sir John and Diana. He most certainly plays the tour de force near the end, far eclipsing the reunion of Sir John and Diana, first a somewhat cold affair and then succumbing to the artifice of the theater. We may of course wonder why it took Fane so long to own up to the crime, willing at first to let Diana take the blame; even his admission of guilt he couches as a theatrical response. This no doubt remains among the plethora of ambiguities.

The prelude to *Tristan*, with its tying together of leitmotifs, ambiguous harmony and tonality, climactic surges, and sensuality, appears to function for the film in a way similar to the opera, in which it introduces us musically to all the salient aspects of the work. We should not be distracted by Sir John's voice-over, since this is much less his music (despite some coordination of spoken and musical surges) than Diana's and Fane's, and the tone of the film itself, which Hitchcock sustains masterfully. William Rothman rightly calls it "the masterpiece of Hitchcock's early work," and his discussion of the ambiguities at the psychological and visual levels bears that out.[13] Immediately after the lengthy performance of the Wagner (it lasts close to five minutes), music again plays a role in the order/ambiguity conflict, now in the Markham flat with their young daughter mangling a Clementi sonatina at the piano. Here the music of order gives in to its opposite because of the performance, although the playing of a new sonatina improves markedly after the letter from Sir John arrives inviting the Markhams to visit him. This appears not to be, as has been suggested, a view of a family aspiring to a higher social level; the girl, the piano, and even the score get far too much prominence for that. The more likely aspiration points to order itself, and with practice it will come. For the film, though, order does not arrive.

Lifeboat

One of the most unusual treatments of the classics to underlie conflict occurs in *Lifeboat* (1944), and in this case one finds parallels to the use of popular music. What makes this so unusual is the way in which the diegetic music must be performed, since all the action in this film takes place on a lifeboat in the middle of the Atlantic Ocean, after an American merchant marine ship has been torpedoed by a German U-boat, which also goes down. The few American and British survivors aboard have their own wartime conflict when they rescue a German, who seems in every respect more intelligent, informed, and stronger than any of them. Few opportunities exist in this setting for musical performance, but we occasionally get it, played on a tin flute by Joe (Canada Lee), the lone African American on board, or sung by the German, Willie (Walter Slezak), accompanied usually on Joe's flute by Rittenhaus (Henry Hull), a wealthy industrialist. Since Hitchcock made this film toward the end of the Second World War, the connection between the Nazis and the music of Wagner would now have been reasonably well known. The Nazis regarded Germans as a superior race, and similar kinds of notions appear in some of Wagner's operas, making his music a natural fit for Hitler and his followers. In a film in which Allied survivors in a lifeboat rescue a Nazi from the U-boat which sank their ship, and that Nazi seems stronger and more superior to them in every possible way, the use of Wagner's music has striking implications. Something will be needed to counterbalance the Wagner, and in this case that role falls to Schubert.

Hitchcock initially engaged John Steinbeck to write the script for the film, and Steinbeck opted to start with a scenario, amounting to a short novel; in this scenario Joe plays the flute, but with no indication of the choice of music. Hitchcock and Steinbeck soon ran into disagreements about the plot, and Hitchcock, in his usual fashion, dropped Steinbeck with as little ado as possible, hiring a new scriptwriter, this time Jo Swerling. Swerling identifies some of the music Joe plays in the screenplay, for example "Don't Sit Under the Apple Tree" or "Ach du lieber Augustine," but in the final revised script of 29 July 1943, Willie does not sing, and Joe does little but play randomly on the tin flute.[14] Hitchcock himself appears to have seen potential for the music to underlie the conflict, setting, for example, a German song against an American song. As Gus (William Bendix) drinks brandy to prepare for the amputation that Willie (who turns out to be a surgeon in civilian life) will perform on him, he asks Joe for some music, and Joe obliges with the German drinking song "Du, du, liegst mir im Herzen" (You, you are dear to me), in contrast to Swerling's script, which calls for some fragment of a classical piece. Gus (who has changed his own name from Schmidt to Smith) disapproves, wanting none of that, and tells Joe to "boogie it up," which Joe does with something jazzy that quickly turns into "Don't sit under the apple tree."

The direct juxtaposition of German and American music here works at a more sophisticated level with other musical treatments as well. After Willie has been rescued, over the objections of at least two of the Americans who would prefer to throw him back into the ocean, we quickly learn of his apparent superiority to the others. He claims to be an ordinary sea hand but in fact he is a captain, and as a surgeon he can save Gus's life by removing his gangrenous leg. At first he speaks only German, which Connie (Tallulah Bankhead) translates for the others, but later he speaks perfect English and French as well: late in the film Connie refers to him as an ersatz superman, but earlier he appears to be the real thing. While the boat drifts aimlessly at sea, a conflict arises about which way they should sail, with Willie confidently pointing in one direction; Joe plays the flute while the others argue, and to most viewers his playing sounds like nothing more than the aimless tootling scripted by Swerling. A closer listening reveals it to be Walther's song from act 3, scene 5 of Wagner's *Die Meistersinger* (The master singer), a chilling choice of music in this context. In this opera set in the Middle Ages, a song competition has been elevated to mythic proportions, and Hans Sachs inadvertently leaves the notes he has dictated for Walther at his shop, where Beckmesser discovers and steals them. Elaborate rules exist for the creation of the songs, and when the unoriginal Beckmesser presents his own garbled version of Walther's, it sounds ludicrous, earning the contempt of the judges and laughter from the onlookers. Walther then sings it as it should be sung, breaking the rules of the competition, but in such an extraordinary way that the judges must accept it. He demonstrates not only his superiority over Beckmesser but a superhuman creative capacity, with Wagner giving it his best music, showing what he believed demonstrated the highest level of Germanic achievement in this overtly nationalistic opera; Hitler and the Nazis clearly concurred. If audiences did not know about the adopting of Wagner's music and ideals by Hitler and some other Nazis from news reports, they would have had some inkling from Chaplin's treatment of the prelude to Wagner's *Lohengrin* in *The Great Dictator* (1941). One can only imagine that Hitchcock had something to do with the choice of Wagner's music in *Lifeboat*. The irony that the one African American on board plays the music of Aryan superiority cannot be overlooked.

Before the Americans and British finally see through Willie's deceptions, finding his hidden compass and water supply, they alternate in their views about him. On the one hand they see him as a repugnant Nazi who boasts about his national superiority and takes over the command of their boat, while on the other hand they can observe his highly desirable qualities, an urbane man with education and culture and even a capacity to save a life. In *The Great Dictator* Chaplin plays both the dictator and the Jewish barber, and the latter has as much claim to the great cultural heritage as the former. While

8.1 *Lifeboat* (Canada Lee with Walter Slezak) (Joe plays Wagner for the Nazi)

Chaplin plays out this tension with Wagner alone, Hitchcock does it with Wagner and Schubert's song "Heidenröslein" ("Wild rose"), using Wagner to represent aggressiveness and presumed superiority, and Schubert for the great cultural heritage. Since this song has a text by Goethe, that affinity to the great heritage becomes even stronger, but at the same time this is a song with a simplicity and almost child-like innocence (Schubert treats the subject more innocently than Goethe, avoiding the implicit sexual suggestions of the text). A Nazi officer singing "Heidenröslein" could be a decent human being, and accompanied by an American industrialist (his name happens to be German) who readily knows the song implies that German culture has left a positive mark on the rest of the world, perhaps even offering a bridge for an ultimate uniting of nations. Hitchcock himself had positive feelings about Germany, having made films there in the mid-1920s, learning from the great expressionist directors such as Murnau, and in the bad Nazi–good German scenario may have been thinking wistfully about a return to international civility.

Considering when Hitchcock made this film, optimism was in short supply, and one should not expect solutions or reconciliation in this setting. When the others discover that Willie has not shared his food or water with them after they have saved his life, they do what two of their members had wanted earlier—they brutally beat him to death and throw his body to the sharks. Only one person does not participate, Joe, the African American, also the only person on board who could recite Psalm 23 in full, for the impromptu funeral of a dead infant. At the end an Allied ship sails toward them after sinking a German supply ship, and after Willie has been disposed of, another German pulls himself into the lifeboat, this time a youthful survivor of the supply ship. The same scenario as Willie's has the potential for playing itself out, although this time the German draws a gun, which the others take from him. Before they decide what to do with him, the film ends, and viewers are left to ponder what will happen. In the conflict of this film, not so much between Allies and Nazis as more fundamental human values,[15] musically distinguished by Wagner and Schubert, no solution emerges; to the extent that Wagner represents ambiguity, his music appears to get the last word.

Vertigo as opera

In this perhaps the most discussed of all Hitchcock's films, writers have invoked various myths and legends, including Orpheus and Euridice, Tristram and Iseult, Pygmalion, Persephone, and even Faust. Through much of this writing the presence of illusion as a destabilizing force stands as one of the most persistent themes, and the futile attempts of order to counteract it. Robin Wood expresses this as well as anyone: "The 'vertigo' of the title, then, expands from the man's fear of heights into a metaphysical principle ... The world—human life, relationships, individual identity—becomes a quicksand, unstable, constantly shifting, into which we may sink at any step in any direction, illusion and reality constantly ambiguous, even interchangeable."[16] Here we appear to have the ultimate Wagnerian representation, and Hitchcock and his composer Bernard Herrmann did not go far out of their way to disguise it, making this film so Wagnerian that it can almost be thought of as opera. Numerous writers have made the connection with Wagner, in aspects of the plot, the atmosphere, and certainly Herrmann's music, with some revealing the details of Herrmann's Wagnerisms in great detail.[17] This is not to say that Herrmann plagiarized the music of Wagner: instead, he quickly perceived the underlying tone of the film, and wrote music in the appropriate style that captured that essence, occasionally borrowing more directly from the score of *Tristan und Isolde* to emphasize points that require special attention.

In the lengthy process of developing the script from the novel *D'Entre Les Morts* (translated as *From Among the Dead*), by Pierre Boileau and Thomas Narcejac, the myths and legends just noted readily come to the fore, and some of these emphasize the association with opera. The myth that seems most apparent, of Orpheus and Euridice, explored by Royal S. Brown and others,[18] with Scottie (James Stewart) as Orpheus pursuing Madeleine (Kim Novak) as Euridice, emerges in the second half of the film; after Madeleine's apparent death, Scottie attempts to bring her back from the underworld, at least in his own illusion-possessed mind. A special connection exists between this myth and opera, and one could even make the case that had it not been for this myth, opera itself would never have been born. When opera emerged as an art form at the end of the Renaissance, composers such as Jacopo Peri, Giulio Caccini, and the celebrated Claudio Monteverdi all turned instinctively to this legend as subject matter. Singing had taken a brilliant turn at the end of the sixteenth century, with singers such as Caccini having discovered the art of *bel canto* singing, and placing this new vocal weapon in the mouth of Orpheus proved to be irresistible. In the centuries since the beginning of opera, few composers have been able to resist this subject, not only because of the appeal of the myth itself but because of the opportunity it provides for spectacular singing; Orpheus the singer must persuade the boatman at the river Styx to convey him to the nether region by the sheer force of his singing, and from Caccini onward this song has emerged as the highlight. Reasons for the appeal of this myth to cinema may be a little less clear, but many have embraced it, overtly in the case of Jean Cocteau with his Orpheus trilogy, or Marcel Camus with *Black Orpheus*, but also less directly where the myth gives an underpinning, as in any of the *Phantom of the Opera* films, starting with Rupert Julian's starring Lon Chaney in 1925, and numerous other films from Otto Preminger's *Laura* to Roman Polanski's *Frantic*.

Hitchcock happily embraced it as well, and it runs through some of his most mysterious films, adding a dimension to an already noticeable operatic character. This certainly happens in *Notorious*, in which Ingrid Bergman plays the Euridice-like character Alicia, who needs to be rescued from the clutches of death in a Nazi house in Rio by her Orpheus, played by Cary Grant. At one point they descend together into the lower regions of the house, to the wine cellar, and at the end of the film he spirits the poisoned Alicia out of the house, singing, as it were, persuasively to Sebastien (Claude Rains) of the repercussions if he does not allow them to leave. In the case of *Vertigo*, descent into the underworld inhabited by Madeleine receives not only visual reinforcement with cars going down San Francisco's hills, Madeleine plunging into the bay, vertiginous images from stepladders to building roofs, and swirling vortexes that appear to lead to hell, but Bernard Herrmann's score participates as well, with its falling sequences and modulations at strategic points. In this film Hitchcock remains true to the legend, as the second attempt by Scottie to bring Madeleine back results in failure. While Scottie may not use an Orphic singing voice, both Hitchcock and Herrmann provide it for him, by creating a film with opera deeply embedded into its essence, and by bolstering that with a musical score in which the operatic references cannot be mistaken.

Tracing the development of individual Hitchcock films by observing the evolution of the script has already been noted in other films, such as *Suspicion* and *Shadow of a Doubt*, and in the case of *Vertigo* this proves to be most revealing. Numerous versions of the script still exist, over two dozen at the Margaret Herrick Library alone, and others can be found as well. The script in this case went through the hands of different translators and writers, and in fact had various titles before settling on *Vertigo*. In one of these, titled *Darkling I Listen*, prepared by Maxwell Anderson, the myth receives overt treatment. Roger (who in later versions becomes Scottie) gives Madeleine a cigarette lighter with the inscription "Eurydice," and when she asks who that was, he briefly explains the myth. He then addresses her by that name, beckoning her to come out of that old time, and turn her face to the light.[19]

Of much greater importance to the presence of opera in this film are the references in early versions of the script to opera itself, and a point of special interest here concerns how Scottie should first see Madeleine, settled upon eventually as taking place at Ernie's restaurant, just after Scottie's first meeting with Gavin Elster (Tom Helmore). As the script progressed, going through the hands of Maxwell Anderson, Alec Coppel, and Samuel Taylor, among others, this scene first did not exist at all; when it finally was added, it bore very little resemblance to the one we know from the film. Just prior to production, before Herrmann provided the score, Hitchcock assumed the scene would have a voice-over by Gavin Elster, a very prosaic and wordy treatment which Herrmann's music not only made unnecessary, but without words turned the scene into something it could not have otherwise been.[20] This reminds us of Hitchcock the maker of intertitles for silent films, having to be told not to use so many. It seems at first not to have occurred to him that this scene embodied pure opera, and words would ruin it. The end result indicates that Hitchcock was only as good as the people collaborating with him, and that in this case Herrmann's collaboration proved to be decisive. The same proved true of a later scene, even more operatic than this one, the moment at which Judy, now transformed entirely back into Madeleine, emerges from the powder room with her hair done as Scottie wants it. In scripts up until the shooting, hairpins can be heard falling as she fusses with her hair; in this scene Herrmann's score carries the full emotional burden and the ecstatic climax, music that utterly precludes the tinkling of hairpins.

In an earlier script by Coppel, dated 30 November 1956 (and in others from around this time), the scene at Ernie's restaurant still did not exist, and instead, the occasion for Scottie's first observation of Madeleine actually takes place at the opera.[21] At the end of the first meeting between Madeleine's husband Elster (still Elder in this version) and Scottie, Elster asks Scottie if he can make it to the opera that night which he and Madeleine will attend, and Scottie would be able to get a good look at her there. The next scene takes place inside the San Francisco Opera House, Scottie sitting in the audience with an unidentified opera in progress (which may have been intended to be Wagner's *Die Walküre*[22]), and we see him gazing out in a different direction from the rest of the audience. He scans the front of the grand tier, and sees the silhouetted heads of people below him, and also views the tier of loges; now the camera includes the orchestra as well as the singers on stage. In the grand tier a man turns to whisper to a woman beside him, and for a moment they can both be seen in profile. Scottie casually raises a small pair of opera glasses to his eyes. His view through the opera glasses provides the opportunity for a close-up of the pair in profile, and for the first time we see Madeleine, a young and beautifully elegant woman. At this point in the darkness she appears as a classic silhouette, backlit by light coming from the stage. In a close-up of Scottie, he lowers the glasses and directs his attention to the stage.

The act comes to an end, and Scottie joins the throng moving down the stairs to the lobby. He searches for the husband and wife, and the expression on his face changes when he sees them. As they approach, Madeleine, who does not look about her, turns slowly so Scottie can see both profiles and her full face, and his expression now conveys how struck he is by her beauty. He stares abstractly at her as they pass, and with that the scene ends. This scene modified one from the original novel, which takes place at the theater, also with his first view of her coming through opera glasses. Changing this to the opera signified recognition by Coppel and Hitchcock of how important opera was to the representation of the mysterious Madeleine, and the irrational world that she inhabits. Curiously, though, this scene did not have to be retained in order to keep this aura of opera alive. With Taylor's script of 21 February 1957 the references to opera disappear altogether,[23] but in the final shooting script (and in the film) we have this brief line from Elster: "Look, we're going to an opening of the opera tonight, we're dining at Ernie's first; you can see her there." This very small reminder of opera proved to be useful, but in order to generate opera, we did not need a scene there, one that practically went so far as to put Madeleine on the stage with the positioning of the camera. In the end, the best effect could be achieved without words, and instead with fundamentally operatic music.

In this restaurant scene Scottie seems already to be at the opera, for the woman he sees defies description as an ordinary mortal. She stands much bigger than life, burning into his mind with her beauty, archaic (spiral) hair arrangement, and poise as an untouchable dream of a woman on a stage, a diva that one can admire from afar but not come near and touch. Like a diva, her eyes do not meet his, while the mere sight of her transfixes him, changing his life forever. She need only glide across the floor/stage without saying a word, looking the elegant character from grand opera he cannot resist. To make it real opera, Herrmann provides the score, offering melodrama in the truest sense as his Madeleine leitmotif tells us—along with the expression on Scottie's face—everything we need to know about his innermost thoughts and desires. Herrmann claimed not to be interested in Wagner's notion of the leitmotif, but he used leitmotifs throughout his scores, and certainly in *Vertigo*. In fact, his Madeleine theme bears some similarity to the opening of the prelude of *Tristan und Isolde*, a leitmotif that has been identified as desire in Wagner's opera; the Madeleine theme most clearly has the same function in the film.[24]

Musically it achieves this through dissonances on strong beats that resolve in unpredictable ways, leading in fact to harmonic destabilization that most certainly parallels the bewildered state in which Scottie finds himself. The four-note figure which becomes

8.2 *Vertigo* (Kim Novak at Ernie's restaurant) (Madeleine glides across the floor)

the melodic cell of the Madeleine theme comes through as a variant of the four-note figures which generate Wagner's theme, and the chordal accompaniment parallels Wagner's accompaniment, including the famous "Tristan chord" and its resolution. In fact, at the beginning of the seventh bar of the Madeleine theme, Herrmann actually uses the Tristan chord, and the chord falls on the same notes (with only one tone altered by a semitone) and in the same position as Wagner's first placement of the chord at the beginning of the prelude. Herrmann also adopts Wagner's six-eight meter, and uses rhythmic patterns and suspension that parallel Wagner's. After the initial statement of the motivic material Wagner moves into a distinctive three-note dotted rhythmic figure, and at a similar point Herrmann adds the same dotted three-note figure. Daniel Srebnick nicely sums up the effect of this type of writing: "the harmonic identity of Herrmann's score is often so ambiguous that the music, like the characters in the film, struggles to find a stable tonal identity upon which it and the listener can comfortably rest. As a result, we feel that the film's chaotic world, the characters that it explores, are on the brink of disorder and, perhaps, destruction."[25] From this point on Scottie embarks on an illusory quest from which he cannot be shaken, triggering his descent into ecstasy, despair, and madness.

Other moments in the film have a distinctively Wagnerian aura, and Herrmann underlies these occasionally with other characteristic Tristanesque passages. One stands out especially, this being the climactic moment when Judy fixes her hair to complete the final physical transformation to Madeleine. As she emerges from the powder room their eyes meet in ecstasy, before their passionate embrace. The moment can only be defined as operatic, and Herrmann provides an apt operatic accompaniment. Again he borrows from the *Tristan* prelude, this time the grand and explosive figure at bars 16–17, a rising figure leading to Wagner's first bombardment of the listener with the full orchestral palette. In *Tristan* this passage can be variously associated with longing and desire, and Herrmann knew exactly what he was doing using something like it here. In imagining this scene without music during the entire period of the script's evolution, Hitchcock revealed just how much he often depended on the sound judgment of others.

The film has other associations with Wagner, both *Tristan und Isolde* in particular and Wagner more generally, including in the plot itself. Like Tristan, who is charged with the responsibility of bringing Isolde safely back to King Mark but instead falls in love with her, Scottie receives similar instructions from Elster, but from the moment he sees her, his interest ceases to be dispassionate.[26] Even seeing her has a parallel in the opera, where "the look" has

8.3 *Vertigo* (Kim Novak at Empire Hotel) (Judy transformed to Madeleine)

such potency that it actually receives a leitmotif. Love and death freely intermingle in both works, prompted by what should have been a death potion in the opera which turns out to be a love potion; in the film the bay may be a similar potion, followed by the drinks that Scottie periodically offers Madeleine. Both works require much suspension of disbelief, and this requisite for serious opera becomes central to the unfolding of the film. In Wagner's operas conventional religion gives way to eroticism and ecstasy, where characters such as Tannhäuser can flaunt religion and still find redemption; Scottie's new religion becomes his obsessive love, but traditional religion lurks never far in the background, with important scenes across from churches or in missions. In the end the presence of a nun atop the San Juan Bautista tower triggers the final plunge from the tower.

Wagnerian ambiguity dominates the film, but Scottie does not give up on attempting to find order—the key that will unlock the mystery of Madeleine and his own suspension above and descent into swirling vortexes. He loses all sense of time, and the illusory Madeleine proves to be the perfect companion for this, but his friend Midge (Barbara Bel Geddes) does her best to find the order he lacks, especially during his periods of convalescence. Music plays a therapeutic role in this—the ordered music of the eighteenth century, early on the Sinfonia in E flat, op. 9, no. 2 by J. C. Bach, which Midge plays for him at her apartment, and later the andante of Mozart's Symphony No. 34, prescribed by a music therapist at the sanatorium, but she recognizes the improbability of this therapy working. Even the structure of the film attempts to impose order, with its almost palindrome-like shape revolving around the central point of the film— Madeleine's first plunge from the tower.[27] The defining moments though are the points of greatest disorder and imbalance, of falls from towers, the pursuit of irrational obsession, and descent into illusion and madness. Mozart proves to be no match for Wagner in *Vertigo*.

Other counterbalances

Numerous other films use music in ways similar to the ones just discussed, although in some cases it may not be the music itself but the mere suggestion of it. An example of this occurs in *The Birds*, when Melanie Daniels (Tippi Hedren) spends her first evening in Bodega Bay, first with the Brenner family and then at the home of Annie Hayworth (Suzanne Pleshette), where she stays for the night. When she enters the Brenner home, we see a piano on the left, and after pouring drinks, Mitch (Rod Taylor), the reason for her being there, sits on the piano bench to chat with her. When he leaves the room we hear the piano being played; Melanie has sat down to play Debussy's *Arabesque in E*, which Hedren herself actually plays. While Debussy's music can have an unsettling effect, here, because of the nature of the work, it achieves something much more stable. There may be some aspect of the woman who plays the piano having a seductive effect, but the fact that as she plays she speaks with Mitch's little sister about Mitch, Bodega Bay, and a birthday party, minimizes that. Mitch's mother perhaps senses the more threatening seductiveness of the playing, and quizzes Mitch about Melanie's character, including a news report about her bathing naked in a fountain in Rome. Even in this gentle situation the piano has the potential to prompt different responses, and in contrast to its role here, it later appears both before and during bird attacks. Melanie drives away after a somewhat unpleasant exchange with Mitch, and as she does, the camera takes in the ominous sight of hundreds of birds amassing on the power lines. When she arrives and sits down in Annie's living room, immediately behind her and in full view on a shelf sits an LP of Wagner's *Tristan und Isolde*, a purely visual rather than aural stimulus here. The Wagner may very well invoke darker and more destructive associations, certainly the looming birds, and there may also be an element of tension between the two women since Annie had at one time been in love with Mitch. The two women speak in frank terms with each other, and Wagner appears to have more to do with a premonition of the destructive forces soon to be released in their full fury.

A similar type of prompting occurs in *Psycho*, in the second half of the film, as Lila Crane (Vera Miles) searches the bedroom of Norman Bates (Anthony Perkins) for clues about her missing sister, after Sam Loomis (John Gavin) has diverted Norman's attention. She looks into an open phonograph, and sees on the turntable an LP of Beethoven's *Eroica* Symphony, perhaps an odd discovery—this great musical representation of human striving—in the room of a psychopathic murderer. The Beethoven appears to belong more to her than to him, to her quest for answers and the truth, and the invocation of Beethoven may be part of an attempt to return to order after the grisly scene we witnessed not long before. The LP though does have a death reference, since the side in full view contains the first two movements, the second being the *Marcia funebre* (funeral march). Herrmann's music with its more Wagnerian tone underlies the irrationality and disorder of the film, although in the case of a couple of the musical cues, the score leans toward suggestion of other composers. These happen near the beginning of the film, first with the titles music, and then the music immediately after the titles. The abrasive driving rhythms of the opening music may remind us of passages from Stravinsky's *Rite of Spring*, especially the section near the end in which the chosen maiden must dance herself to death. This could possibly be an eerie premonition about the untimely fate of Marion Crane (Janet Leigh). The much gentler music heard as the camera pans Phoenix on a hot afternoon and moves into the hotel window of the two lovers, with its thick chords rising and falling, suggests Debussy's *Prélude à l'après midi d'un faune*, a work of considerable musical ambiguity based programmatically on Stéphane Mallarmé's poem about a satyr's erotic visions in the heat of the afternoon. Beethoven in this film remains unheard, and certainly cannot overcome the dark forces, even at the end as the psychological explanation must give way to the car being pulled from the swamp; Herrmann's three-note madness theme, as Steven C. Smith reminds us, gets the final word.[28]

Music itself can be used as a weapon, possibly for good but more likely for ill, and Hitchcock's preferred musical instrument of torture appears to have been jazz. This happens explicitly in *Foreign Correspondent* (1940), after the English Nazi collaborators kidnap the aging Dutch diplomat Van Meer and try to extract information from him that only he and one other person know. Instead of using physical torture, they subject him to loudly repeated American swingtime jazz, assuming that this music would be unbearable to a European of his generation. They almost push him to his limit, but in fact it takes physical means to achieve their end. Hitchcock, a great lover of classical music and a newcomer to the US in 1940, may have shared this view about jazz. Elisabeth Weis suspects that he enjoyed irritating his audience with this usage of jazz,[29] although it seems unlikely he would have done this had he not shared at least something of the distaste, perhaps not unlike Mr Drayton in *The Man Who Knew Too Much* (1956), who expresses his dislike for bebop at dinner in Marrakesh. In fact, jazz turns up in other films with perhaps less nefarious intent but still with negative associations, such as in *Young and Innocent* (1937), where it becomes the domain of the murderer, a jazz percussionist. Rhythmic off-beats or syncopations are hallmarks of jazz, and in that film off-rhythms push this even further, allowing the murderer to be identified because his rhythm degenerates into complete disorder. Even *The Wrong Man* has similar implications, since misery befalls a jazz musician who plays the bass at the Stork Club, wrongly identified as a thief, and whose conviction plunges his family into despair. In that film a counterbalance exists—the use of Mozart, which symbolizes order in his family setting as he promises to give his son a piano lesson involving a Mozart piece. One suspects that some of the difficulties Hitchcock had with adapting to the expectations about film music in the 1960s may have had something to do with his own distaste for jazz or other types of popular music.

9

Going popular

For a director with an active career spanning five decades, starting during the era of silent films and lasting until the mid-1970s, one would expect there to be issues about the kinds of music used in the films, and there most certainly were. Generally Hitchcock simply wished to engage excellent composers who could provide the best possible music for his films, but in the 1950s and 60s other considerations arose that needed to be taken into account. As a transatlantic director, with roots in England and Europe and at home in the United States after 1939, he shared some of the aspirations of the European art film directors but never lost sight of his audiences and the need to appeal to them. In his approaches to filmmaking over this time he expanded his horizons in ways that allowed him to appeal to the audience's changing tastes, scoring major hits in each one of the five decades. Along with the films, music also needed to change, and this presented new problems starting in the 1950s. Hit songs had been part of the film landscape from the earliest sound films in the late 1920s, but that landscape changed in the 1950s when it became apparent to the industry that a hit song could radically transform the reception of a film. The song could serve as an audible signature, sparking interest in the film or keeping it alive through relatively small but highly engaging sound bites. At the same time, the song could have a life of its own, although that life would never be entirely separated from the film itself. This happened, for example, in *High Noon* (1952), with music by an occasional Hitchcock collaborator, Dimitri Tiomkin, whose song for the film scored a major hit.

Of course this possibility arose much earlier than 1952, although the earlier successes did not seem to trigger a marketability frenzy with studio executives. In the mid-1940s, David Raksin could write a ubiquitous theme for *Laura* (1944), and that theme clearly did take on a life of its own, as it became one of the most recorded tunes ever, racked up huge sales as sheet music, and was even supplied with a text, which Johnny Mercer first recorded. Neither Raksin nor his director/producer Otto Preminger had any idea what they were unleashing with this tune, since Raksin designed it strictly as *Laura*'s theme—something that would be tightly integrated into the fabric of the film and would give a musical representation of the leading character. Its success outside of the film provided a fortuitous and pleasant surprise, but not one that anybody anticipated. This success, though, probably did make some wheels start to turn in the head offices of Hollywood studios. *Laura*, of course, did not stand alone; one can include "As Time Goes By" from *Casablanca* and numerous other films from the 1940s. Considering the rise of popular music during this time, it should not surprise us that there would be a new merging with film, where two media with popular appeal could come together. When Elvis Presley hit the airwaves in the 1950s and then the Beatles in the 1960s, all of this took on a new urgency.

Not only did hit songs become part of the new film landscape, but so did jazz, which, having established itself as the quintessential American music, took a natural place in American film, not necessarily to create hits, but much more to become the new standard for film music. Jazz could take many forms, and one of these was simply as a style from which composers could borrow, as Raksin did with his Laura theme, writing in a style with strong similarities to Duke Ellington. One soon encounters this new style in numerous films from the time, with even the European-born composers getting in on the act.

Like any director working in Hollywood, Hitchcock had to confront these issues, and the prevailing view intimates that he did so badly, dragged kicking and screaming into something for which he had only distaste. In his book *Hitchcock's Music*, Jack Sullivan sums this view up, putting it in the context of *Rear Window*: "This was the beginning of Hitchcock's increasingly debilitating obsession with hit tunes, something that came largely from studio pressure and that was very much at odds with his deeper instincts about music." He survived the minor distractions of this in the 1940s, but later, when "Lew Wasserman and others were relentlessly demanding hit tunes, [this was] one of the pressures that poisoned Hitchcock's relationship with Bernard Herrmann."[1] These comments raise some fundamental questions about Hitchcock's taste and judgment concerning music in his films, as they seem to suggest he was swept along by the pressure from studio bosses like Wasserman, giving in to something he found disagreeable. Could he really have missed the mark so badly, sacrificing his relationship with a close colleague like Herrmann that lasted more than a decade and ended badly with Herrmann's dismissal from *Torn Curtain*? Perhaps even worse, should we infer that Hitchcock's poor judgment in succumbing to these pressures about music pointed to a larger out-of-touch phenomenon that contributed to his decline as a director from the mid-1960s to the end of his career?

Hit songs

The facts appear to suggest something very unlike what Sullivan calls an obsession. Similarly, Hitchcock was no shrinking violet in his relationship with the likes of Lew Wasserman, and the episode of his collapsed relationship with Herrmann, certainly much written about, remains fairly clouded by the biases toward one of the parties or the other. These will be addressed in the course of this chapter, but first an overview needs to be taken of the use of popular songs throughout his career. The fact that a popular song appears prominently in his first sound film, "Miss Up to Date" in *Blackmail* (1929), suggests that he had no reservations about using this from the earliest possible stage in his career, and that he would readily use it again if and when the occasion arose. Over time the occasion arose surprisingly few times, most likely coming up if a singer played the role of a leading character. Silent film will spare us this; otherwise, Ivor Novello may very well have had songs in *The Lodger* or *Downhill* (1927). That changed in 1950 with Marlene Dietrich in *Stage Fright* and again in 1956 with Doris Day in the remake of *The Man Who*

Knew Too Much, but not with Julie Andrews in *Torn Curtain*. In three of these, the character who sings in the film either plays the role of a singer, or, in the case of Cyril Ritchard in *Blackmail*, a singer plays the role of a character who has a dramatically feasible opportunity to sing. Julie Andrews plays a scientist, and despite the various problems of *Torn Curtain* as well as Hitchcock's concern about the possibility of her singing, the idea of a singing scientist did not seriously cross anyone's radar. In *Rear Window*, the song logically goes to the composer who attempts throughout the film to create it.

During the period of the so-called studio pressures, no songs of extraneous value appeared in his films, and in fact after 1956 we find no songs in his films. They all reveal a consistent approach, which lies in the fact that the songs must be an integral part of the film, woven into the narrative in a way that makes it essential at best, or at the worst, not extraneous. The last one of these, *The Man Who Knew Too Much*, offers the best example of a song essential to the narrative. At the earliest stages of work on the outline for the script by Angus MacPhail in January and February of 1955, the text identified the leading female character as a singer. In these early drafts, still using some of the names from the 1934 version, Jill sings the favorite song of her son (Phil) at their hotel, in part as a reaction against the "deplorable highbrow stuff" by the fictitious Romanian composer Take Jonescu, whose centenary it happens to be.[2] In the next revision of the outline, Jill sings a lullaby at the embassy and the faint voice of Phil joins in; Jill keeps playing and singing to cover her husband Bob as he mounts the stairs in search of Phil (this section ends with a note that the upstairs events remain to be sorted out).[3]

About a month later the names change to Jo, Ben and Hank, and not until 7 May, Hitchcock now having heard and liking the song by Jay Livingston and Ray Evans, does the favorite song get its title "Que Sera, Sera." These scenes had been sketched before Doris Day received her contract, and probably even before Hitchcock anticipated her being hired. Very simply, they needed a singer for the part, and Day turned out to be an excellent choice. Whether a case can be made, as Murray Pomerance has attempted,[4] for the song and its text serving a specific narrative and filmic function, proves much harder to say, but the film as drafted by MacPhail and then fleshed out by John Michael Hayes clearly had to have a song. At first Day did not especially like the song, believing it to be merely a children's song; not only did it become immensely popular, but she also adopted it as her signature song. Herrmann, who composed the music for the film, had nothing but contempt for it, and at his irascible best grumbled, "What do you want a piece of junk like that in the picture for?"[5]

At various points in Hitchcock's career, and especially when David O. Selznick and Lew Wasserman had controlling interests in his productions, the issue of providing a hit song for a film arose, and then for one reason or another vanished. During the 1940s Selznick pursued this vigorously for *Spellbound* and *Notorious*, although since neither one materialized, it remains unclear what the intended role of the song would be. Both of these films came hot on the heels of *Laura*, and Selznick may not have had in mind that the song should appear in the film itself, for example as a replacement for the composers' titles music. The notion of a film leading off with a hit song had not yet gripped Hollywood at this time, although one could point to the example of part of Aaron Copland's titles music for *The Heiress* (1949) being replaced by the song "Plaisir d'amour," which Montgomery Clift uses for the purpose of wooing Olivia d'Havilland during the film. The humiliated Copland only learned of this replacement at the premiere of the film. It seems more likely in the mid-1940s that Selznick had something in mind more along the lines of *Laura*, in which a song could be extracted from the theme music and find a life outside of the film, serving as promotion material and another way of generating income. It appears that the composer for the film, Miklos Rozsa, thought of this possibility; Audray Granville, the head of Selznick's music department, reported that he [Rozsa] claimed "the love theme would lend itself to a popular ballad, using the title 'Spellbound', but that he is unfamiliar with this field of music and would require a popular songwriter."[6] Nothing came of this or other attempts.

During the 1950s the opportunity for leading off a film with a hit song or placing one within the film took on a new urgency, and during the next decade it became a matter of routine. As the titles music it could be somewhat more remote from the film, not having to serve a dramatic function as "Que Sera, Sera" did in *The Man Who Knew Too Much*, and this opened up the possibility of a loosely manufactured merger between a film and a song, one which could have significant financial implications but little or no artistic merit. Those responsible for the bottom line saw this type of merger as a godsend, but serious directors and composers thought of it as the worst possible abuse, with the potential to turn an excellent film into a laughing stock. The issue arose in Hitchcock's films during these years, certainly in *Vertigo* and later in *Marnie*, although one cannot say for certain if the songs in question would be placed in the films or serve an outside promotional function. In the case of *Vertigo* the latter seems most likely, since studio memos actually use the term "exploitation song." The studio accepted the one written by Livingston and Evans with the title "Vertigo," and used it for public relations.[7] The same thing happened with the song "Marnie," recorded by Nat "King" Cole, Tiny Little, and Roland Shaw. Harry Garfield recommended to Hitchcock that $2,000 be spent to promote and publicize the song, clearly intended only for publicity purposes, and Hitchcock agreed to the spending.[8] At a price of 60 cents, and a picture of Sean Connery and Tippi Hedren captioned with "Alfred Hitchcock's Suspenseful Sex Mystery … *Marnie*," this sheet music published by Hawaii Music Company had the potential to give the film some useful promotion, but the dismal music and lyrics killed any chance of that.

Hitchcock and Lew Wasserman

It appears, in fact, that no real danger existed of starting any Hitchcock film with a popular song, since no recorded example can be found of this kind of pressure from a studio executive. A more significant threat arose from the matter of the type of score that should be used, particularly how modern the music should be and what sort of audience it should embrace. In this respect the name Lew Wasserman comes up consistently, and we are led to believe, even by Hitchcock himself, that Wasserman, as Hitchcock's boss and the most powerful mogul in Hollywood, forced Hitchcock to turn away from the kinds of scores he had been using, especially those by Herrmann, and adopt the new jazzy music with a beat. We have probably been much too ready to accept Hitchcock's words on this, words that deflect the casting of any type of aspersions away from himself, as he conveniently did on numerous occasions. For example, when his close colleague Herbert Coleman decided to leave and become a freelancer, Hitchcock's final words to him, "Alma's not happy you're leaving," put the regret in her voice, not his.[9] His words to Herrmann prior to their break-up seem to belong in the same category, and probably reflect very little of his own thoughts on the matter. Since he implies without really saying so that the pressure came from Wasserman, it is worth looking at Hitchcock's relationship with Wasserman to put this into context. At the heart of the matter lies Hitchcock's ability to make judgments about his own films, certainly about the nature of the music to be used, and other issues by implication.

Hitchcock could be cordial and engaging, sufficiently so that many of his colleagues, including Herrmann, believed him to be a friend, but in reality very few fell into that category. Lew Wasserman proved to be one of the few, a man Hitchcock could relate to because of their similar rise from modest origins to the top of the profession as a result of extraordinary perceptiveness and skill. Wasserman's orbit very much included music: not only was his father in the business, but his own work as a promoter started in his home town of Cleveland where he did publicity and booked acts at local nightclubs. His skillful work as an agent drew attention, and by 1940 he had become vice president of the Music Corporation of America's motion picture division, and he eventually became the president of MCA. As a result of the complex web of MCA's acquisitions, Wasserman became the most powerful mogul in Hollywood.[10]

When David O. Selznick brought Hitchcock to the United States, his agent became David's brother Myron, who represented him until his death in 1944. By 1945 Hitchcock found a new agent, Lew Wasserman, and not only did Hitchcock's career thrive with Wasserman's support, but they became close friends. Over the next three decades they frequently dined together, went on vacations together with their spouses, and shared their common interests in art collecting and good wine. As Hitchcock scored successive hits at the box office, Wasserman gave him key advice on how to invest his money, and almost all his suggestions proved to be winners. One could argue, though, that Hitchcock's success in the industry owed much to Wasserman's uncanny sense of promotion, which included putting Hitchcock on television in the mid-1950s. Wasserman proposed the idea, and in such a way that Alfred Hitchcock Presents and later The Alfred Hitchcock Hour would give him maximum exposure to the public but would not take all that much of his time. He could continue his frenetic pace as a screen director with very little input into the television productions; even his appearances at the beginning of shows were scripted by staff writers. Wasserman had calculated correctly: not only did television prove to be very successful financially but this exposure, along with the continuing flow of films during these years, made Hitchcock's name one of the most recognizable at the time, even surpassing that of his leading actors.

Having succeeded at making Hitchcock the most famous filmmaker in the world, Wasserman guaranteed Hitchcock's continuing loyalty to the studio by offering him a business arrangement that no one else in Hollywood could match. As Patrick McGilligan points out, Wasserman's secretiveness has prevented the specific terms of this arrangement from ever being fully disclosed, but with it, Hitchcock enjoyed a secure future. At this point in 1954 the contract covered nine films, five that Hitchcock would both produce and direct, and four to be produced by the studio that he would direct. Not only would he receive a very high salary, but also a percentage of the profits, and for the first four (*Rear Window*, *To Catch a Thief*, *The Trouble with Harry*, and *The Man Who Knew Too Much*) he would also control the rights. In fact, the most financially advantageous clause of this Paramount agreement gave Hitchcock ownership of the first five that he produced and directed for a period of eight years after the initial release.[11] With his wealth assured, as well as his artistic stability, Hitchcock could get on with the most fruitful projects of his career.

By the end of the 1950s, Hitchcock could do whatever he wanted at Paramount, with complete control over every aspect of production, including the music. His control was so complete that one Paramount executive noted in a letter during the production of *North by Northwest* that "Paramount functions practically as a studio setup for him."[12] Hitchcock still had an obligation to make a picture for Universal, also of course part of Wasserman's MCA conglomerate, and to satisfy this obligation, Hitchcock decided to make an inexpensive film using relatively unknown actors and the equally inexpensive production facilities of television. The film that resulted, *Psycho*, turned out to be a staggering financial success, in no small part due to Wasserman's shrewd marketing ideas, such as not allowing entry to the theater after the film began. With Hitchcock now at Universal, Wasserman agreed that he could stay there, and the new arrangement far surpassed what he had at Paramount: he traded the rights to *Psycho* and his television programs for corporate stocks, and in 1962 he became MCA's third-largest stockholder.[13]

Along with Wasserman, Hitchcock now became a co-owner of the world's largest studio conglomerate, and that made him the second most powerful person in Hollywood, with only Wasserman holding more power than himself. As a boss on almost equal footing with Wasserman, Hitchcock did not have to give in on important matters; his ability to make good corporate decisions had been amply demonstrated, and other studio executives regarded him as one of the shrewdest operators they had ever met. His relationship with Wasserman by the early 1960s had been long and warm, but Hitchcock recognized without any prompting how much of his success he owed to Wasserman, not only on purely business matters but artistic ones as well. On numerous matters he would defer to Wasserman, certainly in the selection of actors (although not always willingly), and also in overcoming his own insecurities about the impact of certain scenes. Humor, of course, is one of the hallmarks of Hitchcock's films, although with the exception of specific scenes, little of it was intended in *Psycho*. During the first screenings audiences reacted otherwise, laughing at completely unexpected points, although some of this presumably resulted from nervous laughter at scenes of horror. To correct some of these, Hitchcock tried to persuade Wasserman to agree to some remixing, such as the scene in the hardware store immediately following Norman submerging Marion's car in the swamp. As Anthony Perkins recalled it, "The entire scene in the hardware store [in which a woman is buying rat poison and Lila visits Sam] was practically inaudible because of the leftover howls from the previous scene. Lew Wasserman talked Hitch out of putting more volume into some of the scenes, saying 'You can't do that. We've already made our prints.'"[14] Hitchcock did not have an entirely free hand, and at times resented Wasserman's interference, but to the end they remained strong friends and colleagues.

Jazzing it up

The collapse of the Hitchcock–Herrmann collaboration during the making of *Torn Curtain* has been much discussed in print, but the reason for it has not been adequately demonstrated. Steven C. Smith has provided most of the pertinent documents—the communications between Hitchcock and Herrmann,[15] often with Hitchcock's assistant Peggy Robertson acting as an intermediary—but the generally accepted conclusion that things fell apart because Herrmann disobeyed Hitchcock's directive about the type of music he wanted has something of a hollow ring to it. After all, Herrmann had done this before, most notably for the shower scene in *Psycho*, so we need to be very clear on what made this one different. No one saw this whole affair from a better vantage point than Robertson, not only writing to Herrmann on behalf of Hitchcock, but also in attending some of the sessions where things came unstuck, so we can do no better than to listen to what she has to say on the matter. Her first responsibility lay with Hitchcock, her employer, but also being fond of Herrmann, she took a view as unbiased as possible under the circumstances. The same cannot be said for various others who have weighed in on the break-up, who more often than not sided with Herrmann as the injured party.

Despite the accessibility of the documents, it is worth reiterating some of the main points, in part to determine the credibility of the claims about pressure on Hitchcock. To be sure the relationship had become strained after a decade of collaboration, complicated by Herrmann's personal problems (the separation from his wife) but more from what Hitchcock heard and did not like in their most recent film, *Marnie*, in which too much of the music sounded to Hitchcock tired and recycled. Yet another film with themes that sounded like the Madeleine theme from *Vertigo* or background motifs that had been recycled since *The Man Who Knew Too Much* would not do, and Hitchcock tried to head this off, first by passing along instructions through Robertson, and then in his own communication to Herrmann in London. In a cable dated 4 November 1965, Hitchcock laid down the law, emphasizing "the need to break away from the old fashioned cued-in type of music that we have been using for so long. I was extremely disappointed when I heard the score of *Joy in the Morning*, not only did I find it conforming to the old pattern but extremely reminiscent of the *Marnie* music. In fact, the theme was almost the same." Not only did Hitchcock consider the score for this mediocre film to represent artistic bankruptcy, but he felt Herrmann had stolen property by using material from his own films.

Feeling that Herrmann needed to be educated about keeping up to date, Hitchcock condescended to give this lesson:

> Unfortunately for we artists, we do not have the freedom that we would like to have, because we are catering to an audience and

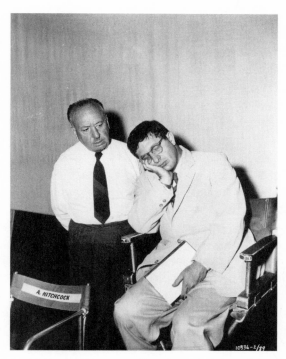

9.1 Hitchcock with Bernard Herrmann (Near the end of the collaboration)

that is why you get your money and I get mine. This audience is very different from the one to which we used to cater; it is young, vigorous and demanding. It is this fact that has been recognized by almost all of the European film makers where they have sought to introduce a beat and a rhythm that is more in tune with the requirements of the aforesaid audience. This is why I am asking you to approach this problem with a receptive and if possible enthusiastic mind. If you cannot do this then I am the loser.

Which European filmmakers he had in mind is less than clear: certainly not a master director such as Fellini, who himself worked consistently with the same composer, one with not the slightest interest in music with a beat. The assumption has been that this was code for studio pressure, and studio pressure meant Lew Wasserman. As a part owner of the studio and close friend of Wasserman, that pressure existed only to the extent that Hitchcock allowed it, and considering the music in the films he made after *Torn Curtain*, apparently he did not let it be too much of a problem.

As the cable continued, Hitchcock got closer to his real concern, and this involved his working relationship with his composer and his own judgment about the nature of the music. His music notes in advance of composition of any given score gave definite cues for the placement of the music and sometimes general suggestions about the atmosphere of the music, but normally he left it to his composers to do their work unobstructed. If he did not like what he heard, changes could be made; sometimes he even anticipated the composer would have ideas about musical placements that he did not, as he did for example in his dubbing notes for *Vertigo* (for the powder room changing scene at the Empire Hotel "Mr. Herrman may have something to say here," or later in the scene, "when Mr. Herrman will be the one to take over"[16]). Now he refused to give any such freedom, and complained about the attempts of composers to manipulate him—composers who thought they knew better than himself:

I have made up my mind that this approach to the music is extremely essential, I also have very definite ideas as to where music should go in the picture and there is not too much. So often have I been asked, for example by Tiomkin, to come and listen to a score and when I express my disapproval his hands were thrown up and with the cry of "But you can't change anything now, it has all been orchestrated." It is this kind of frustration that I am rather tired of. By that I mean getting music scored on a take it or leave it basis.[17]

Herrmann appeared to be on side, replying in his own cable: "Delighted to compose a vigorous beat score for *Torn Curtain*. Always pleased to have your views regarding the music for the film. Please send script indicating where you desire music." Hitchcock seemed to doubt it, asking production associate Paul Donnelly to write again, emphasizing the points about his requirements for a vigorous rhythm and avoiding the old pattern.[18]

After these exchanges, Herrmann ignored Hitchcock completely, and he undoubtedly felt he had precedent on his side. He could easily recognize that the talk about pressure from the audience—the studio—was a ruse, since Hitchcock did not make that sort of film; in fact, he later said he went so far as to tell him, "Look, Hitch, you can't outjump your own shadow. And you don't make pop pictures. What do you want with me? I don't write pop music."[19] After a decade of collaboration without a hint of the need for anything popular, and entries in dubbing notes such as "Mr. Herrman will be the one to take over," Herrmann had good reason to expect the business-as-usual approach. If he added music where Hitchcock said there should be none, he could invoke the experience of *Psycho*, where, after providing music for the shower scene that Hitchcock explicitly said he did not want, Hitchcock had to concede with the words "Improper suggestion, my boy, improper suggestion."[20] He proceeded to write a business-as-usual score and went ahead with recording it on schedule.

Everything changed when Hitchcock arrived at the recording studio to hear the first takes, and Peggy Robertson, who also attended, has furnished the most reliable account of what happened. Hitchcock had not said much in advance about the music, but on a few matters, aside from the points where music should be cued in or out, he made his position absolutely clear. The first of these concerned the titles music: "On opening of *Torn Curtain* I feel that the Main Title should be an exciting, arresting and rhythmic piece of music whose function would be to immediately rivet the audience's attention. Irrespective of the abstract designing of the titles and their background, the music could be, and should be, written before this is achieved."[21] Second, as Robertson later reconstructed it, Hitchcock said, "Benny, there's one spot in reel one right at the beginning when we're talking about the cold weather, where there's an opportunity for humor. I want a light and humorous score, just there." Benny said, "Okay."[22] Third, Hitchcock made it clear there should be no music for the sequence in which Michael (Paul Newman) and the East German farm woman kill the security man Gromek. To the first of these, Herrmann came close to complying, certainly writing music that would arrest the audience's attention. It does, though, lack rhythm, and the possibility exists that Hitchcock used a code here that he thought Herrmann would understand, having to do with the tone of the film. Herrmann did not catch it, and his misreading of the two other scenes bears this out.

The problem with the "cold weather" scene near the beginning, according to Robertson, brought about the swift exit of Herrmann as the film's composer. She arrived at the recording studio before Hitchcock, and Herrmann played reel one for her. Expecting light music to underlie the comic scenes of scientists poking at their drinking glasses to break the ice, followed by quips about the heating not working, and then on to Newman and Julie Andrews in bed, she found it distressing to hear "music that was funereal, dirge-like music, where Hitch had wanted light music." After going through reel one she did not know what to do, and at that point Hitchcock walked in and asked her opinion of the music. Before she could voice her view, he asked what would be heard next, and Herrmann answered reel two. Hitchcock wished to hear reel one, but Herrmann retorted "Don't hear reel one, Hitch. Reel two is the important one." Hitchcock insisted on reel one, and after hearing it, he stopped and said, "That's enough, I've heard enough. I don't want to hear any more." Herrmann asked if he loved it, and Hitchcock replied, "No, I asked for light music there, Benny, and I don't want to talk about it any more."[23] Various accounts exist of what happened next, but it appears, according to John Russell Taylor, that Hitchcock drove back to Universal, and "went straight to the music department to accept responsibility and offer to pay off Herrmann himself."[24] Stanley Wilson noted that Herrmann felt he should have been able to complete recording the score, and then make the changes that Hitchcock wanted, but instead, Gerald S. Barton sent a letter of termination to Herrmann on 25 March 1966.[25] After a search for a new composer (and the opportunistic Tiomkin offered his services), Universal hired John Addison to write a new score.

Hitchcock apparently never did get to hear Herrmann's score for the murder scene at the farm, but it would not be too difficult to imagine what his reaction would have been. Here the comparison with the shower scene in *Psycho* comes into play, since Hitchcock had ruled out music in both cases; if Hitchcock had seen it with Herrmann's score, could it have been possible, as Herrmann assumed would happen, that Hitchcock would again have said "Improper suggestion?" In conceiving the shower scene, Hitchcock believed the images and sounds would make the correct impact, stressing in his dubbing notes that, "Throughout the killing, there should be the shower noise and the blows of the knife. We should hear the water gurgling down the drain of the bathtub ... during the murder, the sound of the shower should be continuous and monotonous, only broken by the screams of Marion."[26] This highly complex scene, with violence and nudity involved, required some original shooting techniques, which Hitchcock described in the following way: "I'm going to shoot and cut it staccato, so the audience won't know what the hell is going on."[27] Saul Bass worked so closely with Hitchcock on the scene that some concluded he actually directed the scene; he came up with a montage approach involving a complex set of angles and shots, and in fact his storyboards required no less than 78 camera setups. With this amount of filmic virtuosity, it seemed unimaginable that music could do anything but blunt the effect of that virtuosity. Herrmann's music does exactly that, but Hitchcock could recognize that the audience would not care about the techniques of making the scene but only the terrifying effect it would have. For that Herrmann's music with its stabbing treatment of strings fit to a tee.

Hitchcock seemed ready to give up on *Psycho*, and considered letting it revert to the type of film its production techniques point toward: a television show scaled down to a one-hour time slot.

Herrmann's music went a long way toward preventing that, and if it could rescue a shabby thriller, then why not a spy picture plagued with problems, not the least of these being the lack of electricity between the two actors in the starring roles. In some ways he imagined the film as having certain similarities to *Psycho*, not as a murder thriller, but nevertheless as a kind of film noir piece with brutality, murder, a hated regime, and attempts to stay one step ahead of menacing forces. Herrmann's dark music, with the exception of the Hotel d'Angleterre scene in Copenhagen, reflects that grimness and menace throughout, certainly in the turbulent music for the titles, again in the dirge-like music as Robertson termed it for the opening droll scenes, but nowhere more forcefully than in the killing scene. Compared to *Psycho*, in which we see the brutal murder of a woman we have come to identify with and whose love life and moral dilemma we care about, with the minor character Gromek in *Torn Curtain* we have an East German security man whose work will not endear us to him, who seems a bit of a bumbler (he can't make his cigarette lighter work), and makes a series of bad jokes about American expressions. Even in the killing scene he does not give up on the expressions, saying he could take Armstrong with one arm tied behind his back, or calling the farm woman "the cookie" when she comes at him with a carving knife.

When Truffaut commented on this scene, noting that "Since it is played without music, it is very realistic and also very savage," Hitchcock explained how he tried to avoid the clichés associated with this type of scene:

In every picture somebody gets killed and it goes very quickly. They are stabbed or shot, and the killer never even stops to look and see whether the victim is really dead or not. And I thought it was time to show that it was very difficult, very painful, and it takes a very long time to kill a man. The public is aware that this must be a silent killing because of the presence of the taxi driver on the farm. Firing a shot is out of the question. In line with our old principle, the killing has to be carried out by means suggested by the locale and the characters. We are in a farmhouse and the farmer's wife is doing the killing. So we use household objects: the kettle full of soup, a carving knife, a shovel, and, finally, the gas oven.[28]

As ever in his descriptions, he omits certain key details. He rightly informs us that it takes a long time to do it, but he neglects to describe the effect that this and the methods used will have on the viewer. The first, a soup bowl flying through the air and smashing against the wall with that night's dinner splattering about will remind us of dozens of slapstick movies from the Keystone Cops onward, and most viewers will find it difficult to restrain the laughter.

If Hitchcock wanted to avoid clichés here he certainly did not in the use of the camera, allowing it to sway back and forth as the farmer's wife aims at her moving target. With a broken knife above his collarbone things have become more serious, but laughter will still be difficult to restrain, now of the nervous variety. She next goes at him with a shovel, and the loud clanging of it against his shins will do nothing to suppress the nervous tittering. Even the attempt to shove his head into the gas oven will do little to change the tone (discussions about the script recognize how unlikely a gas oven would be on an East German farm, to say nothing of the unlikelihood of a family-owned farm). As Armstrong holds his head in the stove, Gromek's hands come up and his fingers dance a little habañera; if we imagine sounds at this point they would be castanets, fading with the motion of his fingers as life slowly ebbs away. Everything about the scene suggests that Hitchcock not only wanted us to squirm but that the squirming should evoke macabre humor. He does not tell Truffaut this but in his music notes for *Frenzy*, he describes something of a similar nature: "The music starts on cut to the hospital ward—it should have a furtive, but humorous quality. 'Dear Mr. Musician—Please do not make the error that this is a heavy dramatic scene of escape—it is a comic one yet a daring one.'"[29]

The same directive applies to this scene, implied by the visual unfolding, and Herrmann missed it completely, making it "heavy" and "dramatic." His music starts immediately after the flying bowl misses Gromek's head,[30] with a jagged and raw motif that has a driving rhythmic pulse. This motif predominates until the knife strikes Gromek after the swaying, now with shrill tremolos overlying a menacing pulse in the percussion section. As Gromek rises after being stabbed, a new urgent motif comes in, again with a tremolo effect. The music cuts out just before Michael drags Gromek to the gas stove, and with its blood-and-thunder intensity, it could not have been further from what Hitchcock had in mind. Clearly Hitchcock wanted the scene to seem as protracted as possible, and without music, it seems to go on unbearably long. Herrmann knew perfectly well that music changes our perception of time, and that with music this scene will seem to go by much more quickly. In the late 1960s I had the good fortune to attend one of Herrmann's lectures, and he started by playing the opening three minutes of *Citizen Kane*, once without his music and then with it, and he then rhetorically asked us how the music changed our perception (no one doubted he was referring, among other things, to time). With the change to the perception of time in the killing scene along with his failure to notice the macabre humor, there seems no chance that Hitchcock would have changed his mind if he had heard it. In *Psycho* the music worked; in *Torn Curtain* it did not.

At stake for Hitchcock lay the soundness of his own judgment about music for his films—whether he recognized the tone of his films and knew what music would be appropriate. He had been

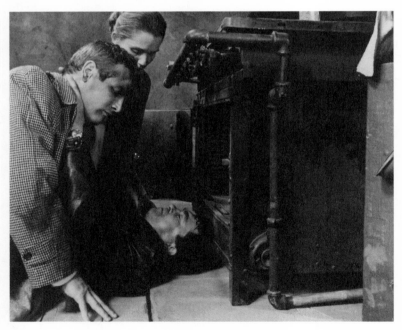

9.2 *Torn Curtain* (Paul Newman with Wolfgang Kieling and Carolyn Conwell) (It's not easy to kill a man)

wrong about such matters before, but it would be absurd to assume, as it appears Herrmann did, that Hitchcock would so completely misjudge his own film. When Herrmann saw the reels as he provided music for them, he may have felt that the film had so few redeeming qualities that its only hope lay in his score. Hitchcock clearly did not agree, although his attitude appeared to change about the film after he saw the rushes. At first he had high hopes for the film, and no doubt when Peggy Robertson at an early stage called this his best film yet, she reflected his own aspirations. He had disagreements with Wasserman about the casting, doubting that he could get a good film from Paul Newman and Julie Andrews, but similar kinds of doubts in the past had proved wrong, most recently with Kim Novak and Doris Day. Even the fact that Newman had an Actors Studio background, the method acting for which Hitchcock felt only contempt, did not necessarily provide an insurmountable obstacle; Eva Marie Saint had the same background, and her work in *North by Northwest* helped to make it one of his best films to that point. Newman, though, proved to be all but impossible to work with,[31] and Newman and Andrews simply could not generate any excitement.

Hitchcock knew the film had little chance of doing well, and in the final stages of postproduction he in all probability simply wished to put out something that would not embarrass him completely. He apparently felt that Herrmann's music, which attempted to turn the film into something it was not, would be an embarrassment, and that he would be much better off simply providing the film with relatively innocuous music, something light and certainly not too serious. He received that with a fairly mediocre score from Addison, and Hitchcock's attitude can be seen in his apparent lack of interest in the score as Addison produced it; as the composer tried passages out on Hitchcock, he never received anything more than one-word positive responses. *Torn Curtain* proved to be the flop that everyone thought it would be. Hitchcock could walk away from it confident that his judgment on key points remained intact.

Over the course of his career, Hitchcock's judgment involving music appeared, with a few exceptions, to be remarkably sound. When he wanted composers to take the lead, he let them do so, often saying as much in his notes on music, and on occasions he acknowledged that composers had better ideas than his own.

Coming from the silent era, when music played such a fundamental role in the conception of a film, he recognized the role that music could play, both as something audible and even more importantly as a constructive force behind a given film. This could have a profound bearing on the most crucial constructive elements, such as *mise en scène* and montage, and it allowed him to be aware of what he needed from his composers. Lacking the verbal wherewithal of explaining that, he sometimes had to accept what he received even though he knew it did not meet the standard, as happened with *Rear Window*; in the case of *Torn Curtain* the music missed by such a wide margin that he could not accept it. In virtually every work the music, whether heard or underlying, had a major role to play in finding the primary tension in the film, which more often than not involved the conflict between order and disorder. Even waltzes and pianos could take a leading role in this, and so could popular music or source music of the classics. Perhaps not a musician in a literal sense, Hitchcock had a most perceptive ear, and he used that in a potent way in transforming music into the visual techniques which give viewers the most basic emotions and impressions that a filmmaker can convey.

Appendices

Appendix 1. a. Beethoven, Piano Sonata in F minor, Op. 2, no. 1, mv't. 1, bars 1–11

Appendix 1. b. Harmonic rhythm pattern

2		2		1		1	½	½	¼	¼	(rate of change of harmonic rhythm)
|i	|i	|V	|V	|i	|V	|i	ii	|*V |			(the harmony, *appoggiatura*)
p			sf	sf	ff		p				(dynamics)
1	2	3	4	5	6	7	8				(bar numbers)

Appendix 2. Chopin, Prelude No. 15 in D flat, bars 1–9

Appendix 3. Beethoven, Piano Sonata in D major, Op. 28, mv't. 1, bars 1–33

Appendix 4. Debussy, "Jardins sous la Pluie," from *Estampes*, bars 1–9

Pattern of beats per chord
|2 1 1|1 1 1 1|2 2|2 2|2 2|4|2 1 1|1 1 1 1|1 1 1 1| (beats per chord)
1   2   3   4   5   6 7 8   9   (bar number)

Appendix 5. *Blackmail*, Alice's walking montages (length of shots in seconds)

1   Leaves Crewe's studio: 27, 5, 3, 3, 2

2   By theatre patrons: 8, 16, 4, 3, 3, 2, 2

3   Big Ben: 8, 4, 9, 7, 2

4   Trafalgar Square to the falling arm: 19, 2, 2, 7, 2, 5, 3, 1

Appendix 6. Structure of Ravel's *La Valse* (with rehearsal numbers)

In two parts, with introduction and an interlude separating the 2 parts

Introduction: starts as a low rumble, fragments of waltz come in (1), but nothing definite; some ominous sounds

Part 1: the waltz enters (9), with four-bar phrases—at first one could imagine dancing to it

Musical foreground and background—the foreground is the waltz, the background is the musically extraneous passages which increase in number as part 1 goes on; these become disruptive, but not enough to completely upset the waltz: rumbling cello (11), harp glissandi (13), woodwind runs (14), loud brass interjections (17)

Interlude: return to material from the introduction (54)—low rumble, indefinite

Part 2: waltz now has difficulty establishing the phrasing pattern (57) Roles of foreground and background become reversed: three orchestras (69), short chromatic scales (76), long chromatic passage enters (78), this crescendos (79), *accélérez jusqu'a* 85 (82), Pace quickens (83), climax of long rising chromatic line, completely forcing out the waltz (85) Eventually complete musical chaos takes over (94) Piece ends with cadence on D major (the original key of the waltz) Is that a credible closure after the chaos?

Appendix 7. Dinner table montage

.02   young Charlie hums waltz, sets table
.08   close-up of her; she sits
.13   told not to hum at the table

.28 Uncle Charlie will put money in the bank
.32 close-up of him: $30-40,000
.35 Joe stunned by the amount
.41 young Charlie in close-up: "what's that tune...what waltz"
.54 Uncle Charlie, close-up, worried look
.59 young Charlie, close-up, tunes can jump from head to head
1.04 Uncle, close up, furrowed brow, doesn't know, Emma thinks Victor Herbert
1.17 Roger says Victor Herbert is not a waltz
1.19 Uncle, close-up, suggests "Blue Danube"
1.21 young Charlie, close-up, yes of course, then no
1.27 Uncle, close up even closer
1.29 "It's the Merr..." close-up of milk glass spilled by Uncle
1.30 Uncle stands, all leave the table

Montage pattern: 2, 6, 7, 15, 4, 3, 6, 3, 5, 5, 13, 2, 2, 6, 2, 1

Appendix 8. Attempted murder of niece montage

.10 farewell to community members
.19 Uncle Charlie with Emma
.25 young Charlie with concerned look; train becomes background
.31 he asks children to come onto the train
.43 boards train, more goodbyes
1.09 on train
1.16 waves at window
1.19 with children and porter
1.35 Uncle alone with young Charlie (music starts)
2.01 train moves
2.10 he holds her back
2.12 she looks away
2.14 she tries to free herself
2.17 at train coach door (waltz starts, distorted)
2.28 his hand over her mouth
2.29 their feet
2.32 her hand on door catch beside open door
2.33 Uncle from back
2.34 her hand on door catch
2.35 they struggle

2.37 he waits for train to speed up, hand over her mouth
2.38 ground (adjacent track), a blur as train gains speed
2.40 hand over her mouth
2.41 ground
2.41 hand over mouth
2.42 ground
2.43 their heads, struggle
2.45 her hand on door catch (opposite side)
2.46 struggle
2.47 full bodies, struggle
2.49 he falls out (pushed?)
2.53 double image as waltz dissolves in

Montage pattern: 10, 9, 6, 6, 12, 26, 7, 3, 16, 26, 9, 2, 2, 3, 11, 1, 3, 1, 1, 1, 2, 1, 2, 1, ½, 1, 1, 2, 1, 1, 2, 4

Notes

Introduction

1 Stephen Watts (1933–4), "Alfred Hitchcock on Music in Films," *Cinema Quarterly* [Edinburgh] 2, no. 2: 83. Reprinted in Sidney Gottlieb ed. (1995), *Hitchcock on Hitchcock: Selected Writings and Interviews*. Berkeley, Los Angeles, and London: University of California Press, 245.

2 François Truffaut with the collaboration of Helen G. Scott (1984), *Hitchcock*, rev. ed. New York: Simon and Schuster, 367.

3 *Hitchcock on Hitchcock*, 298.

4 Truffaut, *Hitchcock*, 335.

5 *Hitchcock on Hitchcock*, 216.

6 Peter Bogdanovich (1963), *The Cinema of Alfred Hitchcock*. New York: The Museum of Modern Art Film Library, 11.

7 Murray Pomerance (2004), *An Eye for Hitchcock*. New Brunswick, NJ: Rutgers University Press, 7.

8 Quoted in Patrick McGilligan (2003), *Alfred Hitchcock: A Life in Darkness and Light*. New York: Regan Books, 8.

9 John Russell Taylor (1978), *Hitch: The Life and Times of Alfred Hitchcock*. London: Faber and Faber, 150.

10 *Ibid.*, 110.

11 I would like to thank the staff of the Margaret Herrick Library in Los Angeles, and especially Barbara Hall for her interest in and prompt attention to my requests, and for placing material of the Hitchcock Archives at my disposal.

12 McGilligan, *Alfred Hitchcock*, 28.

13 *Ibid.*, 297.

14 Truffaut, 319.

15 Watts, "Alfred Hitchcock on Music in Films," 80–1.

16 *Ibid.*, 82.

17 *Ibid.*, 83.

18 *The Man Who Knew Too Much*, Script Outline, 14 March 1955, Margaret Herrick Library.

19 Murray Pomerance (2000), "Finding Release: 'Storm Clouds' and *The Man Who Knew Too Much*," in James Buhler, Caryl Flynn, and David Neumeyer (eds), *Music and Cinema*. Hanover and London: Wesleyan University Press, 207–46.

20 Of these, the most recent book, Jack Sullivan's (2006), *Hitchcock's Music*. New Haven and London: Yale University Press, stands out. Other books include Jean-Pierre Eugène (2000), *La Musique dans les Films d'Alfred Hitchcock* (Paris: Dreamland éditeur); Eva Rieger (1996), *Alfred Hitchcock und die Musik: Eine Untersuchung zum Verhältnis von Film, Musik and Geschlecht*. Bielefeld: Kleine Verlag; and Josef Kloppenburg (1986), *Die dramaturgische Funktion der Musik in Filmen Alfred Hitchcocks*. Munich: Wilhelm Fink. A detailed study of one work has been offered by David Cooper (2001), *Bernard Herrmann's Vertigo: A Film Score Handbook*. Westport: Greenwood Press. Of other composer studies, Steven C. Smith's (1991), *A Heart at Fire's Center: The Life and Music of Bernard Herrmann*. Berkeley, Los Angeles, and London: University of California Press is especially useful. There are also numerous articles, some of which will be cited in the following chapters.

21 *The Silent Scream: Alfred Hitchcock's Sound Track*. Rutherford: Fairleigh Dickinson University Press (1982); "Music and Murder: The Association of Source Music with Order in Hitchcock's Films," in Peter Ruppert ed. *Ideas of Order in Literature and Film*, 73–83. Tallahassee: University Presses of Florida (1980); "The Sound of One Wing Flapping," *Film Comment* 14 (September–October 1978): 42–8; "The Evolution of Hitchcock's Aural Style and Sound in *The Birds*," in Elisabeth Weis and John Bolton (eds), *Film Sound: Theory and Practice*, 298–311. New York: Columbia University Press (1985).

22 Robin Wood (1969), *Hitchcock's Films*, 2nd ed. London: A. Zwemmer and New York: A. S. Barnes and Co., 59.

23 *Ibid.*, 69, 82, 83, 101, and 102.

24 Royal S. Brown (1994), "Herrmann, Hitchcock, and the Music of the Irrational," chapter 6 in *Overtones and Undertones: Reading Film Music*. Berkeley, Los Angeles, and London: University of California Press, 148–74. First published in *Cinema Journal* 21, no. 2 (1982): 14–49.

25 Sullivan, *Hitchcock's Music*, 279.

26 "Rear Window: The Redemptive Power of Popular Music," chapter 13 in *ibid.*, 169–82. First published in *Hitchcock Annual* 12 (2003–4): 83–99.

Chapter 1

1 Sidney Gottlieb ed. (1995), *Hitchcock on Hitchcock: Selected Writings and Interviews*. Berkeley. Los Angeles, and London: University of California Press, 142.

2 Dennis R. Perry (1996), "Imps of the Perverse: Discovering the Poe/Hitchcock Connection," *Literature/Film Quarterly* 24: 394.

3 *Hitchcock on Hitchcock*, 143–5.

4 Perry, "Imps of the Perverse," 395; Perry (2003), *Hitchcock and Poe: The Legacy of Delight and Terror*. Lanham, MD: The Scarecrow Press; and DeLoy Simper (1975), "Poe, Hitchcock and the Well-Wrought Effect," *Literature/Film Quarterly* 3: 226–31.

5 Quoted in Perry, "Imps," 395.

6 Perry, "Imps," 395.

7 Edgar Allan Poe (1985), *The Brevities*, ed. Burton R. Pollin. New York: Gordian Press, 472.

8 François Truffaut (1984), *Hitchcock*, rev. ed. New York: Simon and Schuster, 269.

9 *Hitchcock on Hitchcock*, 144.

10 Poe, *The Brevities*, 153.

11 *Ibid.*, 153–4.

12 *Ibid.*, 154.

13 Sidney Gottlieb ed. (2003), *Alfred Hitchcock: Interviews*. Jackson: University Press of Mississippi, 157.

14 *Ibid.*

15 *Ibid.*, 158.

16 Quoted in Lotte H. Eisner (1973), *Murnau*. Berkeley: University of California Press, 84.

17 See my (2002) *Cinema's Illusions, Opera's Allure: The Operatic Impulse in Film*. New York and London: Continuum, 151–67.

18 Jo Leslie Collier (1988), *From Wagner to Murnau: The Transposition of Romanticism from Stage to Screen*. Ann Arbor: UMI Research Press, 5.

19 *Ibid.*, 147–8.

20 John Russell Taylor (1978), *Hitch: The Life and Times of Alfred Hitchcock*. New York: Da Capo Press, 110.

21 Quoted in Eisner, *Murnau*, 72.

22 *Ibid.*

23 Sidney Gottlieb (1999–2000), "Early Hitchcock: The German Influence," *Hitchcock Annual*: 109.

24 Truffaut, *Hitchcock*, 27.

25 Pat Hitchcock O'Connell and Laurent Bouzereau (2003), *Alma Hitchcock: The Woman Behind the Man*. New York: Berkley Books, 25–6.

26 Sidney Gottlieb (2005), "Hitchcock on Griffith," *Hitchcock Annual* 14: 40–1.

27 *Hitchcock on Hitchcock*, 211 and 213.

28 Truffaut, *Hitchcock*, 56–7.

29 *Hitchcock on Hitchcock*, 242.

30 *Ibid.*, 244.

31 Patrick McGilligan (2003), *Alfred Hitchcock: A Life in Darkness and Light*. New York: Regan Books, 84.

32 Paul M. Jensen (2000), *Hitchcock Becomes "Hitchcock": The British Years*. Baltimore: Midnight Marquee Press, 121.

33 *Hitchcock on Hitchcock*, 222.

34 V. I. Pudovkin (1976), *Film Technique and Film Acting*, trans. and ed. Ivor Montagu. New York: Grove Press, 186.

35 *Ibid.*, 82–3.

36 *Ibid.*, 133–4.

37 *Ibid.*, 157–8.

38 *Ibid.*,178.

39 *Ibid.*, 48.

40 *Ibid.*, 166.

41 *Ibid.*, 201.

42 *Ibid.*, 289.

43 *Ibid.*, 131.

44 *Ibid.*, 199 and 171.

45 *Hitchcock on Hitchcock*, 213.

46 Peter Bogdanovich (1997), *Who the Devil Made It: Conversations with Legendary Film Directors*. New York: Ballantine Books, 522.

47 Truffaut, *Hitchcock*, 227.

48 Charles Samuels (1972), *Encountering Directors*. New York: G. P. Putnam's Sons, 234.

49 Bogdanovich, *Who the Devil Made It*, 544.

50 Truffaut, *Hitchcock*, 319 and 256.

Chapter 2

1 François Truffaut (1984), *Hitchcock*, rev. ed. New York: Simon and Schuster, 44.

2 Quoted in Patrick McGilligan (2003), *Alfred Hitchcock: A Life in Darkness and Light*. New York: Regan Books, 84.

3 Sidney Gottlieb (1999–2000), "Early Hitchcock: The German Influence," *Hitchcock Annual*: 107–8.

4 "Films We Could Make," in Sidney Gottlieb ed. (1995), *Hitchcock on Hitchcock: Selected Writings and Interviews*. Berkeley, Los Angeles, and London: University of California Press, 165.

5 *Ibid.*

6 *Ibid.*, 166–7.

7 *Ibid.*, 167.

8 See my (2002), *Cinema's Illusions, Operas Allure: The Operatic Impulse in Film*. New York and London: Continuum, 22–3.

9 *Hitchcock on Hitchcock*, 298.

10 Truffaut, *Hitchcock*, 335.

11 *Ibid.*, 276.

12 Peter Bogdanovich (1997), *Who the Devil Made It: Conversations with Legendary Film Directors*. New York: Ballantine Books, 544.

13 This proved not to be as evident as he hoped in would be. See Truffaut, *Hitchcock*, 45.

14 Truffaut, *Hitchcock*, 47.

15 Ken Mogg (1992), "Hitchcock's *The Lodger*: A Theory," *Hitchcock Annual*: 116–17.

Chapter 3

1 Charles Barr (1999), describes the richness of the silent films in *English Hitchcock*. Moffat: Cameron & Hollis, 22–77, as does Marc Raymond Strauss (2004), in *Alfred Hitchcock's Silent Films*. Jefferson, NC and London: McFarland & Company.

2 In "A Columbus of the Screen," *Film Weekly* (1931). This article says very little about Abraham Lincoln but focuses on the larger debt he owed to Griffith. See Sidney Gottlieb (2005), "Hitchcock on Griffith," *Hitchcock Annual* 14: 34–5.

3 Quoted in Richard Schickel (1984), *D. W. Griffith: An American Life*. New York: Simon and Schuster, 497.

4 Tom Ryall (1993), reminds us that it was preceded in Britain by the talkie *The Clue of the New Pin*, in *Blackmail*. London: BFI Publishing, 9.

5 See Charles Barr (1983), "Blackmail: Silent & Sound," *Sight & Sound* 52: 123–6 and John Belton (1999), "Awkward Transitions: Hitchcock's Blackmail and the Dynamics of Early Film," *The Musical Quarterly* 83: 227–46.

6 Sidney Gottlieb ed. (2003), *Alfred Hitchcock: Interviews*. Jackson: University Press of Mississippi, 158.

7 Sidney Gottlieb ed. (1995), *Hitchcock on Hitchcock: Selected Writings and Interviews*. Berkeley: University of California Press, 242.

8 Barr, "Blackmail: Silent & Sound," 123–6.

9 *Hitchcock on Hitchcock*, 167.

10 I have argued elsewhere, especially concerning the music of Franz Schubert, that these signs have little or nothing to do with dynamics, and this is certainly not a new idea. See my "Schubert the Singer," *The Music Review* 49: (1988) 254–66.

11 McGilligan, *Hitchcock*, 8.

12 *Hitchcock on Hitchcock*, 298.

13 Sergei Eisenstein (1974), *The Film Sense*, trans. and ed. Jay Leyda. San Diego: Harcourt Brace Javanovich, 174–216.

14 I would like to thank the British Film Institute for placing the silent version of *Blackmail* at my disposal.

15 Barr, "Blackmail: Silent & Sound," 124.

16 Quoted in Ryall, *Blackmail*, 52.

17 For a good discussion of this music, see Elisabeth Weis (1982), *The Silent Scream: Alfred Hitchcock's Sound Track*. Rutherford: Fairleigh Dickinson University Press, 53–4.

Chapter 4

1 See Patrick McGilligan (2003), *Alfred Hitchcock: A Life in Darkness and Light*. New York: Regan Books, 37.

2 Other films with waltzes, usually seen as well as heard, include *The Ring, Rich and Strange, Waltzes from Vienna, The Man Who*

Knew Too Much (1934), *Young and Innocent, The Lady Vanishes, Rebecca, Saboteur, Strangers on a Train, Rear Window, To Catch a Thief, The Wrong Man,* and *Torn Curtain.*

3 Francesca Draughon (2003), "Dance of Decadence: Class, Gender, and Modernity in the Scherzo of Mahler's Ninth Symphony," *Journal of Musicology* 20: 396.

4 *Ibid.,* 397.

5 Quoted in *ibid.*

6 Otto Weininger (1917), *Geschlecht und Charakter,* 16th ed. Vienna and Leipzig: Wilhelm Braumüller, 310.

7 Arthur Schnitzler (1953), *Merry-Go-Round* [*Reigen*], trans. Frank and Jacqueline Marcus. London: Weidenfeld and Nicolson, 5–6.

8 Paul Hoffmann (1988), *The Viennese: Splendor, Twilight, and Exile.* New York: Doubleday, 109.

9 See Edward Timms (1986), *Karl Kraus: Apocalyptic Satirist.* New Haven and London: Yale University Press, 226–7.

10 Edward Crankshaw (1963), *The Fall of the House of Habsburg.* London: Longman, 317.

11 Timms, *Karl Kraus,* 229.

12 Henry Schnitzler (1954), "Gay Vienna—Myth and Reality," *Journal of the History of Ideas* 15: 111–12.

13 Quoted in Roger Nichols (1977), *Ravel.* London: J. M. Dent, 107.

14 Carl E. Schorske (1981), *Fin-de-siècle Vienna: Politics and Culture.* New York: Vintage Books, 3.

15 See Patrick McGilligan (1997), *Fritz Lang: Nature of the Beast.* New York: St Martin's Press, 24.

16 Sidney Gottlieb ed. (2003), *Alfred Hitchcock Interviews.* Jackson: University Press of Mississippi, 157.

17 See my (1999), "Berg," in *Schoenberg, Berg, and Webern: A Companion to the Second Viennese School,* ed. Bryan R. Simms. Westport and London: Greenwood Press, 240.

18 Uli Jung and Walter Schatzberg (1999), *Beyond Caligari: The Films of Robert Wiene.* New York and Oxford: Berghahn Books, 77–8.

19 François Truffaut (1983), *Hitchcock,* rev. ed. New York: Simon and Schuster, 85–7.

20 Although it was sold commercially, it lacks production information.

21 Eric Rohmer and Claude Chabrol (1979), *Hitchcock: The First Forty-four Films,* trans. Stanley Hochman. New York: Frederick Ungar, 37.

22 Quoted in Charles Barr (1999), *English Hitchcock*. Moffat: Cameron & Hollis, 127.

23 "On Music in Films, An Interview with Stephen Watts," in Sidney Gottlieb ed. (1995), *Hitchcock on Hitchcock: Selected Writings and Interviews*. Berkeley, Los Angeles, and London: University of California Press, 241.

24 *Ibid.*, 244.

25 Margaret Herrick Library.

Chapter 5

1 "Uncle Charlie," Story Outline, Gordon McDonell, 5 May 1942. Margaret Herrick Library.

2 "Notes on Possible Development of Uncle Charlie Story for Screen Play," Alfred Hitchcock, 11 May 1946. Margaret Herrick Library.

3 "Some Notes about the Small Town Atmosphere," Hitchcock, 11 May 1946. Margaret Herrick Library.

4 See Patrick McGilligan (2003), *Alfred Hitchcock: A Life in Darkness and Light*. New York: Regan Books, 308.

5 George Turner (1993), "Hitchcock's Mastery is beyond Doubt in Shadow," *American Cinematographer* 74, no. 5. May: 67.

6 Dimitri Tiomkin and Prosper Buranelli (1959), *Please Don't Hate Me*. New York: Doubleday and Company, 224–6.

7 Christopher Palmer (1984), *Dimitri Tiomkin*. London: T. E. Books, 35.

8 Quoted in Martin Blank (1999), "Wilder, Hitchcock, and Shadow of a Doubt," in Martin Blank, Dalma Hunyadi Brunauer, and David Garrett Izzo (eds), *Thornton Wilder: New Essays*, West Cornwall, CT: Locust Hill Press, 410.

9 Blank, "Wilder, Hitchcock, and Shadow of a Doubt," 410.

10 Diaghilev believed the work to be a masterpiece, but not a ballet, and he rejected it. See Arbie Orenstein (1975), *Ravel: Man and Musician*. New York: Columbia University Press, 77–8.

11 William Rothman (1982), *The Murderous Gaze*. Cambridge, MA: Harvard University Press, 181.

12 Script, 28 July 1942, pp. 94–5. Margaret Herrick Library.

13 Script, 10 June 1942, p. 140. Margaret Herrick Library.

14 Quoted in McGilligan, *Alfred Hitchcock*, 317.

15 Quoted in *ibid.*, 316.

16 Sidney Gottlieb ed. (1995), *Hitchcock on Hitchcock: Selected Writings and Interviews*. Berkeley, Los Angeles, and London: University of California Press, 216.

17 This breakdown is accurate only to the second, even though fractions of a second come into play.

18 The noir character of this and other films has been discussed by James Naremore (1999) in "Hitchcock at the Margins of Noir," in Richard Allen and S. Ishii Gonzalès (eds), *Alfred Hitchcock: Centenary Essays*. London: British Film Institute, 263–77.

19 See Edward Timms (1986), *Karl Kraus: Apocalyptic Satirist*. New Haven: Yale University Press, 227–8.

20 "Amusements," *The New Englander* 26 (July 1867): 408–9. My thanks to Steven Baur for this reference and his thoughts about the waltz in nineteenth-century America.

21 Quoted in Roger Nichols (1977), *Ravel*. London: J. M. Dent and Sons, 108.

22 François Truffaut (1984), *Hitchcock*, rev. ed. New York: Simon and Schuster, 151.

23 Pat Hitchcock O'Connell and Laurent Bouzereau (2003), *Alma Hitchcock: The Woman Behind the Man*. New York: Berkley Books, 119.

24 Margaret Herrick Library.

Chapter 6

1 François Truffaut (1984), *Hitchcock*, rev. ed. New York: Simon and Schuster, 222.

2 Patrick McGilligan (2003), *Alfred Hitchcock: A Life in Darkness and Light*. New York: Regan Books, 481.

3 Steven DeRosa (2001), *Writing with Hitchcock: The Collaboration of Alfred Hitchcock and John Michael Hayes*. New York and London: Faber and Faber, 18.

4 This is covered in detail by Elisabeth Weis (1982) in *The Silent Scream: Alfred Hitchcock's Sound Track*. Rutherford: Fairleigh Dickinson University Press, 107–14, and Jack Sullivan (2006), *Hitchcock's Music*. New Haven and London: Yale University Press, 170–81.

5 Truffaut, *Hitchcock*, 216.

6 Quoted in Weis, *The Silent Scream*, 115.

7 Sullivan, *Hitchcock's Music*, 176.

8 *Rear Window*, DVD, directed by Alfred Hitchcock. 1954. Universal City, CA: Universal Studios, 2001.

9 DeRosa, *Writing with Hitchcock*, ix and xi.

10 Herbert Coleman (2003), *The Hollywood I Knew: A Memoir, 1916–1988*. Lanham, MD: The Scarecrow Press, 176–8.

11 Truffaut, 222.

12 McGilligan, *Alfred Hitchcock*, 483.

13 John Michael Hayes, *Rear Window*, final white script, 1 December 1953, 10.

14 Truffaut, 215–16.

15 *Ibid.*, 216.

16 *Ibid.*

17 See Robin Wood (1989), *Hitchcock's Films Revisited*. New York: Columbia University Press, 247 and 378.

18 Wood (1969), *Hitchcock's Films*. London: Zwemmer and New York: A. S. Barnes, 69–70.

19 *Ibid.*, 70.

20 *Rear Window*, Cutting Continuity, 21 June 1954. Swedish Film Institute.

21 John Fawell (2001), *Rear Window: The Well-Made Film*. Carbondale and Edwardsville: Southern Illinois University Press, 101.

Chapter 7

1 Craig H. Roell (1989), *The Piano in America: 1890–1940*. Chapel Hill: University of North Carolina Press, 5.

2 Ronald V. Ratcliffe (1989), *Steinway & Sons*. San Francisco: Chronicle Books, 52.

3 See Richard Leppert (1992), "Sexual Identity, Death, and the Family Piano," *19th-Century Music* 16: 116–23.

4 Arnaud d'Asseau, *Before the Fact*. Yellow Script, 9 November 1939, pp. 30, 31 and 53. UCLA Arts Special Collections.

5 See Jack Sullivan (2006), *Hitchcock's Music*. New Haven and London: Yale University Press, 7; Tom Ryall (1993), *Blackmail*. London: British Film Institute, 46–7; and Elisabeth Weis (1982), *The*

Silent Scream: Alfred Hitchcock's Sound Track. Rutherford: Fairleigh Dickinson University Press, 53–5.

6 *Notorious*, script accompanying 16mm release, (1961). British Film Institute, 17.

7 Sullivan, *Hitchcock's Music*, 127.

8 See Jeffrey Kallberg (1994), "Small Fairy Voices: Sex, History and Meaning in Chopin," in John Rink and Jim Samson (eds), *Chopin Studies 2*. Cambridge: Cambridge University Press, 50–71.

9 See Michael Anderegg (1986), "Hitchcock's *The Paradine Case* and Filmic Unpleasure," *Cinema Journal* 26, no. 4: 49–59.

10 *The Paradine Case*. Final shooting script, 10 December 1946, 1. UCLA Arts Special Collections.

11 *The Paradine Case*, adaptation of the novel by Muriel Elwood, 12 February 1946, pp. 4 and 20. Margaret Herrick Library.

12 Farley Granger (2007), *Include Me Out: My Life from Goldwyn to Broadway*. New York: St Martin's Press.

13 In University of Southern California Warner Brothers Archives.

14 See Patrick McGilligan (2003), *Alfred Hitchcock: A Life in Darkness and Light*. New York: Regan Books, 413.

15 Richard Allen (2007), *Hitchcock's Romantic Irony*. New York: Columbia University Press, 142.

16 Quoted in *ibid.*, 62.

17 See Sullivan, 151.

18 *Topaz*, production notes, 1–5. Margaret Herrick Library.

19 François Truffaut (1983), *Hitchcock*, revised ed. New York: Simon and Schuster, 269.

Chapter 8

1 Elisabeth Weis (1980), "Music and Murder: The Association of Source Music with Order in Hitchcock's Films," in Peter Ruppert ed., *Ideas of Order in Literature and Film*. Tallahassee: University Presses of Florida, 73.

2 John Russell Taylor (1978), *Hitch: The Life and Times of Alfred Hitchcock*. London: Faber and Faber, 110.

3 Pat Hitchcock O'Connell and Laurent Bouzereau (2003), *Alma Hitchcock: The Woman Behind the Man*. New York: Berkley Books.

4 Patrick McGilligan (2003), *Alfred Hitchcock: A Life in Darkness and Light*. New York: Regan Books, 8.

5 See Barry Millington (1991), "Nuremberg Trial: Is there Anti-Semitism in *Die Meistersinger?*" *Cambridge Opera Journal* 3: 247–60.

6 Cambridge: Polity, (2000).

7 Sidney Gottlieb argues there is a strong connection with E. A. Dupont, whom Hitchcock met in the late 1920s, in "Early Hitchcock: The German Influence," *Hitchcock Annual* (1999–2000): 111–13.

8 Jack Sullivan (2006), *Hitchcock's Music*. New Haven and London: Yale University Press, 11–12.

9 Nietzsche quoted by Tania Modleski (1988) in *The Women Who Knew Too Much*. New York and London: Routledge, 35.

10 Elisabeth Weis (1982), *The Silent Scream: Alfred Hitchcock's Sound Track*. Rutherford: Fairleigh Dickinson University Press, 41.

11 See Raymond Durgnat (1974), *The Strange Case of Alfred Hitchcock*. Cambridge, MA: The MIT Press, 111–15. Richard Allen (2004–5), takes a more generous view of Sir John in "Sir John and the Half-Caste: Identity and Representation in Hitchcock's *Murder!*", *Hitchcock's Annual* 13: 93.

12 Allen shows in detail the differences between the film and the source novel, in which the term does have racial implications, in "Sir John and the Half-Caste," 111–16.

13 William Rothman (1986), "Alfred Hitchcock's *Murder!*: Theater, Authorship, and the Presence of the Camera," in Marshall Deutelbaum and Leland Poague (eds), *A Hitchcock Reader*. Ames: Iowa State University Press, 90–1, and (1982), *Hitchcock: The Murderous Gaze*. Cambridge, MA: Harvard University Press, 58–107.

14 *Lifeboat*, screenplay by Jo Swerling, revised final version, 29 July 1943, p. 54. Margaret Herrick Library.

15 Robin Wood (1989), explores this in *Hitchcock's Films Revisited*. New York: Columbia University Press, 75–6.

16 *Ibid.*, 123–4.

17 Especially David Cooper (2001), in *Bernard Herrmann's Vertigo: A Film Score Handbook*. Westport and London: Greenwood Press, 88–90 and 105–7.

18 Brown (1986), "*Vertigo* as Orphic Tragedy," *Literature/Film Quarterly* 14: 32–43.

19 The Margaret Herrick Library.

20 For example in a script dated 21 February 1957, in The Margaret Herrick Library.

21 The Margaret Herrick Library, pp. 27–32.

22 A cryptic production note during the making of *Vertigo* identifies the production of Wagner's *Die Walküre* by the San Francisco Opera Company, giving dates, the outline of the scenes in act 1, including how the act ends, and notes that the "Wagner opera involves no rights." Margaret Herrick Library, n.d.

23 The Margaret Herrick Library.

24 See Cooper, *Bernard Herrmann's Vertigo*, 88–9.

25 Daniel Antonio Srebnick (2004), "Music and Identity: The Struggle for Harmony in *Vertigo*," in Richard Allen and Sam Ishii-Gonzáles (eds), *Hitchcock: Past and Future* London and New York: Routledge, 151.

26 See Cooper, 90. I have discussed these various similarities at length in (2002) *Cinema's Illusions, Opera's Allure: The Operatic Impulse in Film*. New York and London: Continuum, 237–43.

27 See my description in *Cinema's Illusions, Opera's Allure*, 243–4.

28 Steven C. Smith (1991), *A Heart at Fire's Center: The Life and Music of Bernard Herrmann*. Berkeley, Los Angeles, and London: The University of California Press, 199–200.

29 Weis, *The Silent Scream*, 95.

Chapter 9

1 Jack Sullivan (2006), *Hitchcock's Music*. New Haven: Yale University Press, 176.

2 Skeleton outline, 7 February 1955. Margaret Herrick Library.

3 Revised skeleton, 12 February 1955. Margaret Herrick Library.

4 Murray Pomerance (2001), "'The Future's Not Ours to See': Song, Singer, Labyrinth in Hitchcock's *The Man Who Knew Too Much*," in Pamela Robertson Wojcik and Arthur Knight (eds), *Soundtrack Available: Essays on Film and Popular Music*. Durham and London: Duke University Press, 53–73.

5 *Ibid.*, 56.

6 Quoted in Sullivan, *Hitchcock's Music*, 118.

7 Note by William R. Stenson, 3 March 1958, Margaret Herrick

Library. Sullivan's assumption (p. 120) that it could have replaced the titles music seems unfounded.

8 Memo to Hitchcock from David Golding, 8 July 1964, Margaret Herrick Library.

9 Herbert Coleman (2003), *The Hollywood I Knew: A Memoir, 1916–1988*. Lanham, MD: The Scarecrow Press, 291.

10 For the details of this complexity, see Dennis McDougal (2001), *The Last Mogul: Lew Wasserman, MCA, and the Hidden History of Hollywood*. New York: Da Capo Press, and Connie Bruck (2003), *When Hollywood had a King*. New York: Random House.

11 Patrick McGilligan (2003), *Alfred Hitchcock: A Life in Darkness and Light*. New York: Regan Books, 479.

12 Stephen Rebello (1998), *Alfred Hitchcock and the Making of Psycho*. New York: St. Martin's Griffin, 16.

13 Donald Spoto (1999), *The Dark Side of Genius: The Life of Alfred Hitchcock*. New York: Da Capo Press, 417.

14 Quoted in Rebello, *Alfred Hitchcock*, 163.

15 Steven C. Smith (1991), *A Heart at Fire's Center: The Life and Music of Bernard Herrmann*. Berkeley, Los Angeles, and London: University of California Press, 267–75.

16 Hitchcock's Dubbing Notes for *Vertigo*, 15 January 1958, Margaret Herrick Library.

17 Smith, *A Heart at Fire's Center*, 268–9.

18 *Ibid.*, 269–70.

19 Royal S. Brown (1976), "An Interview with Bernard Herrmann," *High Fidelity* 26, no. 9 (September), 65.

20 Smith, 240.

21 *Ibid.*, 271.

22 *An Oral History with Peggy Robertson, Interviewed by Barbara Hall*. Beverly Hills: Academy Foundation, (2002), 294.

23 *Ibid.*

24 John Russell Taylor (1996), *Hitch: The Life and Times of Alfred Hitchcock*. New York: Da Capo Press, 278.

25 Memo from Gerald S. Barton to Peggy Robertson, 25 March 1966, Margaret Herrick Library.

26 Rebello, 138.

27 *Ibid.*, 101.

28 François Truffaut (1985), *Hitchcock*, rev. ed. New York: Touchstone Books, 311.

29 Hitchcock's Music Notes to *Frenzy*, 1 January 1972, p. 3, Margaret Herrick Library.

30 "Scenes Scored by Composer Bernard Herrmann," *Torn Curtain*, DVD, directed by Alfred Hitchcock, 1966, Universal City, CA: Universal Studios, 2000.

31 McGilligan, *Alfred Hitchcock*, 664–5.

Bibliography

Allen, R. (2004–5), "Sir John and the Half-Caste: Identity and Representation in Hitchcock's *Murder!*" *Hitchcock Annual* 13: 92–126.

—(2007), *Hitchcock's Romantic Irony*. New York: Columbia University Press.

Anderegg, M. (1986), "Hitchcock's *The Paradine Case* and Filmic Unpleasure." *Cinema Journal* 26, no. 4: 49–59.

Anon. (1867), "Amusements." *The New Englander* 26 (July): 408–9.

Antony, J. (2001), "'The Moment that I Dreaded and Hoped for': Ambivalence and Order in Bernard Herrmann's Score for *Vertigo*." *The Musical Quarterly* 85: 516–44.

Barr, C. (1983), "Blackmail: Silent and Sound." *Sight & Sound* 52: 123–6.

—(1999), *English Hitchcock*. Moffat: Cameron & Hollis.

Belton, J. (1999), "Awkward Transitions: Hitchcock's *Blackmail* and the Dynamics of Early Film." *The Musical Quarterly* 83: 227–46.

—ed. (2000), *Alfred Hitchcock's* Rear Window. Cambridge: Cambridge University Press.

Blank, M. (1999), "Wilder, Hitchcock, and *Shadow of a Doubt*." In M. Blank, D. H. Brunauer, and D. G. Izzo (eds), *Thornton Wilder: New Essays*, 409–16. West Cornwall, CT: Locust Hill Press.

Bogdanovich, P. (1963), *The Cinema of Alfred Hitchcock*. New York: The Museum of Modern Art Film Library.

—(1997) *Who the Devil Made It: Conversations with Legendary Film Directors*. New York: Ballantine Books.

Brill, L. W. (1983), "Hitchcock's *The Lodger*." *Literature/Film Quarterly* 11: 257–65.

Brown, R. S. (1976), "An Interview with Bernard Herrmann." *High Fidelity* 26, no. 9 (September), 64–7.

—(1982), "Herrmann, Hitchcock, and the Music of the Irrational." *Cinema Journal* 21, no. 2: 14–49.

—(1986), "*Vertigo* as Orphic Tragedy." *Literature/Film Quarterly* 14: 32–43.

—(1994), *Overtones and Undertones: Reading Film Music*. Berkeley, Los Angeles, and London: University of California Press.

Bruck, C. (2003), *When Hollywood had a King*. New York: Random House.

Cavell, S. (1979), *The World Viewed: Reflections on the Ontology of Film*. Cambridge, MA: Harvard University Press.

—(1981), "North by Northwest." *Critical Inquiry* 7: 761–6.

Coleman, H. (2003), *The Hollywood I Knew: A Memoir, 1916–1988*. Lanham, MD: The Scarecrow Press.

Collier, J. L. (1988), *From Wagner to Murnau: The Transposition of Romanticism from Stage to Screen*. Ann Arbor: UMI Research Press.

Cooper, D. (2001), *Bernard Herrmann's Vertigo: A Film Score Handbook*. Westport: Greenwood Press.

Crankshaw, E. (1963) *The Fall of the House of Habsburg*. London: Longman.

DeRosa, S. (2001), *Writing with Hitchcock: The Collaboration of Alfred Hitchcock and John Michael Hayes*. New York and London: Faber and Faber.

Draughon, F. (2003), "Dance of Decadence: Class, Gender, and Modernity in the Scherzo of Mahler's Ninth Symphony." *Journal of Musicology* 20: 388–413.

Durgnat, R. (1974), *The Strange Case of Alfred Hitchcock*. Cambridge, MA: The MIT Press.

Eisenstein, S. (1974), *The Film Sense*. Translated and edited by Jay Leyda. San Diego: Harcourt Brace Javanovich.

Eisner, L. H. (1973), *Murnau*. Berkeley: University of California Press.

Eugène, J.-P. (2000), *La Musique dans les Films d'Alfred Hitchcock*. Paris: Dreamland éditeur.

Fawell, J. (2000), "The Sound of Loneliness: *Rear Window*'s Soundtrack." *Studies in the Humanities* 27: 62–74.

—(2001), *Rear Window: The Well-Made Film*. Carbondale and Edwardsville: Southern Illinois University Press.

Gottlieb, S. (ed.) (1995), *Hitchcock on Hitchcock: Selected Writings and Interviews*. Berkeley, Los Angeles, and London: University of California Press.

—(1999–2000), "Early Hitchcock: The German Influence." *Hitchcock Annual*: 100–30.

—ed. (2003), *Alfred Hitchcock: Interviews*. Jackson: University Press of Mississippi.

—(2005), "Hitchcock on Griffith." *Hitchcock Annual* 14: 32–45.

Granger, F. (2007), *Include Me Out: My Life from Goldwyn to Broadway*. New York: St Martin's Press.

Hitchcock, A. (1995), "Films We Could Make." In S. Gottlieb ed., *Hitchcock on Hitchcock: Selected Writings and Interviews*, 165–7. Berkeley, Los Angeles, and London: University of California Press.

Hitchcock O'Connell, P., and L. Bouzereau (2003), *Alma Hitchcock: The Woman Behind the Man*. New York: Berkley Books.

Hoffmann, P. (1988), *The Viennese: Splendor, Twilight, and Exile*. New York: Doubleday.

Jensen, P. M. (2000), *Hitchcock Becomes "Hitchcock": The British Years*. Baltimore: Midnight Marquee Press.

Jung, U., and W. Schatzberg (1999), *Beyond Caligari: The Films of Robert Wiene*. New York and Oxford: Berghahn Books.

Kallberg, J. (1994), "Small Fairy Voices: Sex, History, and Meaning in Chopin." In J. Rink and J. Samson (eds), *Chopin Studies 2*, 50–71. Cambridge: Cambridge University Press, 1994.

Kloppenburg, J. (1986), *Die dramaturgische Funktion der Musik in Filmen Alfred Hitchcocks*. Munich: Wilhelm Fink.

Köhler, J. (2000), *Wagner's Hitler: The Prophet and His Disciple*, translated by R. Taylor. Cambridge: Polity.

Leppert, R. (1992), "Sexual Identity, Death, and the Family Piano." *19th-Century Music* 16: 105–28.

McDougal, D. (2001), *The Last Mogul: Lew Wasserman, MCA, and the Hidden History of Hollywood*. New York: Da Capo Press.

McGilligan, P. (2003), *Alfred Hitchcock: A Life in Darkness and Light*. New York: Regan Books.

McGilligan, P. (1997), *Fritz Lang: Nature of the Beast*. New York: St Martin's Press.

Millington, B. (1991), "Nuremberg Trial: Is there Anti-Semitism in *Die Meistersinger?*" *Cambridge Opera Journal* 3: 247–60.

Modleski, T. (1988), *The Women Who Knew Too Much*. New York and London: Routledge.

Mogg, K. (1992), "Hitchcock's *The Lodger*: A Theory." *Hitchcock Annual*: 115–27.

Naremore, J. (1999), "Hitchcock at the Margins of *Noir*." In Richard Allen and S. Ishii Gonzalès (eds), *Alfred Hitchcock: Centenary Essays*, 263–77. London: BFI Publishing.

Nichols, R. (1977), *Ravel*. London: J. M. Dent.

An Oral History with Peggy Robertson, Interviewed by Barbara Hall. Beverly Hills: Academy Foundation, 2002.

Orenstein, A. (1975), *Ravel: Man and Musician*. New York: Columbia University Press.

Palmer, C. (1984), *Dimitri Tiomkin*. London: T. E. Books.

Perry, D. R. (1996), "Imps of the Perverse: Discovering the Poe/Hitchcock Connection." *Literature/Film Quarterly* 24: 393–8.

—(2003), *Hitchcock and Poe: The Legacy of Delight and Terror*. Lanham, MD: The Scarecrow Press.

Poe, E. A. (1985), *The Brevities*, edited by Burton R. Pollin. New York: Gordian Press.

Pomerance, M. (2000), "Finding Release: 'Storm Clouds' and *The Man Who Knew Too Much*," in J. Buhler, C. Flynn, and D. Neumeyer (eds), *Music and Cinema*, 107–46. Hanover and London: Wesleyan University Press.

—(2001), "'The Future's Not Ours to See': Song, Singer, Labyrinth in Hitchcock's *The Man Who Knew Too Much.*" In P. Robertson Wojcik and A. Knight (eds), *Soundtracks Available: Essays on Film and Popular Music*, 53–73. Durham and London: Duke University Press.

—(2004), *An Eye for Hitchcock.* New Brunswick, NJ: Rutgers University Press.

Pudovkin, V. I. (1976), *Film Technique and Film Acting*, translated and edited by I. Montagu. New York: Grove Press.

Ratcliffe, R. V. (1989), *Steinway & Sons.* San Francisco: Chronicle Books.

Rebello, S. (1998), *Alfred Hitchcock and the Making of Psycho.* New York: St Martin's Griffin.

Rieger, E. (1996), *Alfred Hitchcock und die Musik: Eine Untersuchung zum Verhältnis von Film, Musik und Geschlecht.* Beilefeld: Kleine Verlag.

Roell, C. H. (1989), *The Piano in America: 1890–1940.* Chapel Hill: University of North Carolina Press.

Rohmer, E., and C. Chabrol (1979). *Hitchcock: The First Forty-four Films*, translated by Stanley Hochman. New York: Frederick Ungar.

Rothman, W. (1982), *The Murderous Gaze.* Cambridge, MA: Harvard University Press.

—(1986), "Alfred Hitchcock's *Murder!*: Theater, Authorship, and the Presence of the Camera." In M. Deutelbaum and L. Poague (eds), *A Hitchcock Reader*, 90–101. Ames: Iowa State University Press.

Ryall, T. (1993), *Blackmail.* London: BFI Publishing.

Samuels, C. (1972), *Encountering Directors.* New York: G. P. Putnam's Sons.

Schickel, R. (1984) *D. W. Griffith: An American Life.* New York: Simon and Schuster.

Schnitzler, A. (1953), *Merry-Go-Round [Reigen]*, translated by Frank and Jacqueline Marcus. London: Weidenfeld and Nicolson.

Schnitzler, H. (1954), "Gay Vienna—Myth and Reality." *Journal of the History of Ideas* 15: 94–118.

Schorske, C. E. (1981), *Fin-de-siècle Vienna: Politics and Culture.* New York: Vintage Books.

Schroeder, D. (1988), "Schubert the Singer." *The Music Review* 49: 254–66.

—(1999), "Berg." In B. R. Simms (ed.), *Schoenberg, Berg, and Webern: A Companion to the Second Viennese School*, 185–250. Westport and London: Greenwood Press.

—(2002), *Cinema's Illusions, Opera's Allure: The Operatic Impulse in Film.* New York: Continuum.

Sharff, S. (1997), *The Art of Looking in Hitchcock's Rear Window.* New York: Limelight Editions.

Simper, D. (1975), "Poe, Hitchcock and the Well-Wrought Effect." *Literature/Film Quarterly* 3: 226–31.

Sloan, J. E. (1993), *Alfred Hitchcock: A Filmography and Bibliography*. Berkeley, Los Angeles, and London: University of California Press.

Smith, S. (2000), *Hitchcock: Suspense, Humor, and Tone*. London: BFI Publishing.

Smith, S. C. (1991), *A Heart at Fire's Center: The Life and Music of Bernard Herrmann*. Berkeley, Los Angeles, and London: University of California Press.

Spoto, D. (1979), *The Art of Alfred Hitchcock: Fifty Years of His Motion Pictures*. 2nd ed. New York: Doubleday.

—(1999), *The Dark Side of Genius: The Life of Alfred Hitchcock*. New York: Da Capo Press.

Srebnick, A. (2004), "Music and Identity: The Struggle for Harmony in *Vertigo*." In R. Allen and S. Ishii-Gonzáles (eds), *Hitchcock Past and Future*. London and New York: Routledge.

Sterritt, D. (1993), *The Films of Alfred Hitchcock*. Cambridge: Cambridge University Press, 1993.

Strauss, M. R. (2004), *Alfred Hitchcock's Silent Films*. Jefferson, NC and London: McFarland & Company.

Sullivan, J. (2006), *Hitchcock's Music*. New Haven and London: Yale University Press.

Taylor, J. R. (1978), *Hitch: The Life and Times of Alfred Hitchcock*. London: Faber and Faber.

Timms, E. (1986), *Karl Kraus: Apocalyptic Satirist*. New Haven and London: Yale University Press.

Tiomkin, D., and P. Buranelli (1959), *Please Don't Hate Me*. New York: Doubleday and Company.

Truffaut, F., with the collaboration of H. G. Scott (1984). *Hitchcock*. Rev. ed. New York: Simon and Schuster.

Turner, G. (1993), "Hitchcock's Mastery is beyond Doubt in *Shadow*." *American Cinematographer* 74, no. 5 (May): 62–7.

Watts, S. (1933–4), "Alfred Hitchcock on Music in Films." *Cinema Quarterly* [Edinburgh] 2, no. 2: 80–3. Reprinted in S. Gottlieb (ed.) (1995), *Hitchcock on Hitchcock: Selected Writings and Interviews*, 241–5. Berkeley, Los Angeles, and London: University of California Press.

Weininger, O. (1917), *Geschlecht und Charakter*. 16th ed. Vienna and Leipzig: Wilhelm Braumüller.

Weis, E. (1978), "The Sound of One Wing Flapping." *Film Comment* 14 (September–October): 42–8.

—(1980), "Music and Murder: The Association of Source Music with Order in Hitchcock's Films," in P. Ruppert ed., *Ideas of Order in Literature and Film*, 73–83. Tallahassee: University Presses of Florida.

—(1982), *The Silent Scream: Alfred Hitchcock's Sound Track.* Rutherford: Fairleigh Dickenson University Press.

—(1985), "The Evolution of Hitchcock's Aural Style and Sound in *The Birds*," in E. Weis and J. Bolton (eds), *Film Sound, Theory and Practice*, 298–311. New York: Columbia University Press.

Wood, R. (1969), *Hitchcock's Films.* 2nd ed. London: A. Zwemmer and New York: A. S. Barnes and Co.

—(1989), *Hitchcock's Films Revisited.* New York: Columbia University Press.

Selected DVDs
and VHS

Hitchcock

The Pleasure Garden, 1925. UK: Network, 2008.
The Lodger, A Story of the London Fog, 1926. Beverly, Hills, CA: Twentieth Century Fox, 2008.
Downhill, 1927. PR Studios, 2010.
Easy Virtue, 1927. Los Angeles, CA: Delta Entertainment Corporation, 1999.
The Ring, 1927. Los Angeles, CA: Delta Entertainment Corporation, 1999.
Champagne, 1928. Sunnyvale, CA: AFA Entertainment, 2011.
Blackmail, 1929 [silent]. Non-commercial VHS tape available at BFI, London.
Blackmail, 1929 [sound]. Los Angeles, CA: Delta Entertainment Corporation, 1999.
Murder!, 1930. Los Angeles, CA: Delta Entertainment Corporation, 1999.
Waltzes from Vienna, 1933. PR Studios, 2009.
The Man Who Knew Too Much, 1934. Los Angeles, CA: Delta Entertainment Corporation, 1999.
Secret Agent, 1936. Los Angeles, CA: Delta Entertainment Corporation, 1999.
Young and Innocent, 1937. Los Angeles, CA: Delta Entertainment Corporation, 1999.
The Lady Vanishes, 1938. Los Angeles, CA: Delta Entertainment Corporation, 1999.
Suspicion, 1941. Burbank, CA: Warner Home Video, Inc., 2004.
Shadow of a Doubt, 1943. Universal City, CA: Universal Studios, 2006.
Lifeboat, 1944. Beverly Hills, CA: Twentieth Century Fox, 2005.
Notorious, 1946. The Criterion Collection, 2001.
The Paradine Case, 1948. Beverly Hill, CA: Twentieth Century Fox, 2008.
Rope, 1948. Universal City, CA: Universal Studios, 2000.

Under Capricorn, 1949. Chatsworth, CA: Image Entertainment, Inc.,
   2003.
Stage Fright, 1950. Burbank, CA: Warner Home Videos, Inc., 2004.
Strangers on a Train, 1950. Burbank, CA: Warner Home Videos, Inc.,
   1997.
I Confess, 1951. Burbank, CA: Warner Home Video, Inc., 2004.
Rear Window, 1954. Universal City, CA: Universal Studios, 2001.
The Man Who Knew Too Much, 1956. Universal City, CA: Universal
   Studios, 2000.
Vertigo, 1957. Universal City, CA: Universal Studios, 1999.
The Wrong Man, 1957. Burbank, CA: Warner Home Video, Inc., 2004.
Psycho, 1960. Universal City, CA: Universal Studios, 1999.
The Birds, 1963. Universal City, CA: Universal Studios, 2000.
Torn Curtain, 1966. Universal City, CA: Universal Studios, 2000.
Topaz, 1969. Universal City, CA: Universal Studios, 2006.

Other directors

Berlin, Symphony of a Great City, 1927. Directed by Walther Ruttmann.
   Chatsworth, CA: Image Entertainment, Inc., 1999.
Die Büchse der Pandora, 1929. Directed by Georg Wilhelm Papst.
   Criterion Collection, 1929.
Faust, 1926. Directed by F. W. Murnau. New York, NY: Kino
   International, 2009.
The Last Laugh, 1924. Directed by F. W. Murnau. Burbank, CA: Triton
   Multimedia, 2001.
Metropolis, 1927. Directed by Fritz Lang. New York, NY: Kino
   International, 2002.
Phantom, 1922. Directed by F. W. Murnau. Los Angeles, CA: Flicker
   Alley, 2006.
The Phantom of the Opera, 1925. Directed by Rupert Julian. Narberth,
   PA: Alpha Video Distribution, 2001.

Index